DEATH ON THE PRAIRIE

PRAIRIE

The Thirty Years' Struggle
for the Western Plains

BY

PAUL I. WELLMAN

University of Nebraska Press
Lincoln and London

Copyright © 1934 by Paul I. Wellman, Jr.
Renewal copyright © 1962 by Paul I. Wellman
All rights reserved
Manufactured in the United States of America

First Bison Book printing: 1987
Most recent printing indicated by the first digit below:
5   6   7   8   9   10

Library of Congress Cataloging-in-Publication Data
Wellman, Paul Iselin, 1898–1966.
  Death on the prairie.
  Reprint. Originally published: New York: Macmillan,
1934.
  "Bison book."
  Bibliography: p.
  Includes index.
  1. Indians of North America—Wars—1866–1895.
2. Indians of North America—Wars—1863–1865. I. Title.
E83.866.W35   1987   973.8   87-10886
ISBN 0-8032-4747-8
ISBN 0-8032-9721-1 (pbk.)

Reprinted by arrangement with Paul I. Wellman, Jr.

∞

To

LYDIA I. WELLMAN

pioneer on two continents

ACKNOWLEDGMENTS

MANY books have of a necessity been consulted in the writing of this one. I wish to acknowledge particularly my indebtedness to the following:

Houghton-Mifflin Company, Boston, for permission to use quotations and references from Stanley Vestal's "Sitting Bull, Champion of the Sioux."

Charles Scribner's Sons, New York, for permission to quote and use material from George Bird Grinnell's "The Fighting Cheyennes."

Mrs. Olive K. Dixon, Amarillo, for permission to use data, names and incidents from her biography "The Life of Billy Dixon."

Bobbs-Merrill Company, Indianapolis, for permission to quote from Colonel Homer W. Wheeler's "Buffalo Days."

Mrs. Alice V. Schmidt, of Houston, and Charles A. Maddux, of Los Angeles, for permission to use material from John R. Cook's "The Border and the Buffalo."

Captain Robert G. Carter, U.S.A., retired, Washington, D. C., for information and the permission to use material from his "The Old Sergeant's Story; Winning the West from Indians and Bad Men in 1870–76."

The State Historical Societies of Kansas, Nebraska and Minnesota for their generous furnishing to me of material from their records.

A. C. McClurg and Company, Chicago, for the use of quotations and incidents from E. B. Bronson's "Reminiscences of a Ranchman."

Hunter-Trader-Trapper Company, Columbus, for permission to use certain statistics from E. A. Brininstool's "Fighting Red Cloud's Warriors."

The Century Company, New York, for quotations from magazine articles, "Besieged by the Utes," by Colonel E. V. Sumner, and "Chief Joseph the Nez Perce," by Major C. E. S. Wood, published in Century Magazine.

Thanks are also extended to the Bureau of American Ethnology, the War Department, and Professor C. W. Grace, Wichita, for valuable photographs used, and hereby acknowledged.

PAUL I. WELLMAN

FOREWORD

In the old West the beginnings of the Machine Age met the last vestiges of the Stone Age. The white man had just embarked upon the great industrial era; the red man still used the flint arrow point.

Between these two extremes of human culture there was no common ground. The Indian could not understand the Anglo-Saxon's land hunger. To him the earth and its creatures belonged to all, the free gift of the Great Mystery. That one should build a fence about a little corner of it and say "This is mine," was repugnant.

His ideas on war were equally at variance with those of the white man. To him war was a dangerous game, but still a game. It was a glorious, exciting field of honor, as it was to the knights-errant of medieval Europe. The grim, dour Anglo-Saxon attitude that war was something unpleasant to be gotten over quickly by scientifically exterminating the enemy, was new and often appalling.

The white man's greed added to the tension. Seeing the fair land, he reached forth to take it. His conquest of the West was iniquitous in its conception and its execution. Not even the excuse that it permitted the spread of civilization is moral justification.

In the inevitable wars which followed this clash of ideas and interests, the Stone Age was foredoomed to defeat. The white man had the repeating rifle, the telegraph, and the railroad. The Indian had only his primitive weapons and his native courage. Remorselessly the Machine Age engulfed the wilderness.

But it was not without a struggle. There was manhood in the red race. For thirty years the Indian fought a sometimes heroic, often spectacular, always futile war for the possession of his hunting grounds. And it is the purpose of this volume to try to picture for the reader the moving panorama of that struggle; to catch for him a little of the glamour of those days, the action, the vivid color, the heroism and the despair.

PAUL I. WELLMAN

CONTENTS

I.

MASSACRE IN MINNESOTA
1862–1863

Chapter I

THE STORM BREAKS

A SABBATH IN THE BACKWOODS

The soft green hills of Minnesota lay placid in the August sun. Oak and birch and pine scarcely stirred in the breeze which brought a hint of coolness to the drowsy atmosphere, and the woodland lakes, which are the northland's chief charm, were barely ruffled.

Quiet was the forest which stretched its leagues on leagues of feathery tops to the northward. Even the birds were silent, for this was August. In the few small fields which the industry of the backwoodsmen had cleared out of the woods, no farmer moved. Scythe and hoe hung idle on their hooks. It was Sunday.

At the Lower Sioux Agency near Fort Ridgely, the morning of August 17th, 1862, services were held as usual in the little Episcopal church. The rector addressed his simple words of faith to a mixed congregation—English and German farmers, a few agency employees and traders, and a handful of converted Sioux Indians. But his eyes probably wandered most frequently to a single dark figure which sat, morose and alone, in the shadows at the back of the church.

We have a photograph of him as he must have looked then—that silent communicant. He was a tall and splendid figure in his neat black broadcloth, with white collar and dark cravat; dressed as well as the best garbed white man

3

among them. Only his head and feet were in sharp contrast. His feet were covered with doe-skin moccasins, beaded according to the highest art of the Indian race. His head was bare and the swarthy bronze of his face was framed in two gleaming black braids of hair which swept downward over his shoulders, to fall across his broad chest in front.

If anybody in the church felt a shrinking from his dark presence, they gave no sign, for they all knew him. He was Little Crow, the great chief of the Santee Sioux, the steadfast friend of the white man, their guarantee of peace with the dark people of the forests.

The service ended. With perfect courtesy he greeted the white men and women assembled. Suavely he complimented the rector's eloquence; shook hands with everybody; strode out, mounted his horse and rode off—never to return.

Little Crow attended church that Sunday morning. By evening of the next day he was elbow-deep in the blood of those with whom he had worshipped.

THE BEGINNING OF THE MASSACRE

Why did Little Crow attend that last service? Nobody will ever know. Many have held it was for the purpose of cloaking the treachery which must already have been planned and ordered. But the reason may have been more human. Perhaps the dark chief came to be once more with the friends from whom he was to part forever.

Little Crow was an unusual Indian. He affected the white man's garb and ways, but was at heart an utter barbarian. His manners were those of a refined gentleman. His diplomatic talent and oratorical ability were very marked. And events were to prove him a patriot.

His friendship for the whites had once been genuine, but it was blasted long ago. An endless list of his people's grievances cried out to him. Rascally traders, using government red tape to withhold food from the starving red men, to sell them wormy flour and spoiled bacon at exorbitant prices; the seduction of Indian women by degenerate white men and the multiplication of halfbreed children, a reproach and indignity to every honorable Sioux; Inkpaduta in the north, counting the spoils of his Spirit Lake raid and inciting to the war path; these and many other things fanned the smouldering flame.

Above all his tribe, Little Crow felt the wrong and the dishonor. A son and grandson of chiefs, he had known the days of his people's glory. Then came the shameful Mendota treaty of 1851, when the Sioux ceded most of their hunting grounds. He played his own part when, after a drunken fight with his brother, he nursed a crippled wrist and swore to banish firewater from the tribe. He sent for a Christian missionary to "teach the people the white man's way." Reverend Williamson, the man of God, won a place in Little Crow's heart, but now his goodness was all forgotten in the rascality of those other white men, the traders.

Only a week before the Sioux received the final insult. Their chiefs went to the agency to plead for the long-promised government stores. Andrew J. Myrick, a trader, listened with a sneer.

"If they're hungry, let them eat grass for all I care," was his callous reply.[1] The Sioux heard—and remembered.

. . . .

Forty miles from the agency three German farmers and the wife and daughter of one of them, sat at Sunday din-

[1] William Watts Folwell, "A History of Minnesota," p. 233, by permission of the Minnesota Historical Society.

ner. Four Indians entered the cabin. A crash of rifles, a
flurry of knives—the happy dinner party lay dead. The
Indians rode into the forest.

It was a signal. Up and down the Minnesota River
stealthy bands of warriors set forth.

Monday dawned. With the first peep of the sun, the
little community of traders at the Lower Agency was awakened by a gunshot, followed by a hideous war whoop. The
people ran out of their homes into the streets to be shot
down at their doors by Sioux posted in ambush. Myrick,
whose cruel taunt had stirred the Indians' hatred, was
killed in front of his store. When his body was found, days
later, the mouth was stuffed full of grass.[2]

Other traders met ends as bloody. Francois La Bathe was
slain on his counter. Henry Belland, James W. Lyndy and
five other traders and clerks died similarly. Every soul in
the agency would have perished but the Sioux began looting the ammunition stores and food boxes, permitting about
fifty to reach the river. There a heroic ferryman, Hubert
Millier,[3] plied his boat until as he returned for the last
load he was killed. Those cut off from crossing were all
massacred and the Indians pursued the refugees, slaying
seven more in the terrible fifteen-mile race to Fort Ridgely.

The arrival of the haggard vanguard of that fleeing
band must have been a terrific shock to the people of the
fort. The whole world was shocked by the events which
followed.

The agency massacre was not the only tragedy of the
morning.[4] While the Sioux were killing the traders,

[2] Folwell, "A History of Minnesota," p. 233.
[3] The name is also given as Mauley.
[4] There are tales of frightful brutality during these raids. Governor Ramsey
said in a speech: "But massacre itself had been mercy if it could have purchased
exemption from the revolting circumstances with which it was accompanied—
infants hewn into bloody chips of flesh, or nailed to doorposts to linger out their

smaller parties swept through the surrounding settlements. The country was a shambles. The Indians took the farms as they came, slaughtering the men, carrying the young women off as captives, and butchering the children or allowing them to follow their mothers, according to the whim of the moment.

Lake Shetek and Renville County were especially bloody. In the first day alone more than two hundred white persons were killed in the vicinity of the Lower Agency. How anybody escaped is a mystery. Some of the experiences of the refugees are almost unbelievable. Tales of heroism also come down to us from that massacre. Men and women, even children, sacrificed themselves to save their friends.[5]

The exact number massacred will never be known. Min-

---

little lives in mortal agony . . . rape joined to murder in one awful tragedy . . . whole families burned . . ."

The above statement sounds like some of the anti-German propaganda circulated in this country during the World War. It is only fair to the Indians to say that these atrocities occurred only in isolated instances if at all. Most of the settlers were mercifully killed at once. The Indian viewpoint is well summed up by Dr. Folwell: "From the white man's point of view these operations amounted simply to massacre, an atrocious and utterly unjustifiable butchery of unoffending citizens . . . The Indian, however, saw himself engaged in war, the most honorable of all pursuits, against men who, as he believed, had robbed him of his country and his freedom . . . He was making war on the white people in the same fashion in which he would have gone against the Chippewa or the Foxes. There are a few instances of . . . mutilation . . . There are also cases of tenderness and generosity to captives." ("A History of Minnesota," p. 125.)

[5] The story of 11-year-old Merton Eastlick and his devotion to his baby brother Johnny is worth re-telling. When the Indians struck Lake Shetek settlement, the Eastlick family hid with other settlers in the rushes of a stream bed. The Sioux found them, killed John Eastlick, the father, and three of the five boys. Mrs. Eastlick was captured. Before they found her, she hid her baby, Johnny, and charged his only surviving brother, Merton, never to leave him until he died. Mrs. Eastlick eventually escaped from the Indians and was found by August Garzine, a mail carrier, crazed with the belief that her whole family was dead. He took her to New Ulm. On the way, forty miles from the scene of the massacre, they found Merton and Johnny! The lad had carried the baby every foot of the way, hiding from Indians and subsisting on berries. He was an emaciated skeleton, with the flesh worn off his bare feet and was unable to speak for days afterward. But the baby was safe and sound.

nesota state records list six hundred and forty-four.[6]
There were hundreds, mostly women, taken captive. After
the Battle of Wood Lake, two hundred and sixty-nine of
these were recovered. Scores were rescued at other times.
And the record of those who were never heard of again
will never be complete.

CAPTAIN MARSH'S DEBACLE

And what were the soldiers at Fort Ridgely, fifteen
miles from the Lower Agency, doing all this time?

Captain John S. Marsh, 5th Minnesota, was in command. As the first of the refugees burst into the fort with
their frightened story, Marsh acted quickly. Sending a
courier to Fort Snelling for help, he started promptly for
the agency with forty-six men and the post interpreter,
Peter Quinn, leaving only a skeleton guard behind. They
went in wagons but dismounted a mile from their destination. On the way they met a stream of fugitives. Here and
there they passed dead bodies. They began to realize that
they were in the midst of a great disaster—an Indian uprising of nightmare proportions.

---

[6] The Minnesota Historical Society's figures on the massacre are as follows:

Citizens Massacred

In Renville County (including reservations)	221
In Dakota Territory (including Big Stone Lake)	32
In Brown County (including Lake Shetek)	204
In all other frontier counties	187
	644

Soldiers Killed in Battle

Lower Sioux Ferry, Capt. Marsh's command	24
Ft. Ridgely and New Ulm	23
Wood Lake	17
Birch Coulie	26
Other engagements	23
	757

Unused to Indian fighting but supremely confident, young Marsh led his men down to the ferry. The Agency opposite was in flames. Not a soul could be seen. Had the Sioux left? No—at the very moment more than two hundred warriors were hiding behind saw logs and bushes with rifles cocked and aimed, ready to pull the triggers at a signal.

Now an Indian appeared among the burning buildings, walking toward the ferry. The soldiers recognized him— White Dog, a sub-chief and a frequent visitor at the fort. He motioned them to come across. Marsh hesitated. While he parleyed, a party of Sioux crossed unobserved farther down the river, and crept up on his flank.

Then White Dog made a gesture which must have been a signal. Clouds of smoke sprang up from a hundred apparently untenanted places. Marsh and his men suddenly found themselves fighting for their lives.

Half a dozen soldiers were killed in the first volley, including Quinn who was pierced by at least a dozen bullets. At the same moment the Indians on the flank opened fire. Marsh tried to charge into the thicket, saw it was useless, and ordered a volley fired instead. His men were falling fast. A retreat was finally ordered. They threw themselves into the timber near the river and for an hour fought an unequal battle with overwhelming numbers of Sioux, gradually retreating down the stream.

At length the captain decided to cross over. To show his men it was feasible, he tried to swim the swift current himself. The eddies caught him and he drowned—youthful, gallant, but utterly unfit to cope with Indian warriors.

The Sioux harried the rest of the soldiers almost to the fort. What was left of the command which had marched out so gallantly that morning, straggled in late in the eve-

ning. Of the forty-eight men who started, exactly half,
including the captain, were dead.

HOW RUSTY CANNON SAVED FORT RIDGELY

That was a night of terror at Fort Ridgely. Lieutenant
Thomas P. Gere, now commanding, had only a handful
of soldiers left and scores of women and children to protect. The women hysterically begged their friends to shoot
them rather than let the Indians get them. There were a
dozen alarms which set the post frantic with fear. But
nothing happened that night.

Next morning refugees still poured in, demoralized
with fright. Should Little Crow attack now, nothing could
prevent the massacre of every soul in the fort. But for
some reason the attack was delayed. Why? The nervous
young lieutenant paced the fort with anxious steps. About
noon a challenge from a sentry changed to a shout of joy.
Coming down a road from the north, at the double-quick,
was a detachment of soldiers—Lieutenant Timothy J.
Sheehan with the first reinforcements. Five hours later a
second detachment came in from the south, after an all-
night march of forty miles. There were more than two
hundred and fifty refugees at the fort now. Among them
were some resolute men who would make good fighters.
Including these settlers, Sheehan, now the senior officer,
marshaled about one hundred and eighty men, mostly raw
recruits.

Still the Indians did not attack.[7] Every moment was
used in strengthening the defenses.

Without warning on the morning of the 20th, a tall
warrior, mounted on a splendid horse, rode up from the

[7] Sioux Indians afterward said Little Crow could not get his warriors to stop
plundering long enough to follow him to the attack. Whatever the cause, the delay was fatal to the Indian plans.

west and demanded a conference. It was Little Crow himself. He wanted to divert attention from his attack which was forming on the opposite side.

A sudden burst of firing announced the onslaught and the Sioux leader rode for cover. With wild yells the Indians stormed the first line of defenses, outside the regular limits of the fort. Helter-skelter fled the soldiers for safety, with Sioux tomahawks flashing in their rear. So fierce was the charge that the redskins actually burst through the second line of defense, a row of log houses which formed the north wall of the fort and took possession of these barracks.

Still the defense reeled. Working like mad, Sheehan rallied his men on the parade ground. If they did not hold fast here, the fort was doomed. Two or three soldiers, hit, fell thrashing on the ground. The undisciplined troops began to waver. Simultaneously the Sioux came out from the buildings and formed for another charge. Sheehan's men began to retreat. The day seemed hopelessly lost.

And then came aid—aid so unexpected as to seem miraculous.

Among the few veteran soldiers at the fort was an old artillery sergeant with the unromantic name of Jones. Fort Ridgely had once been an artillery post and a few old cannon of various patterns and calibres were still parked there. Like all old gunners, Sergeant Jones loved his field pieces. To vary the monotony of garrison life, he had asked and received permission to drill some of the infantrymen in the principles of artillery practice. The soldiers took it up for fun. None of them had any idea that their lives and the lives of hundreds of others would ever hang upon their skill.

At this critical moment in the Sioux attack, Jones bethought himself of his amateur artillerymen and rusty old cannon. Here and there he hastily collected members of his gun squads and ran to where the ancient field pieces stood. There was some delay in getting things ready. The men were, after all, only infantrymen, and the old sergeant probably did some royal swearing before three guns were loaded. This was finished just as Sheehan's line began to melt before the Sioux fire and the threatened attack.

Now was the time. Everything depended upon the old artilleryman. His own wife and children were among the helpless non-combatants crowded in the south buildings of the fort.

"Aim in their center and fire as rapidly as possible," was the order.

Just as Sheehan, in despair, saw his recruits breaking for cover; just as Little Crow's warriors, with triumphant yells, began their final advance; just as the women in the south fort gave a concerted cry of terror, the ancient cannons spoke.

"*Boom! Boom! Boom!*"

Across the parade ground hurtled a heterogeneous collection of misfit cannon balls, canister and solid shot. Dismayed, the Indians halted.

Working like mad, the sergeant and his men rammed home a second round. Again the rusty field pieces spoke. It was too much for the Sioux. They could stand rifle fire —had done so right bravely. But the "wagon guns" appalled them. They wavered, began to retreat, and as a third discharge thundered among them, fled in panic, followed by the hysterical cheering of the soldiers.

Fort Ridgely was saved and Sergeant Jones was the hero of the day. The Sioux kept the fort surrounded, and even attempted another attack the following morning. But the age-worn cannon now were masters of the situation. Before the charge was well started, Sergeant Jones sent several shots among the hostiles and scattered them.[8] Little Crow had been wounded the first day. A sub-chief, Mankato, led that final abortive assault. The Indians quickly withdrew.

The defeat at Fort Ridgely was a solar-plexus blow to the Indians' hope of sweeping the white man out of Minnesota. They had suffered serious losses and the moral effect had been most discouraging.

[8] Jones was mentioned in the dispatches for his spectacular part in the battle. As for the modest hero himself, however, his only thought was of the workmanlike manner in which the guns were handled. In his terse report, still preserved, he stated that his amateur artillerymen and rusty cannon "gave much satisfaction . . . to all who witnessed the action."

CHAPTER II

THE WHITE MAN STRIKES BACK

THE DEFENSE OF NEW ULM

SHARING the post of greatest danger with Fort Ridgely was the little German frontier town of New Ulm, a few miles down the river. The morning after the agency massacre a small party of Indians were seen near the town but were driven off in a brief skirmish. Not much damage was done on either side but it threw New Ulm—already panic-stricken because of the inpouring hundreds of refugees with their tales of horror—into still greater terror.

Judge Charles E. Flandreau of the supreme court and Ex-sheriff Boardman of St. Peter's rode with a company of volunteers to the threatened settlement. The Indians had gone when they arrived, and next day the town was not molested for Little Crow was busy with his attack on Fort Ridgely. But the Sioux had by no means forgotten New Ulm. In spite of their defeat at the fort they moved toward it. Early Saturday the smoke of burning buildings up the river showed that they were on their way.

Judge Flandreau, a man of great force of character, was elected commander of the defending forces. At the approach of the Sioux he formed his two hundred and fifty fighting men on the prairie a half mile west of the town. By ten o'clock they were skirmishing with Little Crow's advance guard.

Suddenly a brilliant spectacle unfolded itself. Five hundred Sioux warriors, in all the color and movement of feathered head dresses, war paint and brilliant bead work, rode out of the woods and spread like a giant fan over the prairie. As they reached long rifle shot, they charged. The Sioux, yelling like fiends, looked so horrible that Flandreau's rookies began to retreat. A few more whoops and, in spite of the judge's efforts, the whole line fell back leaving the outer tiers of houses of the town undefended. The Indians were soon shooting at New Ulm's citizens from the shelter of their own homes. Flandreau rode wildly up the hill and succeeded in rallying his men. There they halted the Sioux advance. The crackling of rifle fire became incessant. The white men were hard pressed, but they held.

Then smoke came floating up from the lower end of the town. The Indians had slipped behind the defense and set some buildings ablaze. Now they advanced through the smoke. In a few minutes the whole lower part of New Ulm was burning. Bullets whined, in ever increasing chorus, up the streets. Captain William Dodd, Flandreau's second in command, was killed. Captain Saunders was critically wounded with a ball through his body.

Under cover of the smoke, Little Crow massed his warriors in the shelter of some houses near the river. The charge in the morning had been so nearly a complete success that the Sioux believed a second attack would crush the whites. But by now New Ulm had been under fire for several hours and the men were steadying down.[1] The Sioux charge came, but a withering fire drove them back. Then, as the Indians withdrew, Flandreau led a fiery counter-charge. It caught the Indians by surprise and

[1] "White men fight under a great disadvantage the first time they engage (the Indians). There is something so fiendish in their yells and terrifying in their appearance when in battle that it takes a good deal of time to overcome the sensation that it inspires"—Judge Flandreau's story of the battle.

drove them clear out of the city limits. Evening was falling and the firing shortly stopped.

During the night Flandreau ordered more than forty outlying buildings on the outskirts burned to the ground to prevent them from becoming rallying places for the savages on the morrow. A system of trenches was dug, and a large brick house made into a redoubt, garrisoned and munitioned. But there was no battle Sunday. The Sioux contented themselves with some long-range shooting. By noon Little Crow's warriors were in retreat.

SIBLEY TAKES COMMAND

Fort Ridgely and New Ulm definitely ended any probability that the Sioux would push the settlers out of eastern Minnesota. But Little Crow was not discouraged. The northeast, the north and even the south, down into Iowa where Inkpaduta had left a trail of blood years before at the Spirit Lake massacre, offered an unlimited field for his operations.

He withdrew his war parties into the wilderness for the present, content for a time to count his scalps and gloat over his booty. They had been repulsed, it is true, but, even so, the success of the weeks' raiding exceeded the Indians' most sanguine dreams. At one swoop the Sioux had won back much of their richest hunting country. Their camps were full of prisoners and plunder. Little Crow was a bigger man than ever among his people.

But a new figure was entering the picture. Colonel Henry H. Sibley, an old soldier in middle life, took command of the Minnesota troops. He had had wide experience, spoke French and the Dakota tongue and possessed a profound knowledge of Indian character.

Sibley reached the frontier in three days, and in four

Bureau of American Ethnology

Bureau of American Ethnology

Left: Cutnose, one of Little Crow's subordinates in the Minnesota uprising. Center: Little Crow (Cetan Wakan Mani), chief of the Santee Sioux in the Minnesota uprising in 1862. Right: Gen. H. H. Sibley, commanding U. S. forces opposed to the Sioux in Minnesota, 1862.

Red Cloud (Mahkpiya Luta), leader of the Sioux in their siege of Fort Phil Kearny.

more his call for volunteers was answered by fourteen hundred men. They were raw, undisciplined and ill-equipped, but they were the only force on which Sibley could lay his hand. With them he marched toward Fort Ridgely. It took several days to reach the fort. On the way he kept his fatigue details busy burying the bodies of slaughtered settlers. He reached the fort on the afternoon of August 28th, to be received with transports of joy by the people, who, he said, "seemed mad with excitement."

Next day he moved toward the Lower Agency, reaching it the last of August. His men buried Marsh's soldiers, together with more than twenty dead citizens. Traces of the handiwork of the Sioux were plentiful, but thus far not an Indian had been seen. Major J. R. Brown with two hundred men moved west along the river looking for hostiles and burying the dead. They camped at Birch Coulie the night of September 1st.

Little Crow was not asleep. His scouts watched, unseen, every movement of the army. Brown's movement was a beautiful opportunity for the Sioux. As dawn broke there was a war whoop, followed by a sudden volley which swept into the camp from the birch woods near at hand. Dead and dying men, and kicking, screaming horses, littered the ground. The survivors of that deadly volley threw themselves behind their wagons and fought back. It was a short but terrific little battle. The Sioux poured into the camp such a storm of bullets that nearly every horse was killed or disabled, and annihilation threatened the whole command.

But Sibley at the agency heard the distant firing and marched immediately to Brown's assistance. The reinforcements reached Birch Coulie in the nick of time. As Sibley's column appeared, the Sioux withdrew up the valley. A picture of bloody wreckage was presented by

Brown's camp. It was strewn with dead and dying men
and horses. Some of the wagons were riddled like sieves.
Of Brown's two hundred soldiers, twenty-four were dead
and sixty-seven wounded, nearly fifty percent. Sibley retreated to Fort Ridgely to care for the wounded.

Birch Coulie wiped out the sting of New Ulm and
Fort Ridgely for the Sioux. They considered honors even
now. Sibley, on the other hand, saw that his raw levies
were not ready for the job before them and went into
camp to drill them into some sort of a coherent military
body. It was a big task and took time. Meanwhile Little
Crow ranged far and wide.

He led one marauding expedition deep into northeast-
ern Minnesota, with Hutchinson as its objective. Captain
Richard Strout and a company of soldiers met him and
were chased for miles, the Sioux almost riding into Cedar
Mills on the strength of the wild retreat. But Hutchinson, now a fortified post like every frontier town, was too
strong for the Indians. Little Crow, with more scalps and
loot, returned to the old reservation camp.

THE BATTLE OF WOOD LAKE

While Sibley's army was learning its business, its commander took up wearisome days in a long-drawn negotiation with Little Crow. Hundreds of prisoners, mostly
women and children, were in the hostile camp and great
fear was held for their safety. Sibley, knowing Indians,
feared that these helpless hostages would be murdered
wholesale should he march against the Sioux.

The wily red chief proved more than his match in diplomacy, and Sibley finally gave up the negotiations.[2] Lit-

---

[2] Sibley was the center of a storm of abuse and criticism as he waited. The
newspapers grew restive. One dubbed him a "a snail who falls back on his authority and assumed dignity and refuses to march." Another referred to him as

tle Crow was making constant raids and keeping all Minnesota in an uproar. Finally, on September 18th, with sixteen hundred men and two pieces of artillery, Sibley marched northwest toward the Yellow Medicine River where the hostile village was reported to be.

Little Crow knew this march was in deadly earnest. He felt his handicaps. His warriors were fine natural fighters, but they completely lacked organization. They would not stand up to artillery fire. To maneuver them in battle was practically impossible. On the other hand, they were superior in mobility and were expert in scouting and ambush. In planning the fight with Sibley, the chief kept all these things in mind.

The road to the Sioux village lay through the deep timbered gorge of the Yellow Medicine. Sibley had to pass through it. As he marched past Wood Lake down this canyon, a volley of shots rang out half a mile ahead. Indians had fired into a party of foragers. Three men were down, one mortally wounded.

Major Welsh's command went at the double to the rescue. The foragers were saved, but heavy firing which broke out from the woods ahead showed that they were swarming with Sioux. Bullets were cutting the leaves from the trees overhead so that they fell in showers.

Little Crow had thrown a cloud of warriors across the road in front. Although the whites did not yet know it, two other large bodies of Indians lay hidden in ambush— one along the east side of the road, the other in a ravine to the right.

It was strange fighting for Sibley's men. The woods ahead looked deserted except for the spurts of rifle smoke and the sight of an occasional flitting figure. The constant

"the state undertaker with his company of grave diggers," an allusion to his burial of hundreds of dead settlers.

piping of bullets overhead and the occasional smack as one found its mark, made the raw troops nervous. Welsh decided to charge. Into the woods went his men but the foe they expected to meet had disappeared. Using the same tactics which were so fatal to Braddock a hundred years before, the Sioux slipped away from the direct front and poured in their fire from the flank. Welsh was forced to halt.

A staff officer came riding like the wind across the field with an order from Sibley to retire, but the stubborn major did not at once comply. Sibley sent another, this time peremptory, message to fall back at once. Then Welsh ordered a retreat.

Sibley's main body was formed on a low hill. Toward it Welsh started, carrying his wounded. The Sioux leaped in pursuit. There was a moment of hand-to-hand fighting. Then the soldiers began to run. Here was Little Crow's big chance. Had he been able to press home a charge at the backs of the fleeing troops, he might have cut Sibley's line in two. But Sibley rushed forward five companies under Colonel Marshall and the Indians were beaten back.

Then, too late, after the soldiers were formed and ready, the Sioux attacked in deadly earnest. For two hours they tried valorously to take the hill. Once a headlong charge on the extreme left came very near carrying home, but Major R. N. McLaren, with two companies of recruits, repulsed it.

Just then the Indians in the ravine were discovered. Backed by shells from the two guns, Marshall charged and drove them out. The Sioux had been roughly handled and were losing their zest for the fight. As the day wore on, the fire from the woods slackened. Finally, as if at a signal, the Indians disappeared.

Sibley, hampered by his many wounded, camped where he was.[3]

THE END OF LITTLE CROW

That must have been a gloomy night in the Sioux village. Little Crow recognized the completeness of his defeat in a final stand on a chosen battle ground. He could no longer hold his people together. The Sioux broke up their great camp and scattered all over the plains. Sibley said he permitted their escape because he knew that if pressed too closely they would slaughter their white captives. As a matter of fact, Little Crow did try hard to have the prisoners killed after the battle. But the chiefs saw their doom and wanted to soften the punishment. They refused. Little Crow's influence had ended.

Days passed. Through friendly Indians, Sibley got in touch with three trustworthy chiefs, offering amnesty and pardon if they would bring the prisoners to him. The offer was accepted. On the afternoon of September 26th, two hundred and sixty-nine captives were delivered, most of them women and children. All wore Indian clothing. There were some refined and educated women among them. Others were ignorant immigrant settlers. But their consideration for each other was beautiful to see as they helped the sick and assisted with the young children. Most of them cried with joy and relief. But some merely gave vacant stares. The scenes and experiences through which they had passed had left them dazed and stolid.

[3] An interesting sidelight, showing the character of Sibley, is the following: Several dead Sioux were found after the battle, although most of them were carried away. Next day Sibley published a general order expressing extreme pain and humiliation over the scalping of these Indians and threatening punishment for a repetition of the offense. "The bodies of the dead," read the order, "even of a savage enemy, shall not be subjected to indignities by civilized and Christian men."

That night the rescued captives slept in the tents of the soldiers, the men taking the hard ground outside. They were sent down to Fort Ridgely the following day and their relatives—if any were left living—claimed them.

.   .   .   .

The war in Minnesota was over. But there still remained to be written the punishment of its chief figures.

Sibley rounded up fifteen hundred of the Sioux and placed them in prisons at Fort Snelling and Mankato. The rest scattered far and wide over the plains, carrying the seeds of their grievance to the other tribes, the results of which will be noted later.

At a great court martial, three hundred and ninety-two prisoners, accused of extreme barbarity, were tried. Of these three hundred and seven were sentenced to death and sixteen to prison. President Lincoln commuted the death sentences of all but thirty-nine whose cruelties had been too clearly shown, and on December 28th a great concourse witnessed the execution of these unfortunates on a special gallows built for the purpose.

Little Crow was still at large. Although his followers had all deserted him, there were reports that he was gathering new strength and preparing for another invasion. Every day or so fresh rumors were printed in the newspapers and so much fear was attached to his name that it was practically impossible to get the settlers to return to their homes.

Nathan Lampson and his son Chauncey were deer hunting in the north woods on July 3rd, 1863. Stealing through the thickets, they surprised two Indians picking berries. Hostiles were still scattered all over the country. No Sioux was a friend. The elder Lampson fired, wounding one of the Indians. The other tried to help him on a horse. As the wounded Sioux attempted to fire at his father, Chauncey Lampson shot him dead. The other Indian mounted and escaped.

The Lampsons scalped the body and carted it to the neighboring town of Hutchinson. Nobody could identify it. Some claimed they noted a resemblance to Little Crow, but the complexion seemed too light. The mortifying corpse was thrown into the offal pit of a slaughter house.

Then came an unexpected revelation. A party of Indians was captured on Devil's Lake, among whom was a sixteen-year-old boy. He said he was a chief and asking for the commander of the troops by whom he was captured, made a statement of which the following is a part:

"I am the son of Little Crow; my name is Wo-wi-nap-sa. I am sixteen years old. . . . Father hid after the soldiers beat us last fall. He told me he could not fight against the white men, but would go below and steal horses from them . . . and then he would go away off. Father . . . wanted me to go with him to carry his bundles. . . . There were no horses . . . we were hungry . . . Father and I were picking red berries near Scattered Lake. . . . It was near night. He was hit the first time in the side, just above the hip. . . . He was shot the second time . . . in the side, near the shoulder. This was the shot that killed him. He told me he was killed and asked me for water. . . . He died immediately after."

Sibley read the statement and at once concluded that the Indian killed by the Lampsons was Little Crow. The corpse was hauled out of its noisome resting place and there was observed a mark of identification which could not be mistaken. A deformity of his right wrist, caused by a gunshot wound received in a family feud when he was a youth, was the mark.

So died Little Crow, at the height of his power the most

feared red man in America; leader of the greatest massacre in history; a scholar and a gentleman after his way. He started on the white man's path but left it when his people's wrongs cried out to him. Reduced to stripping red berries to keep life in his frame, he was at last shot by wandering hunters and his body thrown into the stinking offal pit of a slaughter house.

II.

WAR SPREADS TO THE PLAINS
1864–1869

CHAPTER III

A CHIEF OF THE OGALALLAS

IN THE BEGINNING

LIFE was good on the high plains of the Dakotas before the white man came. The Teton Sioux wandered in leisurely, light-hearted fashion wherever the whim moved them. Buffalo moved in dark masses on the grasslands; the Black Hills and the Rockies were populous with deer, beaver, bear and other game. The Sioux were great hunters, and starvation was usually far from their teepees. They were great warriors and near at hand were their traditional enemies, Crows, Pawnees, Flatheads, Shoshones and Blackfeet, who were so necessary to them, for how else should the Sioux braves win honor? Everything was ideally arranged for the simple happiness of this people. The skill of the squaws provided every necessity. The world was full of pleasant valleys; Wakan Tanka, the Great Mystery, smiled on his children.

In an Ogalalla teepee, about 1822, was born a baby boy. His father had no particular distinction, except that he died a drunkard. What the boy, Red Cloud, made of himself was due to his own personal traits, not to any family influence. There has never been a satisfactory explanation of how he got his name. No matter; he made it notable in history. His early years were typical of the boys of his tribe. He became a skillful hunter, a magnificent horseman, and could hold his own with any in feats of skill, speed, strength and agility. Very early he gained fame as a warrior and leader. Even in his early twenties he had his following.

The Teton Sioux loved fighting. Their five great tribes, the Ogalallas, Unkpapas, Sans Arcs, Brulés and Minneconjous, had frequent war parties in the field. Red Cloud had plenty of chances to distinguish himself.

The whole theory of war among the Sioux was different from that of the civilized white man. It resembled in many respects the feudal system of the middle ages. There was a certain wild chivalry, for example. A brave enemy was often spared rather than ruthlessly killed.[1] The warriors looked upon war as an opportunity to win honor. There was always greater rivalry to do some deed of stark daring, than merely to inflict damage upon the enemy.

Some of their exploits seem quixotic to our modern standards. The brave who charged into battle and struck his armed, unwounded enemy with his coup-stick or open hand, received more distinction for it than did the man who killed and scalped his enemy. The man who stole into a hostile camp and crept out leading a single horse whose lariat he had cut among the teepees was applauded more than the man who ran off a whole herd of ponies grazing unguarded outside of the village.

The analogy goes farther. Instead of definite military divisions, such as regiments, companies and squads, each with its appropriate officers, the Sioux fighting units were based on the prestige of various chiefs, exactly as medieval lords ranked according to the number of retainers they could muster. Renowned Sioux leaders had big bands of

---

[1] Sitting Bull's preservation of Frank Grouard and Little Assinboine (Jumping Bull) are good examples of this frequent habit among the plains Indians. Yellow Nose, one of the most famous of the Northern Cheyenne warriors, was a Ute who had been captured and adopted into the tribe.

warriors. Each of these bands operated separately and retained the characteristics of an autonomous nation. It levied its own wars, moved to suit itself and was generally independent. Occasionally two or three bands would combine in a grand war party. But the idea of massing three or four thousand fighting men in the field and keeping them at it for months at a time was yet to come.

Living in this atmosphere of constant action, few of the Sioux noticed the black cloud, heavy with portent, which loomed on the horizon. The white man was beginning to seep across the plains in his strange, hysterical stampede over the mountains; was beginning to wander among the hills grubbing in the dirt, spoiling the little springs, for the dull yellow metal he prized above food and drink, above the love of his women, above honor even. There would be fighting—bitter, bloody fighting, not the glamorous, exciting battling of the Indian paladins—and the Sioux were to learn a new name, Red Cloud.

There had been war for some time in the south. The settlers in Kansas resented the presence of the Cheyennes and Kiowas on their frontier. The Indians were angered by the constant streams of immigrants who moved down the Santa Fe and Platte River trails on their way to California and Oregon. The caravans of covered wagons made much noise, what with the creaking wheels, the shouts of mule skinners, the cracking of whips, the bellowing of cattle, and the general hubbub which always accompanies the white man wherever he goes. As a result the buffalo and antelope moved out of the country. It was ruined as a hunting ground.

The exasperated Indians made more than one attack on these wagon trains. And the white men in revenge fired upon the next band they met—often killing Indians who knew nothing of any former attack and who approached them with the friendliest of intentions. This aroused still deeper enmity among the Indians and the vicious circle continued until all of western Kansas and Colorado were in a state of warfare.

In the summer of 1857, Colonel E. V. Sumner campaigned against the Cheyennes. There were several clashes with troops in later years. And on the morning of November 29th, 1864, Colonel J. M. Chivington, a fanatical ex-preacher, with a regiment of "hundred days men," led the notorious Sand Creek massacre, in which he destroyed the friendly Cheyenne villages of Black Kettle and White Antelope, although they were under the protection of Major Wynkoop of Fort Lyon.

The Sand Creek massacre had far-reaching effects. The Cheyennes carried the war pipe to the Sioux, and Sitting Bull and other Sioux chiefs smoked it with them.[2] But Red Cloud was already definitely on the war path. Streaming westward, harried out of Minnesota, had come the Santee Sioux by hundreds, telling of Little Crow's war and the causes of it. Red Cloud and the Tetons heard and sympathized.

When, in the summer of 1865, Major General G. M. Dodge, commanding the Department of the Missouri, sent four columns of troops up the Missouri to further punish the Santees, the Teton Sioux joined their relatives in the war. Red Cloud rode and skirmished with the soldiers under Generals Sully, Conner, Cole and Walker. He joined the Cheyennes in an attack on Colonel Sawyer's military train which was marching up the Niobrara River to open a wagon train to the Montana gold fields. The fight was inconclusive. Sawyer paid Red Cloud an indem-

---

[2] Stanley Vestal, "Sitting Bull, Champion of the Sioux," p. 70. References to this work hereafter are by permission of the publishers, Houghton-Mifflin Co.

nity of a wagon load of sugar, coffee and rice on his promise to withdraw. The chief was true to his promise but some other Sioux came up who had not shared in the provisions and the soldiers had to fight in spite of the indemnity.

The Harney-Sanborne treaty was signed in 1865. Spotted Tail, Man-Afraid-of-His-Horses [3] and other chiefs conceded the white man a safe passage through their lands. Red Cloud was not present. He was in his teepee critically wounded by a Crow arrow. Shortly before, on a raid against the Crows, an arrow fired from ambush had struck him squarely in the middle of the back and passed completely through so that its barbed head stuck out from his breast. He was carried out of danger and a medicine man had tried to draw the arrow out. The feather at the back and the barbs in front prevented the shaft from being withdrawn. At length the medicine man had cut off the head, after which the arrow was drawn out. By a miracle no vital organs were pierced and Red Cloud eventually recovered.

He was set against allowing the provisions of the Harney-Sanborne treaty to be carried out. More far-sighted than his fellows, he saw the inevitable disaster to his country if ever the white man were allowed to set foot firmly in it. With Red Cloud urging them on, the turbulent younger warriors of the Sioux kept up a series of depredations which at length forced the government to send out a second treaty commission in the spring of 1866 to offer the Sioux new terms.

[3] "His Sioux name, Tashunka Kokipapi, is not properly interpreted; it really means that the bearer was so potent in battle that the mere sight of his horses inspired fear."—Frederick W. Hodge, "Handbook of American Indians," Bureau of American Ethnology Bulletin 30.

RED CLOUD'S DEFIANCE AND THE FOUNDING OF
FORT PHIL KEARNEY

The great council was held at Fort Laramie. Red Cloud was present. He was now the foremost warrior of his nation and his influence was steadily thrown against the white man's proposals.

A spectacular incident broke up the council, precipitated war, and made Red Cloud, for the time at least, supreme arbiter of his people. While the council was in session, a column of troops, led by General Henry B. Carrington, rode up. They were on the way to the Powder River Country, in defiance of the very spirit of the peace council, to erect a row of forts, and apparently did not even know the council was in session.

Carrington rode up, dismounted, and was being introduced to the members of the commission, when Red Cloud dramatically leaped on the platform under the shade of the pine boughs, pointed to Carrington's colonel's shoulder straps [4] and shouted that he was the "White Eagle" who had come to steal a road through the Indians' land. The dramatic suddenness of the gesture riveted the attention of the Indians. Then he turned and, followed by every eye, sprang from the platform, ordered his teepees struck and led his band out on the prairie, openly announcing he was going on the war path.

That broke up the council. For some days the older chiefs of the other Sioux bands remained sullenly in conclave, but their young men were melting away like snow in summer, to join the standard raised in such spectacular manner by Red Cloud. Finally in sheer self-defense, to

[4] Although a general officer in the Civil War, Carrington held a colonelcy in the regular army. As everybody knows the colonel's insignia is a silver eagle on the shoulder strap. This was the figure to which Red Cloud alluded in his dramatic charge.

protect their own prestige, the older chiefs followed. Red Cloud was the greatest figure in the Sioux Nation. He had made the Sioux come to him. Now they looked to him for orders.

In the meantime Carrington marched into the Powder River country looking for a spot to erect a fort. The government wanted a string of posts built to protect the Bozeman trail over which thousands of emigrants were ready to travel to the new gold districts of Idaho and Montana. Carrington found an ideal location on the banks of Piney Creek, a branch of the Powder River and began construction of Fort Phil Kearney. Later a second post, known as Fort C. F. Smith was built ninety-one miles to the north.

The establishment of Fort Phil Kearney was equivalent to a declaration of war, if any such declaration was needed. Red Cloud smoked with many chiefs and tribes in those days. He was the prime mover in the hostilities against the white man. But there were many who saw eye to eye with him in the matter. Crazy Horse, the young paladin of the Ogalallas was one. There were Black Shield and High Backbone of the Minneconjous, who were just as eager as he to fight. They knew that the white man was eating up their land, driving away their buffalo, destroying their forests.

The Sioux gathered in magnificent response to Red Cloud's call. At times their huge encampment extended for miles up and down the Little Goose River. Estimates of as high as fifteen thousand Indians were made for this camp, with upward of four thousand fighting men. This number is probably too high. But, even so, it was the most imposing fighting force the Sioux had ever put into the field.

CHAPTER IV

FORT PERILOUS

THE CIRCLE OF DEATH

No FINER natural cavalry ever existed than the Sioux, according to such authorities as General George Crook and General Frederick Benteen. Yet they were unfitted for conducting a sustained siege. Their ideas of organization were the most rudimentary, discipline was utterly lacking as our modern armies know it, and they had no knowledge of scientific warfare. In spite of this, the Sioux, largely because of the leadership of Red Cloud, besieged Fort Phil Kearney for more than two years. There are writers who have denied that Red Cloud played the dominating role ascribed to him in the campaign. It is true that Indians are prone to exaggerate not only their own importance but that of the leaders of their individual bands, so that it is often difficult to discover who was the actual commander in a given encounter. Still the impression of Red Cloud's importance and of the part he played is too well established to be dismissed from history.

General Carrington began building the fort on July 15th. Less than forty-eight hours later, at daybreak of the 17th, the Indians made their first attack. Part of the post horses were stampeded, and in a brisk little fight two soldiers were killed and three wounded. Later that day, the same war party scooped up the outfit of Louis Gazzous, a traveling sutler, and killed six men. In the next twelve

days five wagon trains were attacked, fifteen men killed
and much livestock run off. On July 24th Carrington wrote
for reinforcements. He already knew the implacability of
his enemy.

The Sioux did not formally invest the fort. But they
planted scouting parties everywhere about it. The soldiers
found they had a foe who never slept. Did a herder stray
from his guard? He was cut off and killed. Did a sentry
expose himself on the palisade during a moonlit night?
A bullet from the bush laid him low. Did a detachment of
soldiers set out without an imposing display of power?
They straightway had to fight for their very existence.

Even during the long, bitter cold spells the Indians kept
the circle of death about the post. That was not like the
Sioux, whose custom was to withdraw to their camps during cold weather. Better than anything else that showed
the grim purpose of their leader.

There was an atmosphere of constant dread about the
fort, reflected in the letters the soldiers wrote home. And
the feeling was justified by the circumstances. In the first
six months from August 1st to December 31st the Sioux
killed one hundred and fifty-four persons at or near Fort
Phil Kearney, wounded twenty more and captured nearly
seven hundred head of livestock. Fifty-one times they
made hostile demonstrations. It was a hectic existence for
the garrison.

In spite of this constant pressure the men worked on the
building of the fort with dogged courage. The country
about was hilly but barren, and the nearest forests from
which stockade posts could be obtained were seven miles
away. An enormous amount of wood was required for the
huge rectangular palisade, sixteen hundred feet long by
six hundred feet wide, to say nothing of the corral for several hundred horses and mules and the forty-two build-

ings in the post. Large parties of men continuously felled timber and hauled it to the fort. At times this "wood train" numbered one hundred and fifty members.

All through those six months not a man left the stockade without knowing that he might never see it again. They worked with their rifles close at hand and a guard stood constantly under arms. Even so, men were frequently cut off and killed. Sometimes soldiers disappeared and no trace of them was ever found. That meant one thing: they had been captured and carried away for torture.[1]

CAPTAIN FETTERMAN'S BOAST

Captain William J. Fetterman was a soldier by birth, instinct and profession. His Civil War record was brilliant. He went to Fort Phil Kearney because it promised plenty of action. From the first he disapproved of Carrington's tactics. Fetterman arrived in November. On December 6th he had a chance at the action he craved and an opportunity to test the mettle of his tawny foe.

On that day frantic signalling from the lookout on nearlooming Pilot Hill showed that the wood train was attacked two miles from the fort and forced to corral. Fetterman, with forty men, including Lieutenants Grummond, Bingham and Wands, and Captain Fred H. Brown, dashed to the rescue, while Carrington and twenty-five troopers rode over the Piney to take the Indians in the rear.

---

[1] "A favorite method of torture was to 'stake out' the victim. He was stripped of his clothing, laid on his back on the ground and his arms and legs, stretched to the utmost, were fastened by thongs to pins driven into the ground. In this state he was not only helpless, but almost motionless. All this time the Indians pleasantly talked to him. It was all a kind of a joke. Then a small fire was built near one of his feet. When that was so cooked as to have little sensation, another fire was built near the other foot; then the legs and arms and body until the whole person was crisped. Finally a small fire was built on the naked breast and kept up until life was extinct."—Colonel Richard I. Dodge, "Our Wild Indians," p. 526.

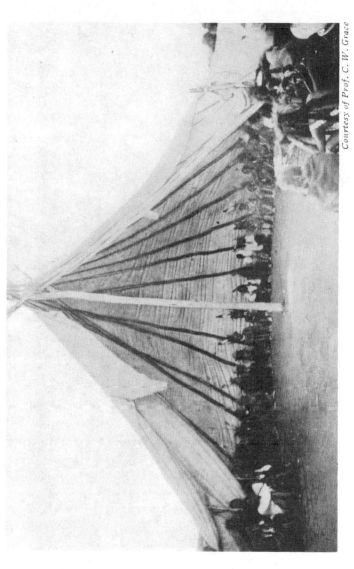

A Big Sioux council in session. This gives a good view of the chiefs and head men in the council lodge of the old days. The rank and file sat outside.

Sioux in council with government representatives. Note the flag flying over the council lodge.

Down the valley galloped the eager Fetterman. Dust rose ahead and they saw horsemen—Sioux. Guns began to speak and bullets kicked up little clouds of dirt around their horses' feet. But Fetterman's carbines were crackling too. The Sioux whipped their horses and rode hard down the valley. Five miles Fetterman chased them, his men shooting but not hitting any of the Indians. The wood train made its way on in to the fort unmolested.

Thus far the affair was fun. The pursuit turned a spur of the Sullivant Hills and the fort was shut out of view. In a twinkling the whole aspect of things changed. The Sioux stopped running. Other mounted warriors joined them. And now, yelping and shooting, they turned and charged.

At the Indian rush some of Fetterman's troopers whirled their horses and spurred as hard as they could for safety. He had only about twenty-five men left and the Sioux were four to one, but he held his ground. It looked as if it would be hand-to-hand in a minute, with the odds in favor of the enemy, when there was a clatter of hoofs, and Carrington, his sabre flashing, galloped around the spur at the head of his detachment.

Not knowing how many soldiers were following Carrington, the Sioux rode off. Fetterman was saved. But for the timely arrival of the post commander it would have been all over but the scalp dance. As it was, Lieutenant Bingham and Sergeant Rogers were dead. Lieutenant Grummond barely escaped with his life from the circle of barbaric foes. Five other soldiers were wounded.

It was a clever ambuscade and almost worked. The plan was a favorite one with the Sioux and Cheyennes—a small decoy party to lead the foe into the reach of the main body of warriors. In this case Indian lookouts were observed on the hills signalling the troop movements. Red Cloud's plans miscarried but were later put into effect.

As for the fire-eating Fetterman, it would be supposed that he should have derived some wisdom from the episode. But the opposite appears to have been the case. Only a short time after the fight he said: "Give me eighty men and I'll ride through the whole Sioux Nation."

If that remark ever got to Red Cloud's ears, it probably caused him considerable grim amusement.

WHERE IS FETTERMAN?

Two weeks passed. The morning of Friday, December 21st, dawned bright and cheery, the sun gleaming on the snow in the hills. Carrington surveyed the almost completed fort with a creator's pride. One more consignment of logs, he estimated, would finish the hospital building, the last structure to be built.

That morning a wood train of fifty-five men started to the hills. At eleven o'clock the Pilot Hill lookout began violently signalling. The wood train had been attacked again.

"Boots and Saddles," sounded the bugles. Carrington quickly told off forty-nine men from the 18th Infantry and twenty-seven from the 2nd Cavalry for the relief. He ordered Captain James Powell, experienced and cool-headed, to take command, but Fetterman came up and begged so hard for the assignment, urging his seniority, that the general gave in. Lieutenant Grummond volunteered to lead the cavalry. Captain Brown, soon to be transferred to Fort Laramie, asked to go along. He considered Indians a sort of game to be hunted and was crazy "to get a scalp." A couple of old Indian fighters, Wheatley and Fisher, likewise went, with their new Henry breech-

loading rifles which they "wanted to try on the red-skins."
Every man was mounted, including the infantry, and they
carried Spencer carbines and revolvers or Springfield muskets. Ammunition was low so they were not very well supplied. Still, they looked formidable enough as they rode
out of the fort, eighty-one officers and men. Now was the
time for Fetterman to "ride through the Sioux Nation."

Carrington, who knew his reckless subordinate, seems to
have feared that some such thought was in his mind. He
gave Fetterman specific orders: "Relieve the wood train,
drive back the Indians but on no account pursue the Indians beyond Lodge Trail Ridge." To make sure he was
not misunderstood, he repeated the orders to Grummond.

Instead of heading south of the Sullivant Hills where
he heard the firing, Fetterman rode north of the hills
toward Lodge Trail Ridge, which he occupied with his men
in skirmish order shortly after noon. As he did so, the
lookout signalled the wood train was no longer being attacked.

Now an alarming thing happened. Fetterman's command, after a brief halt on the ridge, disappeared on the
other side. He had deliberately disobeyed orders.

·   ·   ·   ·   ·   ·   ·   ·   ·

Fetterman perhaps merited all the censure that has been
heaped on his head for that disobedience. But a wiser man
than he might well have fallen victim to the uncanny skill
of the trap which was prepared for him.

As he mounted the ridge he saw a handful of Indians
below him, riding so daringly near that the hot impulse to
pursue could not be denied. How was he to know that, in
the ravines running from each side of the draw, hid the
Sioux and Cheyennes in hundreds, their mounted men
clustering at the mouth of the ravine, to close the door of

the trap, while others in scores lay in the grass across the line of march?

The handful of warriors who so tantalized Fetterman were ten picked men, chosen as a high honor for this tremendously dangerous post. One of them was the famous Big Nose, brother of the great Cheyenne chief Little Wolf. As the soldiers started after the audacious decoys, Big Nose, greatly daring, whipped his horse back and forth in front of the troops, so close he seemed to be right among them, yet escaped from the hail of bullets unscathed.

At last the ten Indians divided into two groups, riding apart then criss-crossing. It was the signal to close in.

A wild whooping, a rush and the Cheyennes charged. Then the whole mass of Indians swept around the little band of soldiers. Some rode clear through the blue line. The troops grew rattled. Fetterman, Brown and the infantry stopped and became separated from Grummond's cavalry. These men died in the first fierce rush of the savages, stabbed and clubbed to death as they stood. But Grummond gathered his troopers around him on the ridge, surrounded by the yelling horde. Arrows glinted like a swarm of grasshoppers flashing across the sky.[2]

Suddenly, according to the Indian account, the officer commanding the cavalry (Grummond) went down, shot or beaten out of his saddle. The troopers grew panicky. Remorselessly the Indians followed them as they tried to retreat up the ridge. There was a final great rush, a desperate smother of flashing lances, tomahawks and clubs. Then all was quiet except for the whooping of the victors.

---

[2] Most of the Indians in this battle were armed only with bows and arrows. A few had old smooth-bore muskets. A very few must have had rifles. Only six of Fetterman's men died from bullet wounds. The rest were killed by arrows, lances or clubs.

Fetterman's command was dead to a man. His boast had proved empty and bitterly tragic.[3]

THE BLOODY TRAIL OF DISASTER

Back at the fort, Carrington, noting with alarm that Fetterman had disobeyed orders, looked around for somebody to send after him. Five minutes after the command disappeared heavy firing broke out. The roar of many guns was continuous and increased in volume. Everyone knew a hard battle was in progress. Surgeon Hines was sent with an orderly, with instructions to join Fetterman if possible. Hines quickly returned. There were too many Indians in the hills.

At that Carrington ordered Captain R. Ten Eyck, with every man who could be spared, to follow Fetterman. Followed by fifty-four soldiers, the captain galloped down the trail and began to ascend the ridge. It was noticed that the firing was diminishing in volume. What had happened? Were the Indians driven off? Or were the soldiers beaten? Carrington was nearly crazed with anxiety. He knew the men were ill supplied with ammunition. Then, just before Ten Eyck reached the summit, with three or four scattered shots the firing abruptly ceased altogether.

Ten Eyck in turn disappeared beyond the ridge. In a few minutes an orderly came spurring down the hill at the dead run. He rode into the fort with a message which filled every listener with dread.

"The valley on the other side of the ridge is filled with Indians, who are threatening me," wrote Ten Eyck. "The

[3] George Bird Grinnell gives the Indian story of this battle in full, "The Fighting Cheyennes," pp. 230-235. References to and quotations from this book used hereafter are with the permission of and by arrangement with the publishers, Charles Scribner's Sons.

firing has stopped. No sign of Fetterman's command. Send
a howitzer."

Back went the orderly with word that reinforcements
were coming. Forty men followed hard at his heels. At
the same time Carrington armed every non-combatant man
in the post, even released prisoners from the guard house
to man the palisades. No howitzer could be sent for lack
of horses.

When Ten Eyck crossed the ridge, more than two thousand Indians were in the valley he estimated. There was
no fighting going on. The warriors were dashing back and
forth, yelling, their war bonnets flying in the breeze, the
dust rising. It was cold. The temperature was falling,
presaging the blizzard soon to come. Ten Eyck did not
descend the hill until the reinforcements arrived. By that
time the Indians were gone.

Cautiously Ten Eyck moved down the road. Quite
without warning he came upon the ghastly evidence of a
terrible disaster. In a little space enclosed by huge rocks
were the bodies of Fetterman and Brown and forty-seven
of their men. This was where the infantry had been over-
whelmed. It was a horrible sight. The bodies of the dead
were stripped, scalped, shot full of arrows and mutilated.[4]

Fetterman and Brown had bullet holes in their left tem-
ples from weapons held so close that the powder had
burned their faces. They had "saved their last shots for
themselves," to escape capture and torture.

Ten Eyck brought the forty-nine corpses to the fort in
wagons. It was now bitter cold and night was setting in.
With darkness, preparations were made to resist the expected Indian attack. Double guards were placed and in

---

[4] "Years afterwards the Sioux showed a rough, knotty war club of burr oak,
driven full of nails and spikes, which had been used to beat the soldiers' brains
out. It was still covered with brains and hair, glued to it in clotted blood."
—J. P. Dunn, "Massacres in the Mountains," p. 495.

every barrack a non-commissioned officer and two men stood watch. The surviving officers did not sleep. But the night passed without attack.

Morning dawned cold and blustery with a blizzard threatening. Carrington, disregarding the advice of his officers, took eighty men and went to learn the fate of Grummond and the thirty-two missing men. As he left, he ordered every woman and child placed in the magazine with an officer sworn not to allow a single one to fall into the Indians' hands alive. If the Indians captured the fort, he was to blow up the magazine.

Evidences of the fight multiplied as Carrington reached the fatal ridge. Dead cavalry horses were scattered along the trail. Here and there they found bodies of slaughtered soldiers. A quarter of a mile beyond the scene of greatest carnage lay Grummond. Still farther were the corpses of a dozen men, grouped together with many empty cartridge shells about them. To one side were the dead frontiersmen, Wheatley and Fisher, with a heap of empty shells as evidence that they had sold their lives dearly.[5] All of the bodies were scalped and mutilated.

Every man was now accounted for. Eighty-one were dead. After the peace treaty the Indians admitted twelve killed and about sixty wounded on their side. But years later the Cheyennes said that the dead warriors, laid out side by side, made two long rows, perhaps fifty or sixty men.[6]

There has been much dispute as to who led the Indians in this battle. Red Cloud said he commanded. High Back-

[5] "Within a few hundred feet of this position were found ten ponies and sixty-five great gouts of blood which had flowed from the death wounds of as many Indians. No ponies and no death spots were found anywhere else."—Dunn, "Massacres in the Mountains," p. 496.

[6] "There is scarcely a doubt that each of the sixty-five bloodspots on the field meant a dead Indian. Wounded Indians leave a battle field with wonderful celerity and one who cannot move until he has bled freely may safely be counted as dead or mortally wounded."—Ibid, p. 500.

bone, the Minneconjou, has also been named as have Black
Leg and Black Shield. But it is probable that the real commander of the Indians was Crazy Horse who was just
beginning to build his reputation as the greatest fighter the
Sioux Nation ever produced.

PORTUGEE PHILLIPS' RIDE

Carrington brought the dead back to the fort. That
night the threatening sky fulfilled its portent. A terrific
blizzard broke loose. The thermometer fell to thirty degrees below zero. Snow piled up so rapidly against the
stockade that details of men had to work constantly to
shovel it away lest it pile high enough to allow the Indians
to climb over. Sentries could stand the intense cold only
twenty minutes at a time. Even with quick reliefs there
were many frozen feet, ears, noses and fingers.

But for the blizzard the Indians might have followed
their advantage by attacking the fort itself. According to
their own account this was a part of the plan.[7] To the people at the fort arrival of cold weather was providential.

Southward, two hundred and thirty-six miles, lay Fort
Laramie, with reinforcements, ammunition and supplies.
Word must be gotten through. There was no telegraph, so
a courier had to take it. Carrington called for volunteers.

Several old plainsmen were in the post and many veteran soldiers, but they shook their heads. That ride, over
a broken, snow-covered country, even in times of peace,
meant almost certain death by freezing, with the temperature where it was and the blizzard raging so it was hard to
see a hundred yards ahead. With the country swarming
with hostile Indians it was odds of a hundred to one against
any man rash enough to attempt it.

---

[7] Grinnell mentions this in "The Fighting Cheyennes," p. 227.

But there was one man willing to take the risk. John Phillips, commonly known as "Portugee," was an Indian fighter, trapper and scout. He knew the country and offered to go.[8] Carrington gave him his own horse, a blooded Kentucky runner, the swiftest animal in the post. Wrapping himself in a huge buffalo coat, with a little hardtack for himself and a sack of grain for his horse, he passed out through a side gate into the swirling storm.

Nobody ever got the full details of that ride but it will always remain one of the epics of the West. At first he walked in the blackness of the night storm. For hours he led his horse, stopping at suspicious noises. He expected to be seen in the first half mile but no Indian yelled. With the howling wind whipping the snow around him, he mounted at last and spurred his horse along, across the Piney and past frozen Lake De Smet. Behind him the lights of the fort grew dim and disappeared.

Gallop—gallop—on through the storm, plunged Portugee Phillips. The miles fell behind him like the snowflakes he shook from his furry shoulders. The Indians were in their teepees, not dreaming that any white man would face the fury of this storm. And Portugee Phillips rode on and on.

Day dawned and still the wind whirled the snow. A short stop to feed his horse and cram a few crackers down his own throat, a handful of snow for a drink, and Portugee Phillips was in the saddle again. How he guided his horse across that wilderness, is explained only by the instinct which is sometimes possessed by those perfectly attuned to the wilds. From the Big Horn Mountains the blizzard swept with unslackened fury, piling in drifts from

[8] Portugee Phillips was moved by sorrow for the widow of Lieutenant Grummond, a young woman freshly out from the east, and perhaps a tenderer emotion, according to her story, "My Army Life." Mrs. Grummond later became General Carrington's second wife.

five to twenty feet deep. The storm prevented his seeing any landmarks. The trail itself was covered by the drifts. Yet on he rode, as unerring as a hound on the slot.

Night fell, and still the good steed breasted the snow. In the homes of civilization happy families gathered around their hearths in the light and warmth of their homes. But alone, a dot in the icy waste, Portugee Phillips was riding for the lives of the women and children at Fort Phil Kearney. Just at dawn he reached Horse Shoe station, forty miles from Laramie, and one hundred and ninety miles from Phil Kearney. He telegraphed his news to Laramie. Fortunately he did not trust the telegraph. The message never got through. After a brief rest he rode on.

Icicles formed from his beard. His hands, knees and feet were frozen. He looked more like a ghost than a man. But still, with indomitable purpose, he urged his failing horse over the trail.

It was Christmas Eve and they were holding high revel at Fort Laramie. A grand ball was in progress at "Bedlam," the officers' club. Beautiful women, garbed in silks and satins, and gallant officers, in brilliant dress uniforms, made the interior a splendid kaleidoscope of changing color. The sound of violins, the laughter of the ladies, and the gay banter of the brave men who were taking holiday from military cares, created a symphony of cheery sound.

Above this happy noise came suddenly the sharp challenge of a sentry. It was followed by the shouting of men in the fort enclosure and a rush of running steps outside, coupled with a ringing call for the officer of the day. The dancing stopped. Officers and ladies grouped themselves at doors and windows, gazing out at the snow-covered parade ground. A horse lay there, gasping its last, fallen from exhaustion. And reeling, swaying like a drunkard, a gigantic, fur-clad figure staggered toward the hall. In through the door he stumbled and stood for a moment, supporting himself on the lintel while his eyes blinked in the unaccustomed light. Then seeing the post commander, he told a story of horror which put a period to the festivities that night—the story of the Fetterman disaster.

As he gasped out his story and appeal for reinforcements, he swayed, then fell crashing to the floor, unconscious from over exposure and exhaustion. Kind hands lifted him and carried him to a bed. Even with his rugged physique it took him weeks to recover from the terrible ordeal. To this day his ride remains unparalleled in American history.

Chapter V

THE LAST DAYS OF FORT PHIL KEARNEY

THE ENEMY OF THE WHITE MAN

The Fetterman disaster shocked the whole United States. Over night the government discovered it had a real war on its hands. Four companies of infantry marched at once to Fort Phil Kearney and fresh supplies of ammunition and other stores were dispatched in response to the message Portugee Phillips had brought.[1]

Fetterman died because he disobeyed his chief, but a scapegoat was needed, and Carrington, who was not remotely to blame, was removed from his post and transferred to Fort Caspar. Colonel Wessells succeeded him. Carrington demanded a military investigation but not until twenty years later was it held. Then he was fully exonerated of any lack of soldierly discretion, courage or foresight.

The long winter dragged on. Red Cloud, the implacable enemy of the white man, stubbornly maintained his grip on the fort. He had plenty of warriors although many Sioux had retired to favorite camp grounds, such as the Crazy Woman canyon and the Powder River valley, to

[1] The sequel to Portugee Phillips' ride is interesting. Records show he was paid $300 by the government for that cruel ride "and other scouting duties." But his exploit was eventually to cost him far more than the peril and suffering. The Sioux swore vengeance. Six years later they killed all his stock, depriving him of his sole property. He died in 1883 at Cheyenne, Wyoming. The government paid his widow $5,000 on her claim for Indian depredations. But Portugee Phillips' grave today remains unmarked.

"hole up." There they spent the time in leisure, with dancing, feasts and other Indian merry-making, while the grim chief sat in his exposed teepee on Little Goose River, or rode with a few of his "Bad Faces" to reconnoitre the fort.

Wessells tried a winter campaign but the cold was too severe. The troops were recalled until spring came.

Red Cloud lacked the united support of his people during this trying period. He had a constant struggle to keep the Sioux interested in his "siege" of the fort. Man-Afraid-of-His-Horses, the real chief of the Ogalallas, was very jealous of Red Cloud's spectacular rise. He hated to play second fiddle. On June 12th he made overtures of peace to the government. At that time he told a peace commission sent out from Washington that his people wished to end the war. Then he spoiled the whole thing by asking for ammunition. It was refused. Chagrined, Man-Afraid-of-His-Horses returned to the wilderness. Red Cloud was still in the ascendancy. That chief's success in the campaign thus far had given him tremendous prestige, a prestige further enhanced by the failure of Man-Afraid-of-His-Horses.

Red Cloud continued to hector the fort through out June and July. As August approached the Sioux planned another decisive blow, similar to the Fetterman victory. Led by High Backbone, Crazy Horse, and other famous fighters, a force of from one to three thousand warriors gathered at Red Cloud's camp. The blow was struck August 2nd. A wood-chopping detail was cutting fuel for the post, with an escort under Captain James Powell. Powell had been forced to divide his meagre detachment to take care of all the choppers. Twelve men under a sergeant were sent to the camp in the forest. Another sergeant with thirteen men escorted the wood train to and from the fort.

Powell, with Lieutenant J. C. Jenness and the remaining twenty-six men, established his headquarters on an open plain about a thousand yards across.

Many Indians had been reported in the woods. Trouble was brewing and Powell made preparations. The wood haulers' wagons were made of inch boards, not able to turn a rifle bullet, but a protection against arrows. Powell had fourteen of these wagon beds dismounted and dragged into an oval corral near the tents where the soldiers slept. Across the openings at the ends stood other wagons on wheels. The supplies and ammunition were placed inside. A recent consignment of the latest type firearms—the new Springfield-Allen rapid-fire rifles—had been received. Powell's men had these guns, together with a supply of Colt revolvers and plenty of cartridges for all.

Powell's premonition of danger was speedily fulfilled. Early in the morning a daring band of young warriors swooped down on the wood-train horse herd and stampeded it. This was the opening blow. The Indians had made elaborate plans to "eat up" the entire detachment.

WHITE MAN'S RETRIBUTION

Through the trees slipped a swarm of Sioux, most of them on foot. Only a small proportion had guns, but they were better supplied in this respect than they had been the winter before.

Wood choppers appeared ahead. The leading warriors began to shoot. Presently they saw men running across the open space to the wagon box corral. These were soldiers and choppers, chased out of the woods. Four bodies, bristling with arrows, lay among the pines, where the Sioux had caught them. But the rest reached the corral, raising the total inside to thirty-two.

The wagon box corral squatted out there in the open, silent, apparently untenanted, but with an air of menace about it. Over the top of the boxes blankets had been thrown, and between them were piled sacks of grain, ox yokes, logs and other objects. Not a movement could be seen. How many men were in there the Indians had no way of knowing. The chiefs decided to take no chances. They had plenty of warriors. It seemed sure that if they all rushed the corral at once, it ought to be easy to ride over it and kill all the white men. The cry went around to form a line at the edge of the woods.

In the little fort, Powell was coolly telling off the best shots, with two or three guns each, while the poor shots were instructed to load rifles. Nobody expected to survive the fight but they were going to make the hostiles pay for every life they took. Some of the men preferred the barricades between the wagons to the wagons themselves. One knelt behind a barrel of beans; another chose a barrel of salt. Some attached loops to their triggers so that at the last moment they could place the muzzles of their rifles at their heads and pull the triggers with their boot toes, escaping capture and torture.

By now the Sioux were ready to charge. There were some famous fighters among them. High Backbone and Crazy Horse have been mentioned. Crow King, American Horse and Big Crow were also present. Of course Red Cloud was the central figure.

A chief—probably Red Cloud himself—was seen giving the signal for the charge by whirling a blanket over his head. Whipping their ponies and yelling their war cries, the Sioux broke out of the woods and bore down on the corral at a dead run. In a charge on a fortification of any kind, there was always great rivalry among the plains Indians as to who should first touch the breastworks, as it counted coup for the warrior. The charging braves expected a volley, then silence while the defenders reloaded, permitting them to reach the corral before a second volley. But a bad thing happened.

The first volley crashed out, knocking many from their saddles. The rest kept on. But to their amazement there was no pause in the firing. A steady stream of lead poured from the wagon boxes—the new repeating rifles. On came the Sioux, howling across the plain, a wave of murder. The withering blast mowed down their best warriors, leaving the wake of the charge strewn with stricken men and horses. The sweeping front broke in two at the center, and the two wings raced around each side of the fort, pouring into the wagon beds a storm of bullets and arrows. More riders dropped, but still they grimly rode around and around the corral in a vain effort to pierce it. There was not one undefended point. From every angle the little fort spat fire and lead. The Indians grew discouraged and retreated to the woods.

The Sioux could not understand the terrible effectiveness of the white man's murderous fire. They finally seemed to have decided that the corral contained many more men than they had at first supposed to keep up such a continuous stream of bullets.

The garrison had time now to catch its breath and to check up losses. Lieutenant Jenness was dead and with him Privates Haggerty and Doyle. Others were wounded. But the survivors were still brimful of fight.

A council of Sioux chiefs was being held out of range, and on top of a near hill some of the warriors began signalling with pocket mirrors to other Indians over the ridge several miles away, telling them to come on. A different plan of attack was decided upon by the council. This time most of the warriors with guns crept up through the grass and bushes and opened a heavy fire on the corral. With their wonderful ability at concealing themselves, many of them got within close rifle range. Most of their guns were old smooth bores, but there were some Spencer carbines, trophies of the victory over Fetterman, and a few other rifles. The old Indian weakness in marksmanship asserted itself and the shooting was all too high. The tops of the wagon boxes were riddled, but little damage was done to the defenders.

To this fire the white men responded only occasionally. Now and again some warrior, growing bold, would expose himself; a rifle would crack from one of the wagon boxes; and he would crumple to the ground, an inert corpse, or else drag himself away, crippled and out of action. But for the most part the defenders were silent.

The Sioux must have concluded at last that they had killed most of the people in the corral. By this time many other Indians had arrived, summoned by the flashing mirror signals. A charge on foot was the plan.

In a huge V or wedge the Sioux ran forward, their naked bodies painted, their war bonnets fluttering, their war cries filling the air. But again the fearful blast of flame and lead burst in their faces. With the highest courage they ran forward in spite of the spray of death which kept eating out their front ranks. They came so close that the defenders said afterwards that they could see the whites of their eyes. Some of the white men seized knives preparing for a last ditch hand-to-hand fight. Then the Sioux had enough. They scattered and ran for cover.

No braver fighters ever lived than those Sioux. Going up against a sustained fire which they did not understand but which left their dead scattered all over the field, the naked warriors prepared for still another charge. This time it was on horseback, the painted riders yelling chal-.

lenges to each other to be the first to touch the corral. Again the explosion of flame from the wagon boxes. Again the stubborn rush in the face of death; the reeling of the line at last; and the final breaking up in flight.

It was late in the afternoon. Red Cloud and his chiefs were through. There was, however, one more duty to perform. All around the corral lay the bodies of the slain. It was a point of honor that these bodies should be removed. A cloud of skirmishers went forward again and put the corral under a hail of lead. All the dead and wounded in easy reach were taken to the hills. Then the bravest warriors crept forward to bring out the bodies near the enclosure. Taking one end of a long rope made out of many lariats tied together, an Indian would wriggle up and fasten the rope to a dead comrade's ankles. The men at the other end of the rope would drag the body back to safety, the rescuing brave returning under the cover of his shield.

While this was going on, the report of a cannon was heard, and over the hill came a line of blue uniforms. Major John E. Smith's relieving force had arrived from the fort. The rescuers could scarcely believe their eyes when the defenders crawled out of the corral as the Indians retreated. Three men were dead and three more lay wounded in the corral. Add to this the four woodchoppers killed, and the white loss was seven dead and three wounded.

There is a striking disparity between the white and Indian estimates of the Sioux loss. Preposterous stories have been told in some accounts of fifteen hundred Indians having been put out of action during the battle. This is plainly ridiculous. According to some estimates there were not even fifteen hundred Indians in the battle. But equally unconvincing are some of the Indian stories. Some of the Sioux accounts say that only five or six were killed and as many wounded on their side during the fight. Indians have the habit of listing only the dead whose names they can remember. This may be the case with these estimates. But I am of the belief that they err on the side of conservatism almost as badly as the wild tales of the whites vary in the opposite direction. Captain Powell estimated one hundred and eighty killed and wounded. This, too, may be high, but it is probably closer to correct than either of the other figures. Remember that Powell was a veteran of the Civil War, and used to the appearance of a stricken field. His estimate is very likely close. The Sioux had charged in battle array and many of the white defenders were expert marksmen. No less than three charges had been broken up by the riflery of the soldiers. Under these considerations Powell's figures do not seem very far out of line.

THE END OF FORT PHIL KEARNEY

The Sioux had regarded Red Cloud as invincible and the Wagon Box affair was an awful blow to his prestige. Hundreds of warriors left his camp and went buffalo hunting. But the grim Ogalalla held to his purpose, to force the evacuation of the fort. As long as he kept his war parties around it, there was no chance for travel on the Bozeman trail. Somehow he held the rest of the Sioux together.

Winter came on again but the following spring Red Cloud's patience was rewarded. The Fetterman disaster had led the government to investigate the situation in Wyoming. In the spring of 1868 a peace commission met with the Sioux chiefs at Laramie on April 29th. The central figure was Red Cloud. His terms were definite and he never abated from them for one minute: The Bozeman trail must be closed. The government forts must be abandoned.

At last the commission agreed to all Red Cloud demanded. In consideration of a promise that the Indians would not interfere in the construction of the Northern Pacific Railroad, far south of their hunting grounds, the government ceded the entire Powder River country including the Black Hills and agreed to abandon all forts and withdraw the troops.

It was a smashing victory for Red Cloud, but he showed his distrust of the white man's word by refusing to be a party to the treaty or signing it until the troops were actually withdrawn. Then, when he had received tangible proofs that the government intended to abide by its promise, he signed, on November 6th.

In the meantime, a memorable event took place on the Piney. On a bright summer day in August, the soldiers, in full view of hundreds of their Sioux foes, hauled down the flag from the masthead of Fort Phil Kearney and marched out of the post they had built and defended at such cost of blood and suffering.

"They knew not the reason why" except that they had their orders. Many a veteran looked with black rage at the hills which hid the dark warriors who had so long besieged them.

No sooner had the soldiers marched out of one side of the fort, than the Sioux entered at the other. Red Cloud, who had fought so long and schemed so constantly for this event, must have been there. If so, it was a moment of supreme triumph for him. How his heart must have swelled as he watched his yelling warriors apply the torch to the palisades. With what an ecstasy of pride must he have looked at the great black pillar of smoke which went rolling up to the sky, carrying with it the last vestiges of the white man—for the time at least.

III.

THE STRICKEN FRONTIER
1864–1869

CHAPTER VI

THE GRIEVANCE OF THE CHEYENNES

CHIVINGTON'S MARCH

NORTH of old Fort Lyon stretched a rugged, barren country, dividing the plains from the mountains. Today it is a smiling vista of green, irrigated Colorado fields, but in November, 1864, it was a sterile waste, covered with monotonous clusters of sagebrush and soapweed.

In spite of its barrenness, the region had for many years been a favorite wintering ground of the Southern Cheyennes. That fall the big bend of Sand Creek, thirty miles north of the fort, was populous with teepees. Here were the villages of Black Kettle, White Antelope and War Bonnet. In their warm buffalo-hide lodges they defied the rigor of the elements. With a sufficiency to eat and limitless time to while away in merry-making, they lived a happy, carefree life.

The Cheyennes were a race of warriors, but now they were at peace with the world. Largely because of Mo-ke-ta-va-ta (Black Kettle), they had kept out of trouble with the white men as much as the ever-aggressive, arrogant paleface would let them.

Only the previous August the chief had written a letter to Major Colley at Fort Lyon, saying: "We received a letter from Bent wishing us to make peace. We held a council . . . All come to the conclusion to make peace with you, providing you make peace with the Kiowas, Comanches,

Arapahoes and Apaches and Sioux . . . We want true news from you in return."

The Bent referred to was William Bent, who with Ceran St. Vrain had built the famous Bent's Fort, a trading post for decades, on the site of Fort Lyon. He it was who had talked to the Southern Cheyennes and induced them to come south to hunt. He it was who had married one of their women and lived with her honorably. He was the only white man the Southern Cheyennes trusted. One of his half-breed sons, George Bent, was in camp with them then, and with Edmond Guerrier, another half breed, wrote the letter just quoted, at the dictation of Black Kettle and other chiefs.

Later Black Kettle, White Antelope and others went to Denver with Major Wynkoop and talked to Governor Evans. On their return they were told to camp on Sand Creek, where they would be under military protection as long as they kept peace. The Cheyennes had every reason to feel secure in these promises of protection. As proof of their good intentions they surrendered half their firearms to Wynkoop, keeping only enough for hunting.

The Platte and Arkansas basins had seen plenty of Indian troubles that year. The Sioux and Kiowas, aided by their allies, the Comanches, Arapahoes and some Cheyennes, scourged the wagon trails so that freight ceased for a time to move. Some helpless settlers had been killed, too. Public feeling was high against all Indians in Denver.

On the other hand the Indians had sufficient grievances of their own. There was the unprovoked attack by Lieutenant George Eayre and his men on a Cheyenne village the April before, in which a score of Indians were killed. And there were plenty of other crimes of a similar nature to be laid at the white man's door. Then there was the old sore point that the wagon trains frightened away all the game.

But the frontier cared nothing about the Indian's side of the case. It wanted the raiding stopped. And so all day on November 28th, a long, trailing splotch of blue—cavalry—had moved steadily across the landscape. Toward night the troops halted. Near the head of the column rode a half-breed, his horse's reins tied to a soldier's saddle-pommel. A group of horsemen spurred up. Their leader, huge, burly, fierce-visaged, rasped out a question. The trooper saluted. It was Colonel J. M. Chivington, of the 2nd Colorado Cavalry.[1]

"The breed won't go no farther, sir," the soldier said.[2]

"Wolf, he howl," said the Indian. "Injun dog, he hear wolf, he howl too. Injun, he hear dog and listen; hear something and run off."

Hopefully he stole a glance at the white man's face—to meet there a look so fell that he shrank back. In a hard voice Chivington spoke.

[1] Colonel J. M. Chivington was in civil life a Methodist preacher. He went west from Ohio where he "got religion" and entered the ministry. In 1850 he was in Colorado but later moved to Missouri, where the anti-slave controversy gave his extraordinarily belligerent nature a better chance to find the strife it enjoyed. He took part in the anti-slavery movement, first as a preacher and later as a member of Jim Lane's free-state bushwhackers. After the border war he again assumed the cloth and at the outbreak of the Civil War was presiding elder of his church in Denver.

In the first days of the war Chivington preached often to the soldiers in the barracks. His fire-eating eloquence pleased them and the upshot was that he was offered the chaplaincy in a Colorado regiment. He refused saying, "if I go with the soldiers I am going to fight." The governor gave him a major's commission instead. He soon received his colonelcy.

Like many religious fanatics Chivington appears not to have had one compunction for the deed he perpetrated at Sand Creek. In fact he gloried in it afterward, and before he set out on this expedition, he made a public speech in which he said: "Kill and scalp all [Indians] big and little; nits make lice." This quotation is contained in the sworn testimony of S. E. Brown, before the Congressional Investigating Committee which later probed—and repudiated—the whole affair.

[2] All direct quotations in this chapter are taken from J. P. Dunn's account of the incident published in 1886.

"Jack," he said, "if you fool with me, and don't lead me to that camp—" he tapped his holster and the half-breed read death in his eyes.

With a sigh the prisoner again took the trail. No use to argue here. To Chivington all Indians looked alike and there was "no good Indian but a dead Indian." He knew of Black Kettle's peaceful village and he had kidnapped the half-breed, Jack Smith,³ to lead him to the camp. Moreover, the prisoner knew Chivington's right-hand man was with him, the baleful Major Downing, who had not hesitated, as he later boasted, to wring information out of a captured Indian "by toasting his shins over a small fire."

Dazedly the guide plodded ahead. All night they marched. At daybreak of the 29th they mounted a rise and saw, stretched along a shallow, sluggish stream, the village they sought, peacefully slumbering.

A squaw in the Cheyenne camp heard the distant rumble of hoofs and cried out that a herd of buffalo was coming. The Indians rushed out and beheld the troops on the ridge. They were badly frightened. In the confusion a white trader who had been sleeping in one of the lodges— pretty good proof in itself that the Indians were peaceful —came out and started toward the troops. At the same time Black Kettle ran up an American flag over his teepee, with a white flag above that. He had been told to do so to show that his camp was friendly. The Cheyennes, believing themselves under protection, and reassured by their chiefs, did not at first run. They clustered in a huddled mob in front of their lodges.

Then there was a shot, followed by two or three more. Firing became general. The trader, half way between the camp and the troops, hesitated and stopped. A cavalryman

³ Jack Smith was the son of the famous John Smith, trader, explorer and trapper, and a Cheyenne woman. His uncle was the great Cheyenne chief Yellow Horse.

An old-time stagecoach crossing the plains. Indians made frequent attacks on these equipages during the sixties and seventies.

Left: Roman Nose (Woquini), also known as Sauts (The Bat), leader of the Cheyennes in the Platte Bridge and Arickaree battles. Right: Jack Stilwell, Indian fighter and scout, who carried a message for help from Forsyth's besieged command to Fort Wallace.

Old Camp Supply, from an early drawing. It was from this post that Custer set out in his Washita campaign.

War Department

War Department

Left: Gen. Eugene A. Carr, conqueror of Tall Bull. Right: Col. George A. Forsyth, famous Indian fighter.

galloped toward him but was shot out of his saddle. At that the troops charged.

It was a massacre. The Indians, bewildered and only partly armed, could not realize at first that the white men actually meant war. When they did finally understand this they fought like demons, but then it was too late.

After the first deadly volley which dropped many women and children, the Cheyennes ran up the bed of the creek. A detachment of soldiers cut off the pony herd. Some of the warriors stayed in the village to cover the retreat of the women and children. Among these were Black Kettle and the fine old chief White Antelope, then seventy-five years old. Black Kettle saw it was useless to remain and urged White Antelope to run with him. But the old chief stood in his tracks, singing his death song, with arms folded. Presently he was shot down.

Meantime the handful of warriors who had fought in the village were all killed. Chivington was in possession of the camp.

Up the creek about three quarters of a mile the Cheyennes scooped holes in the sand for rifle pits and made a stand. Braves, squaws and children were mixed up together. The troops were disorganized. Some lined up and shot at the Indians. The rest scattered widely. Some looted the lodges; others killed stragglers; still others with ferocity never surpassed by the Indians themselves, scalped and mutilated the dead.[4]

THE CHIVINGTON MASSACRE

Some of the scenes which ensued are almost unbelievable except that they were later attested by sworn state-

---

[4] In extenuation of this revolting circumstance, Chivington's men later said they were avenging similar mutilations practiced on white men. Contrast Chivington's attitude with that of Sibley in the Sioux War in Minnesota in 1862.

ments of eye-witnesses. Women and children were killed indiscriminately. In the creek bed fight they fought side by side with the men, but in the village the noncombatants, fleeing for their lives, were slaughtered without pity.[5]

The Cheyennes battled desperately in the creek bed. The firing was at long range and try as they might, the soldiers could not dislodge them. But by noon two howitzers were brought up and began throwing shells into the position. That broke the stubborn line. The Indians fell back to a new position, leaving their dead where they lay. Chivington followed. Again with the dreaded "wagon guns" thundering, the Cheyennes retreated. This program of stand, bombard, and retreat continued all day. The soldiers drove the Indians back five miles.

At nightfall Chivington returned to the village where he camped two days while the survivors escaped. The dead Indians were left to rot where they lay.

A final cap-sheaf was added to the deed of horror when poor, cowering Jack Smith, the unwilling guide, was murdered by the soldiers. An appeal was made to Chivington to protect the poor wretch. He replied: "I have given my orders and have no further instructions to give." A short time later the half-breed was shot.

With only seven prisoners, two women and five children, Chivington returned to Denver. He had "defeated" the Cheyennes as he proved by exhibiting more than a hundred scalps in a theater between acts of a performance.

---

[5] Major Anthony testified as follows before the Congressional Investigating Committee: A little baby, not more than three years old, emerged from one of the lodges after the flight of the Cheyennes from the village. Plump, brown, perfectly naked, it toddled down the pathway where the Indians had fled, crying a little, but not much, in the cold.

It was a sight which should have stirred compassion in a wolf but it stirred none in the men who were sacking the village. A soldier saw the child and fired at seventy-five yards, missing. Another dismounted and said: "Let me try the little — —," and fired, but missed also. A third, with surer aim, shot and this time the innocent crumpled up, dying.

Around three hundred Indians were killed of whom about seventy-five were warriors and the rest women and children. The soldiers lost seven killed and forty-seven wounded, of whom seven afterward died.

The Cheyennes never forgot Chivington's massacre. And bloodily they avenged it in the years to follow.[6]

[6] The government repudiated Chivington's acts and paid Black Kettle's band a heavy indemnity the following year—as if indemnities could bring back murdered wives, children and husbands. In 1868 a commission appointed by Congress and consisting of Generals W. T. Sherman, Alfred H. Terry, and C. C. Augur and Messrs. S. F. Tappan, N. J. Taylor, J. B. Henderson, John B. Sanborn and others, spent seventy-two days hearing evidence on the affair. When all the testimony, pro and con, was gone into, the commission made this sweeping and damning report concerning the massacre:

"It scarcely has its parallel in the records of Indian barbarity. Fleeing women, holding up their hands and praying for mercy were shot down; infants were killed and scalped in derision; men were tortured and mutilated in a way which would put to shame the savages of interior Africa. No one will be astonished that a war ensued which cost the government $30,000,000 and carried conflagration and death to the border settlements. During the spring and summer of 1865 no less than 8,000 troops were withdrawn from the effective forces engaged against the Rebellion to meet this Indian war."

General Nelson A. Miles in his "Personal Recollections" (p. 139) characterizes the Sand Creek massacre as "perhaps the foulest and most unjustifiable crime in the annals of America."

Virtually every military authority who has ever commented on it has referred to it as a massacre, pure and simple. It was universally deplored by army leaders.

Chivington, the central character in the affair, returned to Ohio after the close of the Civil War, started a newspaper, and after two years ran for the legislature. "Sand Creek" was the watchword of his opposition and he was the object of so much execration that he finally withdrew from the race. His political ambitions shattered, he eventually left that part of the country and returned to the mountains.

CHAPTER VII

AN ISLAND IN THE ARICKAREE

MAKING THE WHITE MAN PAY

SAND CREEK cost the Indians heavily in blood and sorrow but it cost the white man more. After the massacre a party of Cheyenne chiefs went north carrying the war pipe. There they offered it to their brothers, the Northern Cheyennes, who smoked it, and afterward to the Sioux, who also smoked it. One of the Sioux chiefs who smoked the war pipe was Sitting Bull, then just coming into prominence. From that time on Sitting Bull was a more implacable foe of the white man than even Red Cloud had been.[1] The Little Big Horn had its roots in Sand Creek.

But the Cheyennes made the paleface pay far more directly than that. Early in January, 1865, a great war party composed of Cheyennes, Sioux and Arapahoes, started north from the Smoky Hill River. On the night of January 6th, they camped near Julesburg, an important point on the Overland Stage route. Close by was Fort Rankin, garrisoned by a troop of the 7th Iowa Cavalry. Early next morning a little party of Cheyennes and Sioux, seven in all, headed by Big Crow, a famous Cheyenne warrior, rode out of a ravine near the fort and charged some post employees who were working outside the stockade.

The men ran inside and the cavalry leaped to horse to chastise the rash hostiles. At top speed the troopers chased the seven Indians toward the sand hills about two miles away. Captain O'Brien hoped to catch the redskins before

[1] See Vestal, "Sitting Bull," p. 70.

66

they reached the safety of those hills. But for some reason, try as they might, they could not catch up with their quarry, although they always seemed *almost* to overtake them. Then, just as they reached the sand hills, the crest suddenly sprouted war bonnets and lances.

It was the old trick. The seven Indians were a decoy. It was a flight for life now. O'Brien's force came within an eyelash of being annihilated. As it was, the Indians killed a sergeant, fourteen privates, and four civilians—eighteen men—in the wild dash for the fort.

Around the stockade rode the red men, yelling and shooting. Then they plundered Julesburg. Nobody was killed in the settlement because all took refuge in the fort before the Indians got there.[2]

On January 28th the Indians again struck the stage line when they surrounded and set fire to Harlow's ranch, killed two men and carried off a woman. On the same day they raided three other places, burning buildings, setting hay on fire, looting stores and paralyzing the whole stage line for weeks.

In this raid the Cheyennes got a signal piece of vengeance. Nine men, recently discharged from the 3rd Colorado Cavalry which took part in the Sand Creek massacre, were caught by a war party. They were on their way east. The Indians killed them all. When their valises were opened, the Cheyennes found two scalps of their own people which they recognized by the hair ornaments. They were so furious that they cut the dead men literally to pieces.

---

[2] The value of goods taken or destroyed at Julesburg was $40,000. One piece of plunder at the stage station was the strong box of the army paymaster containing thousands of dollars in greenbacks, to pay the Colorado troops. Not knowing the value of the "green paper" the Indians had a lot of fun scattering it all over the valley. Next day the paymaster had men detailed from Fort Rankin to hunt the money. They found it strewn for a mile or more, but only recovered about half of it.

In the next two weeks the allied tribes attacked and burned the Beaver Creek stage station; the Morrison ranch where seven men were killed and Mrs. Morrison and her child carried off; the Wisconsin ranch; the Washington ranch; the Lillian Springs ranch; Gittrell's ranch; Moore's ranch, and many other places. Three wagon trains were captured and looted. In a second raid on Julesburg, they burned the place to the ground while the soldiers watched helplessly from Fort Rankin, a mile away.

And so it went. Scores of white men and women paid with their lives for that Sand Creek affair. The Southern Cheyennes furnished much of the worst fighting for the troops in the Powder River campaign of 1865.

THE PLATTE BRIDGE FIGHT

In the middle of that summer the Cheyennes appeared near the Platte Bridge where there was a stockade garrisoned by some Kansas cavalry. There was a skirmish near the fort. Then the Indians drew off and hid on the other side of the Platte.

A wagon train with a small military escort was coming down the river to the post and Lieutenant Caspar Collins, with a detachment, was dispatched to meet it.

Not an Indian was in sight. In fact those at the fort thought they had cleared out of the country. With no thought of immediate danger, Collins led his men across the bridge and up the flat. As if they had risen from the ground, the Cheyennes suddenly appeared, cutting the soldiers off from the bridge. Collins was fearless. He had been ordered to go to the wagon train, so he continued his march. Then a second, even larger mass of warriors rose out of a ravine on his front.

At first the young officer tried to fight his way forward.

The numbers of Indians steadily increased. At last he gave the order to fall back. The Cheyennes still blocked his way to the bridge. Collins tried to cut his way through. Right into the mass of yelling savages his men rode. An arrow struck the lieutenant in the forehead and hung quivering there, but still he fought his way forward. A few yards farther he was beaten from his horse and killed.[3] Only a remnant of his command won their way through to the bridge. The rest were dead, their scalps in Cheyenne hands.

In the meantime the wagon train continued its slow journey toward the fort, ignorant of the painted death ahead. Sergeant Custard, a hard-faced old veteran, was in command. The booming of cannon when they were almost in sight of the fort was their first intimation of danger. Custard had twenty-four men. He sent five of them, under Corporal James W. Shrader, forward to see what was going on.

Scarcely was the detail clear of the wagon train when a swarm of Indians rode out from hiding in a ravine and lashed their ponies after the soldiers. There was no chance to get back to Custard. The troopers raced for the fort. As they jumped their horses into the stream to ford it, Private James Ballew was shot from the saddle and fell into the river. His body was never recovered. The rest got across, but on the other bank Edwin Summers was killed. Corporal Shrader with Privates Bryam Swaim and Henry Smith, after two hours of alternate running and hiding in the brush of the river bottom, finally reached the fort alive.

---

[3] There is some evidence that Collins was tortured to death. A. J. Mokler, of Casper, Wyoming, who probably knows more about this fight than any other one man, says that the lieutenant's face had been blasted off by powder poured in his mouth and then touched off, when the body was found days later. Mr. Mokler has an interesting discussion of this affair in his book "Transition of the West."

In the meantime Custard, seeing his advance guard cut off, corralled his wagons. Many Indians came riding toward him. They were returning from killing Collins and his men. Around the train they swept in a tempest of noise while puffs of smoke spurted from the wagons. Here and there warriors fell to the ground. The Cheyennes drew back out of range.

The soldiers probably breathed more freely. A repulse like that generally meant the end of an Indian attack. But these were not ordinary Indians. They were Cheyennes, seeking still further satisfaction from the white man for Sand Creek.

A gigantic warrior, wearing a handsome war bonnet, now appeared, riding slowly around the train. He was Roman Nose, most noted of all the Cheyennes. His proper name was Sauts (The Bat), but his nose was hooked like the beak of some fierce bird of prey and the white men dubbed him "Roman Nose." His own people accepted the sobriquet and translated it into their own tongue, Woquini, or Hook Nose.

Few savages on the plains were his equal in strength or courage. He towered six feet three inches in his moccasins, and weighed two hundred and thirty pounds without a surplus ounce of flesh. In addition he was a natural leader. Roman Nose habitually took great risks in battle. He believed himself invulnerable, due to the sacred war bonnet which he always wore and which was never put on without elaborate ritual. Because of this belief he had performed so many daring exploits that he was famous throughout the frontier.

The appearance of Roman Nose at once put a different complexion on the fight. After his leisurely survey of the corral, he told his warriors to dismount. Every man with a gun—and due to the recent raids many were now so armed—crept up close to the wagons and opened a devastating fire upon them. The troopers simply melted away.

About three o'clock in the afternoon, Roman Nose stopped the shooting. Spurring forward, he rode all alone around the wagons, very close, to draw fire. Not a shot answered his challenge. Then Roman Nose dared to enter the circle itself. It was a scene of carnage. Every soldier was dead or badly wounded. The Cheyennes rushed in. Of course they killed all who were still living. Why shouldn't they? Chivington had done the same by them.

.   .   .   .

Because the Cheyennes and Sioux went north to carry on their warfare, the summer of 1866 was comparatively quiet in Kansas.

But in the spring of 1867 the Indians were back on the border again. General Hancock with eleven hundred men took the field in April to show the Indians "that the government is ready and able to punish them if they are hostile, although it may not . . . invite war."

His column marched and counter-marched. The Cheyennes and Sioux played will-o'-the-wisp. After four months of this, Hancock returned to Fort Harker. He had burned one empty village and killed two young Cheyennes, said to be friendly. Meanwhile the Indians were raiding far and wide and doing a tremendous amount of damage. It is impossible to enumerate all their activities.

General George Armstrong Custer, fresh from the east, had just arrived on the frontier. A dashing cavalry officer, he pursued the hostiles with great energy, but his achievements were nil. In fact they were less than that, for a promising young officer, Lieutenant Kidder, of the 2nd

Cavalry, journeying with dispatches for Custer from Fort
Sedgwick, was killed with his ten men and the Indian
guide Red Bead. The bodies were discovered by Custer a
few days later.

Late in the summer the Cheyennes wrecked a railroad
train. A war party came upon the newly laid tracks of the
Union Pacific somewhere east of North Platte, Nebraska.
None of them had ever seen the rails before. One suggested that they put some obstruction on them and throw
the train off the tracks.

A log was laid across and the Cheyennes hid. Presently
a hand car, worked by two men, came into view. The men
saw the Indians and pumped desperately at their handle
bars to get past the danger point. When the car hit the
logs it jumped the rails. The Cheyennes killed both unfortunates before they even had time to run.

But a hand car is small game when you are after a train.
The Indians, encouraged by their success, prepared for a
bigger exploit. After pulling out the spikes at the end of
a rail, they bent the rail with levers until it was out of line.
Again they lay in wait.

It was not a long wait. A glaring light appeared in the
east which rapidly grew brighter. As it rushed by, the
engine struck the bent rail, jumped the track and turned
over on its side. Every member of the train crew was
killed in the wreck except one trainman. He got off the
train and ran down the track with a lantern. The Cheyennes surrounded and killed him. Next morning they
plundered the train which was loaded with valuable mer-
chandise. The Indians got their fill of loot that time.

Thus passed the year 1867. But it was tame compared
to the following summer of 1868. In sixty days one hundred and seventeen settlers were slaughtered and seven
women carried off into captivity. There were at least

twenty-five recorded raids in that time. The Cheyennes literally made a desert out of western Kansas.[4]

FORSYTH'S SCOUTS

Things were so critical that General Phil Sheridan, commanding the Department of the Missouri, took the field in person. Sheridan was no fool. He saw how futile it was to try to follow the Indians who knew the country like a book and could make their living off it, with soldiers who had to carry their own supplies, must trust to often inefficient scouts, and were otherwise handicapped.

There were plenty of good plainsmen in the frontier forts those days—men who knew how to trail, shoot, and travel. To Sheridan one day Major George A. Forsyth suggested a free-lance battalion of these frontiersmen to be enlisted for scouting duty, with the hope of meeting the Indians at their own game.

Sheridan approved and authorized Forsyth to recruit the outfit. It was harder to keep the number of men down than to fill the quota of fifty. Bronzed and rugged plainsmen, aching for a chance at the redskins who had driven them from their homes, clamored for admittance. Scarcely were the lists open when they were filled—buffalo hunters, Civil War veterans, gamblers and trappers. On September

---

[4] Following is a partial list of Indian depredations that summer, from official records which do not pretend to be complete:

Aug. 12—Solomon River settlements, 15 killed; Republican River, 2. Aug. 14—Granny Creek, 1 killed, 1 captured. Aug. 23—North Texas, 8 killed; Two Butte Creek, 3; Pond Creek, 2. Aug. 27—Ft. Lyon, 1 killed; Big Spring station, 1. Aug. 28—Kiowa station, 3 killed. Sept. 1—Lake station, 2 killed; Reed's Springs, 3; Spanish Fort, Tex., 8. Sept. 6 and 7—Colorado Territory, 25 killed. Sept. 8—Turkey Creek, 2 killed; Cimarron Crossing, 17. Sept. 9—Ft. Wallace, 6 killed. Sept. 17—Ella station, 1 killed; Fort Bascom, 1. Sept. 29—Sharp's Creek, 1 killed, 3 captured. Oct. 2—Fort Zarah and Larned, 4 killed. Oct. 4—Fort Dodge, 1 killed. Oct. 7—Purgatory Creek, 1 killed; Sand Creek, 2 captured. Oct. 14—Prairie Dog Creek, 1 killed. Oct. 15—Fisher and Yocucy Creeks, 4 killed, 1 captured.

Not an Indian was killed in these affairs.

10th Forsyth rode forth with his half-hundred to scout the hostile Indian country.

It was a ridiculously tiny force, but the white man still had many lessons to learn, and every scout was filled with the sublime faith that they could whip any number of Indians they might meet.

See, then, this cock-sure handful of hard-bitten fighters, riding out of Fort Wallace that bright autumn morning. Watch them as they jingle along, Sharp's seven-shooter rifles slung on their backs, holstered revolvers slapping thighs, dressed in buckskin or nondescript uniforms—the most careless, irresponsible, hard riding, straight shooting company of scapegraces that ever set out under the United States flag.

For two or three days they scouted westward. Then a big trail was struck and Forsyth followed it. The trail, it later developed, was made by the allied war party under Pawnee Killer—who had wiped out Kidder's command—and the Cheyenne chiefs Tall Bull and White Horse. Roman Nose was also in this party.

Soon after the rash white scouts took their trail the Indians knew of it. The Cheyennes and Sioux later said that preparations were made nearly twenty-four hours ahead for the fight which followed.

Forsyth, hot on the trail, reached the Arickaree River. It had a wide, sandy bed with very little water meandering down the middle. A small island covered with plum brush was in the bed. On the bank of this stream the scouts camped.

As the first streaks of dawn lit the sky next morning, a shot and a yell of "Indians!" aroused the command. With flapping blankets and shrill yelps, eight warriors rode at the horse-lines trying to stampede the animals. Seven broke away and the Indians captured them.

As if this was only a prelude, the entire horizon seemed to fill with tossing feathered head dresses on which the first rays of the sun gleamed brilliantly. In a few minutes the bottom was covered with mounted hostiles.

Pell-mell, helter-skelter, Forsyth's men rode for the low island they had noted in the middle of the stream bed. There, under the plum bushes, they began frantically to burrow out small rifle pits.

The Indians had spread out from bank to bank. One warrior, on a chestnut horse, was taken by Forsyth to be Roman Nose. Sharp Grover,[5] his chief of scouts, also thought it was the famous warrior, evidently basing his belief on the Indian's size, as he added "there isn't such another Indian on the plains." They were mistaken. Roman Nose did not appear until later in the day.

By now the Indians were ready to charge. Old plainsmen, able to distinguish the tribes by their head dresses, saw that Brulé Sioux, Arapahoes and both Northern and Southern Cheyennes were there. A black mass of squaws and children gathered on a hill overlooking the valley to watch the battle. This place is now called "Squaw Hill."

The Indians charged; the drumming of their horses' hoofs and their wild yelling rose in a wave of sound. On the island the scouts clenched their teeth as they glanced down the barrels of their rifles. But not a shot was fired. The order was to wait until the charge was within fifty yards. As it crossed that imaginary line, Forsyth uttered a single word:

"Now!"

---

[5] Grover had lived among the Sioux (Turkey Leg's band) and married a Sioux squaw, but he did not know the Cheyennes, according to Grinnell. He was suffering from a recent wound in his back at the time of this expedition. Only a month before he, with William Comstock, another scout, had been shot while leaving a Sioux village. Comstock was killed, but Grover stood off his assailants and reached the settlements. He was later slain by a man named Moody, in a saloon brawl at Pond Creek, Kansas.

A white cloud of smoke burst from the island. A hail of bullets whistled into the Indian ranks. And then the repeating rifles proved their worth. Instead of the usual single volley, followed by silence, the Indians rode into a continuous stream of lead. In the face of this storm their hearts forsook them. Like an angry wave which hurls itself upon a rock and breaks upon its front, they divided on each side of the island and thundered down the river bed, to circle off to safety in the bluffs.

That charge came near carrying home. Some of the Indian dead lay within a few feet of the rifle pits. And the red men were by no means through.

The chiefs galloped around, assembling their warriors out of rifle range. Some braves dismounted and slipped forward on foot. The prairie close to the river was level, but south of the island grew willow bushes. Behind this the Indians got close to the island. The firing redoubled as they exchanged shots with the scouts only a few yards away. A few Indians were killed. The rest drew off.

The scouts counted their losses. Out of fifty-one officers and men, twenty-three were dead or wounded. Among the mortally hurt were Lieutenant Beecher, second in command, who died that evening, and Dr. Moorehead, the surgeon who died three days later.[6] Forsyth himself was wounded in three places.

Like Achilles, Roman Nose had stayed out of the morning battle, and like Achilles, his absence had been keenly felt by his warriors. The day before he had destroyed the charm of his sacred war bonnet. One of the taboos connected with it was that he must not eat food taken from the pot with an iron implement. At a feast given by the Sioux, Roman Nose ate meat served by a squaw with an

---

[6] The island was later named Beecher's Island in honor of Lieutenant Frederick W. Beecher, who died there. The fight is often called the Beecher Island fight.

iron fork. Tall Bull, his friend, called his attention to the error and urged him to take purification ceremonies at once. But that very night Forsyth's command was discovered and Roman Nose had no time for the ceremonies before the battle.

He stayed out of the first charge, saying he would die if he made it. But he was such a power that the other Cheyennes kept urging him. In mid-afternoon he suddenly decided to go into the fight. Putting on the war bonnet, he mounted. With a wave of his great arm, the giant summoned his warriors. A moment later they were charging.

Forsyth's men fought this new danger desperately. At the dead run, Roman Nose thundered down upon them. Just before he reached the trenches, a shot from some bushes to one side, brought him crashing down. Jack Stilwell and two companions were hiding there. Roman Nose's followers scattered.

The place where Roman Nose fell was on the river bank. Painfully he dragged himself out of sight among the bushes. There he was found by his people and carried away. He died in the Cheyenne village that night.[7]

It will never be known how many Indians were killed at the Arickaree. Years later the Cheyennes could remember the names of only seven warriors who died, but this seems preposterous. Forsyth estimated their loss was at least one hundred.

THE JOURNEY OF STILWELL AND TRUDEAU

As evening fell, Forsyth, wounded and nearly helpless, called his men together. He pointed out their desperate situation and the fact that the nearest help was at Fort Wallace, one hundred and twenty-five miles away. Then

---

[7] George Bird Grinnell, "The Fighting Cheyennes," p. 277.

he called for volunteers to make the journey. They had to travel on foot. All their horses were dead.

The answer surprised even Forsyth. Every man able to travel offered. Henry Trudeau, a veteran trapper, and Jack Stilwell, a nineteen-year-old boy, were chosen. At midnight they slipped out into the river bed, to begin their journey. They neglected no precautions. Their boots were taken off and slung about their necks so if the Indians should see their tracks in the morning they would look like moccasin prints and so perhaps escape notice. They wrapped themselves in blankets, so that in the starlit night their silhouettes should be passed as those of Indians.

Down the river they stole. Somewhere off in the bluffs lay the Indian camp, how near they did not know. Later Forsyth's men declared they could hear the thudding of tom-toms and an occasional eery howl as some squaw expressed her mourning for a slain consort.

Hugging the bank Stilwell and Trudeau progressed several hundred yards. Then they left the river and crawled on hands and knees, taking advantage of the cover of each bit of sage-brush or soap weed. Necessarily their progress was slow. Less than two miles were covered in the five hours before dawn, when they crawled into a dry washout.

All day they sat under the blazing sun. Every moment was an agony of suspense. They did not dare to raise their heads to the level of the prairie for fear of being spied by some hawk-eyed Cheyenne. They heard firing at the island and knew that fighting was going on. The country was full of riding Indians. Now and again the thudding hoofs of a warrior's pony would pass near. Yet by some miracle no Indian came directly upon them.

Darkness fell at last and again they set out. Their progress was faster now, but they were in constant danger. Once they hid in the shadow of a rotting buffalo carcass to escape the attention of a passing war party. They made several miles that night and took refuge in the morning under a high river bank.

The next night they set out at speed. Throughout the dark hours they travelled in a bee line for Fort Wallace without seeing a hostile. At dawn they were on a flat plain without a draw in which to hide. They began to think they might now travel with safety in the daylight, but after a conference lay down in a shallow buffalo wallow, a dry mud hole where the bison had wallowed in the rainy season. A few weeds grew around the border, affording scanty cover.

It was a wise decision. Early in the morning a scouting party of Cheyennes rode up and halted within a hundred feet of their hiding place. At almost the same moment a rattlesnake came wriggling through the grass toward them. They could have killed the snake easily but they did not dare move for fear of attracting the attention of the Indians. Even if the serpent rattled, the red men might investigate. Closer crawled the rattler, with its flat, ugly head raised menacingly and its tail already quivering slightly.

Must the crouching men choose the dreadful alternative of being bitten by the reptile or revealing themselves to their enemies? Jack Stilwell solved the dilemma. Like most plainsmen he chewed tobacco. His mouth was full of the juice at the minute. As the snake drew near, he spat a mouthful of the viscous fluid all over its head and eyes. Completely vanquished by the dose, the rattler forgot its belligerent ideas and wriggled a disgusted retreat. The Cheyennes presently moved on, never dreaming of the little drama which had been enacted under their noses.

Early in the evening the scouts started again and made fine progress, but toward morning Trudeau's age began to tell and he weakened rapidly. Stilwell had to lend him the support of a shoulder. They pushed on thus. When it seemed they could progress no farther, Trudeau exclaimed: "By thunder, a road!"

And so it was—the government highway into Fort Wallace. It was not long, then, until they delivered the message which sent a strong expedition to Forsyth's relief.

In the meantime, a second pair of scouts, Pliley and Donovan, left Forsyth on the second night. These men ran into Colonel Carpenter with the 10th (colored) Cavalry. Carpenter reached Forsyth first. He found the scouts suffering terribly. For six days the Indians had stayed in the vicinity. After they left, the men were chained to the island by their wounded as effectually as if they were bound by iron. For a time they ate the flesh of their dead horses. But this putrefied so that not even when covered with gunpowder could they force it down. An unlucky coyote was killed and they divided its carcass. On the sixth day Forsyth, believing all hope of rescue gone, ordered those who could travel to leave him and the wounded and get back to the settlements. But not a man stirred.

On the ninth day a sentry gave the alarm that there was another bunch of Indians moving in the hills. It was the last straw. The new arrivals could mean but one thing —another attack, which they could not beat off. Then a keen-eyed scout sent up a shout: "By heaven—an ambulance!"

The supposed Indians were Carpenter's relieving column. Forsyth's men were saved.[8]

[8] When Carpenter's command was returning with the remnants of the Forsyth scouts, a white teepee was noticed, standing alone in the valley. Two of the scouts rode over to it and found within the body of a dead warrior. They "identified" him as Roman Nose, and robbed him of the arms and finery which had been left with him. But years later the Cheyennes revealed the fact that the dead man was not Roman Nose, but another Cheyenne warrior named Killed-by-a-Bull, who was slain in the last charge. Roman Nose was carried away and buried after the usual custom, on a scaffold. No man knows today the place of his savage sepulcher.

CHAPTER VIII

THE CHEYENNES PAY

CUSTER'S WINTER CAMPAIGN

THE most picturesque, dashing figure in all our military history was General George Armstrong Custer. As a lieutenant fresh out of West Point he distinguished himself in the Civil War and when only twenty-six was a major general of volunteers.

Custer loved theatrical display. He emphasized his eccentricities and dramatized his personality. He wore his golden hair in long curls which fell to his shoulders and caused the Indians to call him "Long Hair." He affected the excessively wide hat, the buckskin coat and other individualized costume features which have remained a part of the Custer tradition.

He had a talent for writing. His articles in various magazines, published later in book form as "My Life on the Plains," painted a vivid picture of Indian fighting and further popularized the author.

Custer arrived on the frontier during the height of the Cheyenne war. He saw some hot campaigning and one of his first experiences was finding the bodies of Lieutenant Kidder and his ten men [1] after they were cut off and killed by Pawnee Killer's Sioux.

[1] Custer's description of the incident shows the impression it made: "A sight met our gaze which even at this remote day makes my very blood curdle. Lying in irregular order, and within a very limited circle were the mangled bodies of poor Kidder and his party, yet so brutally hacked and disfigured as to be beyond

General Sheridan, viewing the failure of the summer campaigns, decided in the fall of 1868 that his best hope was to attack the Indians in their winter camps. His reasons for the decision were as follows:

". . . Not less than eight hundred persons had been murdered, the Indians escaping from the troops by traveling at night when their trail could not be followed, thus gaining enough time and distance to render pursuit, in most cases, fruitless. This wholesale marauding would be maintained during the seasons when the Indian ponies could subsist upon the grass, and then in the winter, the savages would hide away, with their villages, in remote and isolated places, to live upon their plunder, glory in the scalps taken, and in the horrible debasement of unfortunate women whom they held as prisoners. The experience of many years of this character of depredations, with perfect immunity to themselves and their families, had made the Indians very bold. To disabuse their minds of the idea that they were secure from punishment, and to strike them at a period when they were helpless to move their stock and villages, a winter campaign was projected against the large bands hiding away in the Indian Territory." [2]

Custer was given the job. On November 22nd, in the midst of a bitter cold snap, with a foot of snow on the ground, he set out from Camp Supply, I. T., for the Washita River country. Two other columns, General Carr with seven troops of the 5th Cavalry, and Colonel Evans with six troops of cavalry, two companies of infantry, and

recognition save as human beings. . . . Every individual . . . had been scalped and his skull broken . . . some of the bodies were lying in beds of ashes with partly burned fragments of wood near them, showing that the savages had put . . . them to death by the horrible tortures of fire. The sinews of the arms and legs had been cut away, the nose of every man hacked off . . . Each body was pierced by from twenty to fifty arrows . . . bristling in the bodies."—"My Life on the Plains," p. 77.

[2] "Record of Engagements with Hostile Indians," p. 14.

four mountain howitzers, operated on each side of him as beaters. But Custer with the 7th Cavalry, was expected to do the actual fighting.

Marching south, Custer on November 26th struck the hot track of a war party returning from a raid on the Santa Fé trail. This band had killed mail carriers between Dodge and Larned, an old hunter at Dodge, and two of Sheridan's own dispatch carriers. Custer followed the track as rapidly as possible throughout the day, then decided to continue his march that night. Indian signs multiplied. Once they came upon the dying embers of a fire kindled during the day by Indian herd boys. They knew by that they were very close to the village.

Little Beaver, an Osage scout, smelled fire. He told Custer the camp was near. With the Indian, the general crept to the top of a low hill. His straining eyes made out a dark blotch on the snow—an immense pony herd. Significant noises greeted his ears. Far away dogs barked; there was the sound of a bell from the herd; once he heard the shrill wail of an Indian baby just over the hill. Custer realized he was on top of a tremendous camp. Returning, he whispered orders to his troop commanders which sent them to their posts.

THE VILLAGE ON THE WASHITA

It will be remembered that it was Black Kettle's village which Chivington attacked on Sand Creek. Even after that black treachery Black Kettle continued to favor peace, not because he loved the white man, but because he knew the inevitable result to his tribe of continued warfare. Only a few days before Custer reached the Washita, he had talked peace with General Hazen at Fort Cobb. Now

fate was for a second time to play him a scurvy trick. It
was Black Kettle's village which Custer had discovered.

But Black Kettle's camp was not the only one there.
Custer did not know it but all up and down the valley
great encampments stretched. Kiowas, Arapahoes, Comanches, Apaches and other Cheyennes were there. It is a
question if Custer would have attacked had he known the
odds. There were at least two thousand warriors in that
valley, although only a few hundred were in Black Kettle's camp.

Custer divided his men into four detachments. Major
Joel Elliott took three troops, Captain Thompson and
Captain Myers two each, and Custer retained four. The
four detachments quietly surrounded the camp. Throughout the night the men shivered. At the first light in the
east cinches were tightened and weapons examined. A
bugle sounded. Custer and the 7th Cavalry rode down on
the doomed village from every side.

With startled yelps the Cheyennes ran from their teepees. The charging troopers fired once; then they were
among the Indians. Black Kettle and his wife were killed
in front of their own lodge. Many others, both men and
women, died in the village. The rest ran into the river,
where they fought or tried to escape.

Red Bird Black, now living at Concho, Oklahoma, was
a boy of fourteen when the fight took place. He remem-
bers vividly the terrific cold and how the Indians, rudely
awakened, ran naked except for their breech clouts into
the ice-covered stream. Some of them were cut by the
razor edges of the broken ice until the water ran red with
their blood. Children were trampled under the hoofs of
charging horses. A few brave Cheyenne men, behind the
river bank, fought and fought, until all were dead, in

heroic self-sacrifice, so their families might get away. An Indian woman ran out of her teepee, dragging by the arm a little white boy. Seeing escape cut off, she whipped a knife into his body. She was instantly shot dead. The identity of the slain boy was never learned.

By ten o'clock the fight seemed to be over. But to Custer's surprise, hundreds of additional warriors were seen riding up the valley. Custer was puzzled. Then a captured squaw told him there was a string of Indian villages extending ten miles down the river. From these villages men were hurrying to help Black Kettle.

Custer swung the 7th into battle line and, menacing the Indians in the hills, retreated. An officer and five men were dead, and three officers and eleven men wounded. Major Elliott and fourteen men were missing.[3] Of the Indians Black Kettle and Little Rock, chiefs, were dead. With them were killed one hundred and one Cheyennes, including many women and children. Fifty-three squaws and children were captured. Custer destroyed more than a thousand buffalo robes, five hundred pounds of lead, an equal amount of powder, four thousand arrows, all the lodges, and slaughtered seven hundred captured ponies.

THE FATE OF ELLIOTT

Although Elliott was still missing, Custer retreated to Camp Supply. Within a few days he again marched south, this time on an errand of mercy. Two white girls, a Miss White, and a Mrs. Morgan, a bride of a month, had been captured by the Indians in raids up the Solomon and Republican valleys the previous summer. Their capture

[3] In the village later were found the dead bodies of Mrs. Blinn and her child, captured the preceding October in an attack on a wagon train at Sand Creek, Colorado, and murdered to prevent their being recaptured by the whites.

aroused great indignation in Kansas.[4] Governor Crawford got permission from the War Department to organize the 19th Kansas Cavalry. When the regiment was formed, the militant governor resigned his office to take its colonelcy and marched with it to Camp Supply.

On December 7th, although the weather was bitter cold, Custer again took the trail toward the Washita, with this new regiment and his own. Upon their arrival at the deserted site of the village which they had destroyed they learned the fate of Major Elliott and his men.

With fourteen troopers, Elliott followed some Indian women and children down the river. There were three men with them, one of whom was the chief, Little Rock. The three warriors stopped to fight while the women and children cut across a point. Little Rock was killed during this stand. The other two escaped as did the women.

Little Rock's diversion, brief though it was, saved his people, and it was also fatal to Elliott. It gave just enough time for a big band of braves from the allied camps to get behind the white men and surround them. Every man was killed in the short fight which followed.

Custer found all but one of them in a small circle where they had fought back to back. The single exception was Sergeant Major Kennedy. According to a story attributed to the Indians, Kennedy was the last survivor and an attempt was made to capture him alive. Knowing that torture was in store for him if he was taken, Kennedy pretended he was willing to surrender. He left the circle of his dead comrades and advanced toward one of the war-

---

[4] "The treatment of women by any Indians is usually bad, but by the plains Indians especially so. When a woman is captured by a war party, she is the common property of all of them . . . until they reach their village, when she becomes the special property of her individual captor, who may sell her or gamble her away when he likes. If she resists, she is 'staked out.' She is also beaten, mutilated, or even killed, for resistance. . . . No white woman has ever been known to escape this treatment at the hands of plains Indians."—J. P. Dunn, "Massacres in the Mountains," pp. 427-429.

Bureau of American Ethnology   *War Department*

War Department

Upper left: Quanah Parker, chief of the Quahada Comanches during the 1874 uprising, was the son of a white girl, Cynthia Ann Parker, captured by the Indians and later taken as a wife by Peta Nokoni, her captor. Upper right: Gen. Nelson A. Miles, most successful of all army Indian fighters. Center: Billy Dixon, famous scout and Indian fighter, as he appeared during the early seventies.

Left: Lone Wolf (Guipago), leader of the Kiowas in 1874 after the capture of Satanta. Center: Plenty Coups, great chief of the Crows, who fought against the Sioux as leader of Crook's Indian scouts in the Rosebud campaign. Right: Stone Calf, Southern Cheyenne chief, and his squaw. The man who held the German sisters prisoner.

riors with hand outstretched. The Indian approached, but Kennedy suddenly plunged his sabre through his body. Then the other Indians, angered, shot him dead. All of the bodies were stripped, mutilated, and shot full of arrows as was usual in such cases.

Elliott's men were buried, and Custer set out again with a very good stomach for a fight. But the fighting was over for the year. Satanta and Lone Wolf, Kiowa chiefs, were met and arrested. With these as hostages the Kiowas were forced back on the reservation. Then the command went into winter quarters at Fort Cobb.

In the spring they again set out. Guided by a captive Cheyenne woman, Custer located the village where the two girls were held. It would have been easy to ride down and give the Indians a taste of lead but that would have meant the deaths of the prisoners. Diplomacy had to take the place of force. Custer flattered, promised and threatened for tedious days. Then he took the bold step of seizing three Cheyenne warriors as hostages for the safety of the girls. To sugar-coat the pill, he sent presents and promised the release of the warriors on the surrender of the captives. Next day the girls were sent to him, both mounted on a single pony.[5]

THE FRATERNITY OF WARRIORS

In a tribe whose highest ideal and aim of life was war, a society of and for warriors naturally had tremendous prestige. Such a society was the famous Dog Soldier band, which contained the fiercest and most daring of all the Cheyenne warriors in the '60's and '70's. The name is a translation of the Cheyenne name for the fraternity, the

[5] Mrs. Morgan died a few years after her captivity. Miss White, however, is still living. She afterward married and is now a grandmother.

Ho-ta-min-tanio. It had organizations not only among the Cheyennes, but among the Sioux, Arapaho and other plains tribes. It had its own dances, songs, ceremonial costumes and insignia, besides special medicines and taboos. Only picked warriors could belong.[6]

In the war of 1865–68 the Dog Soldiers acquired such fame in the frontier battles that writers of the period frequently refer to the whole Cheyenne tribe as of that name. Tall Bull, fourth of a line of chiefs of the same title, and a close friend of the famous Roman Nose, now dead, was their leader.

After Custer's campaign in the winter of 1868, many Cheyennes went back on the reservation. But the Dog Soldiers remained defiantly hostile. They had not forgotten Sand Creek and now the Washita was added to their grievances. They would have nothing of the white man's peace.

In the spring of 1869 the Dog Soldiers moved their camp to the headwaters of the Republican River. From that point they made almost daily attacks on the settlements in May and June. They killed scores of civilians, captured two women, and ran off more than five hundred head of horses and mules, thus becoming the most serious menace on the frontier. Consequently, on July 1st, General Eugene A. Carr, with five companies of the 5th Cavalry and one hundred and fifty Pawnee scouts under the famous brothers, Major Frank North and Captain Luther North, started out to find and punish the Dog Soldiers.

It was not long until the Pawnees picked up a big Indian trail on the Republican River. That very night a dar-

---

[6] There were several other warrior societies among the Cheyennes, including Fox Warriors, Flint Warriors, Lance Warriors, Coyote Warriors, and others.

ing band of hostiles tried to stampede Carr's horses, but succeeded only in wounding a teamster.

Next morning the pursuit began. But Tall Bull was warned. Carr soon learned the lesson the Cheyennes always taught to pursuing soldiers. Try as hard as they might, they could not gain on the Indians. With their camp equipment, women, children, and aged, the Cheyennes could still show a clean set of heels to the best cavalry in the west.

Doggedly Carr hung on the trail. But it grew gradually dimmer as the Indians who had made it scattered. At last it divided and the scouts gathered for a conference. The trail to the right was plain; that to the left was scattered and dim. It was an ancient Indian trick. The heavy trail was obviously to be followed but the scouts advised following the other instead. Within a few miles the wisdom of this counsel was apparent. The dim trail grew heavier every hour. Before evening they were sure they were on the right track. The following day a decoy detachment, sent out under Major Royall to follow the false trail, rejoined them, reporting the track they had followed had suddenly faded away altogether.

Next day they made a sixty five mile march in spite of the terrific heat. They were approaching White Butte Creek, which has its source in the Summit Springs. The troops were spurred by the discovery of the print of a white woman's shoe among the tracks at one of the Indian camps. About noon a Pawnee from Frank North's scouting party, came galloping to Carr with word that an Indian camp was located a few miles ahead. It was Tall Bull's village. He had thought himself far enough in advance of the soldiers to escape safely across the Platte. But the waters were high and he camped to let them subside.

As Carr caught up with North in mid-afternoon, the Pawnee scouts were unsaddling their horses. They always fought bareback and stripped of their uniforms.

THE FIGHT AT SUMMIT SPRINGS

A little farther and they came to the edge of some bluffs. At their feet was a deep valley, and in it the picturesque panorama of the Dog Soldier village. Carr ordered the "Charge" sounded. Every horse leaped forward. In a minute more they were riding through the camp, led by the Norths and their yelling Pawnees.

A white woman ran from among the teepees with the Indians shooting at her.

"Lie down!" shouted the cavalrymen, for she was in the direct line of the charge. She obeyed. Every horse leaped over her body without a hoof touching her, but she had been shot through the breast. She was Mrs. Weichell, a German immigrant captured in Kansas.

At almost the same instant another white woman was seen. Too far away to save her, the troopers watched a warrior seize her by the hair and brain her with a tomahawk. An instant later they had ridden the murderer down and killed him.[7] This woman was Mrs. Allerdice, also captured in Kansas. Her baby had been strangled by the Indians.

Then the Indians bolted. The fight was over. Carr's men had done fearful execution. In their brief charge they had killed fifty-two Indians and captured one hundred and seventeen more. All the teepees, arms and supplies were destroyed. Only one trooper was wounded and no-

[7] This is the story told by some of the white soldiers who participated in the fight. The Cheyennes, however, say that Tall Bull killed the woman with his own hand. He did not die until later in the battle.

body killed, so complete was the surprise and so demoralized the Cheyennes.

Tall Bull was killed. He was cornered with a few warriors and women in a ravine by the Pawnee scouts under the North brothers. After finding protection for his wife and child behind a bank, he went to the mouth of the canyon and stabbed his horse there. Tall Bull was going to die where he stood. For several minutes the Cheyennes kept the Pawnees at bay. Then as Tall Bull raised his head above the bank for a shot, a bullet from Major Frank North's gun bored through his brain. Thirteen Indians were killed in the ravine. Tall Bull's wife and child were among the captured.[8] The body of Mrs. Allerdice was buried and Mrs. Weichell was taken back to her friends in Kansas. About $1,500 in money was found in the camp. This the soldiers and Pawnee scouts presented to the poor woman. She eventually recovered.

The Battle of Summit Springs ended active warfare for a time on the Kansas and Colorado plains. For a few months the settlers breathed more freely.

[8] Tall Bull's scalp, secured by Major Gordon W. Lillie from the Pawnees, may be seen at Pawnee Bill's Old Town, near Pawnee, Oklahoma. With it is the scalp of Black Kettle, which was obtained by Major Lillie from the Osages who took it in the Washita fight.

IV.

THE SOUTHERN TRIBES RISE
1873–1874

CHAPTER IX

THE IRRECONCILABLES

SATANTA

SMALLEST of the five nations which signed the Medicine Lodge Peace Treaty in 1867, was the Kiowa tribe. The Cheyennes, Comanches, Apaches and Arapahoes were all more numerous but there was an innate deadliness about the Kiowas which made them more dangerous, man for man, than any Indians on the plains. First and last the Kiowas probably killed more white men, considering their own numbers, than any of the other western tribes.[1] They felt the weight of the government's anger but, with ready adaptability they agreed to its demands, signed any kind of a treaty proposed—and then at the first opportunity, danced out on the war path again.

The greatest name in modern Kiowa history is that of Se-tain-te (White Bear) known to the frontier as Satanta. He was born in the atmosphere of constant danger, constant movement and constant war which was the Kiowa village of the early 1800's. He learned in his youth to hunt and fight; to ride a pony, any pony, and get out of it the last mile of service after it was ready to quit; to endure pain, hunger and adversity, without a show of emotion; and to hate all who were not Kiowas.

In his early childhood the Kiowas and Comanches

[1] Frederick Webb Hodge, "Handbook of American Indians," Bulletin 30, Bureau of American Ethnology.

smoked the pipe together and became allies, permitting his people to live south of the Arkansas River.[2] At twenty he was a graduate in the school of bloodshed and allied himself with Se-tan-gya (Satank), then in the first flush of his prominence. With him he fought and hunted, first as a subordinate, then as an equal until Satank's death in 1871.

Satanta rapidly won fame. No one was more fertile in strategy nor more active in warfare than he. One summer he led a harrying band of Comanches and Kiowas clear to Durango, Mexico. He constantly lurked about the base of Pawnee Rock to swoop down on unwary stage coaches and emigrant trains. His Kiowas all but destroyed traffic on the Santa Fé trail at the start of the Civil War and the irritation caused by their constant depredations was largely responsible for the Sand Creek massacre. Afterward, when the Cheyennes went to war they found able and willing allies in the Kiowas. And Satanta was ever the leading spirit.

He had high intelligence and, during the brief periods when he was not on the war path, lived amicably with the white man. He visited army posts with impunity and impudence and his manly directness and good humor made him a favorite with the officers. Satanta was a marvelous orator [3] and when he rose in council he well knew how to

---

[2] This was probably about 1825.

[3] He knew his power and loved to exercise it. And his sense of humor constantly impelled him to play pranks.

"Before a peace commission the old rascal grew very pathetic as he warmed to his subject. He declared he had no desire to kill white settlers or emigrants but that they ruthlessly slaughtered the buffalo (there was truth in the charge) and left their carcasses to rot on the prairie. He also said white hunters set fires which destroyed the grass and cut down the timber on stream margins to make large fires while the Indian was satisfied to cook his food with a few dead and dried limbs.

" 'Only the other day,' said he with the moving power of his voice playing at its finest, 'I picked up a little switch on the trail. It made my heart bleed to think that so small a green branch, ruthlessly torn out of the ground and thought-play on the emotions of his people. It was he, more than any other, who was responsible for the great outbreak of Kiowas and Comanches in 1874.

Although general Indian warfare ended with the destruction of Tall Bull's village in 1869, peace by no means reigned. Isolated white men were killed and scalped daily. Sometimes nobody knew who committed the murders. But on at least one occasion the Kiowas got the blame.

Satanta was a prisoner of Custer's during the winter of 1868, but the guard house had no effect on him. In the winter of 1869 he remained at Fort Dodge so long that he wore out his welcome. He loved liquor and constantly begged for it. One day he asked a stage driver for a drink. The driver was mixing a bottle of medicine to drench a sick mule. The moment he set it down, Satanta seized it and drank most of it before he drew his breath. He then started for an officer's quarters, begging for something to cure the taste in his mouth which "made his heart bad."

The officer at first refused, then succumbed to a mistaken sense of humor. He went to a closet, apparently took a swallow from a bottle containing most nauseating medicine, and placed the bottle on the shelf. Satanta watched his chance. As the officer left the room, he snatched the bottle and drained it. Even his stoical composure would not stand the strain of this jolt without breaking down. Satanta went hopping around, first on one foot, then on the other, holding his mouth and howling, while the sol-

lessly destroyed by some white man would in time have grown to be a stately tree for the benefit of my children and grandchildren.'

"After the pow-wow was over Satanta got a few drinks of liquor into him and his real thoughts asserted themselves.

" 'Didn't I give it to those white men?' he exulted. 'Why I drew the tears from their eyes! The switch I saw on the trail made my heart glad instead of sad for I knew there was a tenderfoot ahead because an old plainsman would have used a quirt or spurs. When we came in sight he threw away his rifle and held tightly to his hat for fear he should lose it.' "—Kansas Historical Society Reports.

diers beat their thighs and laughed until the tears ran down their faces.

But the Kiowa had the last say. Next morning he called his warriors together, crossed the Arkansas and went south to his village. Before leaving he burned all the government contractor's hay on the bank of the river opposite from the post, then went to Crooked Creek where he murdered three wood choppers—all in revenge for what he construed as an attempt to poison him at Fort Dodge.

Continuing south, he entered the Indian Territory and went on the war path. He never again returned to Fort Dodge as a friendly visitor, and in fact never conversed with a white man again—except perhaps with some victims he may have tortured—until he was taken prisoner.

In the latter part of May, 1871, the Kiowas made a bloody raid in the Red River region of Texas. Learning of their parts in the massacre, the government had both Satanta and Satank arrested. The two chiefs, with Big Tree, were sentenced to the penitentiary at Fort Richardson, Texas. Satank was a pathetic figure at the time. The old man had lost his son in Texas. On a spare horse he carried the bones with him wherever he went. After his arrest his son's bones were taken from him and he grew very gloomy. When the Indians were taken to prison, Satank rode in one wagon while Satanta and Big Tree were in another. A Caddo rode past and old Satank called: "I want to send a little message to my people. Tell them I am dead. I died the first day out of Fort Sill. My bones will be lying on the side of the road. I wish my people to gather them up and take them home."

Then he began to chant his death song. A few miles farther, he turned his back to his guards and pulled the shackles off his wrists, tearing the skin and flesh from his hands as he did so. Jerking a knife from under his blanket, he stabbed one soldier. The other jumped from the wagon. Satank seized a carbine and was trying to work the lever when he was shot twice, the second time fatally, by Sergeant J. B. Charlton, 4th Cavalry, in charge of the detail.

Satanta and Big Tree went on to Fort Richardson. Their loss was a heavy blow to the Kiowas who were quiet for two years. In the meantime the Comanches also received a stunning blow.

MC KENZIE'S VICTORY

The Quahada Comanches under Mo-wi had camped on McClellan Creek. There, on September 28th, 1872, Colonel Ranald S. McKenzie, with part of the 4th Cavalry, found them. When he came out on the wooded hills above the creek and saw the size of the village—there were two hundred and fifty lodges in it—it looked dangerous to attack. There were only two hundred and eighty-four officers and men in his command and at least five hundred warriors in that camp.

But two-to-one odds never abashed McKenzie.

"Right front into line!" he shouted. The squadrons swung into battle front. Hundreds of horses could be seen in the valley with herders frantically trying to rush them to camp so the warriors could mount.

"Charge!" was the next order. With guidons streaming, three troops dashed down toward the camp. The remaining troop went tearing off at a tangent, to cut off the horse herd. McKenzie knew the quickest way to whip an Indian was to dismount him.

The Comanches, taken completely by surprise, did not stay to fight. After a few volleys they bolted for the hills. One troop tried to head them off but it was too late. McKenzie lost three killed and seven wounded. Twenty-three

Comanches were dead and more than a hundred captured. Their entire pony herd was in McKenzie's hands and their village burned with all its stores.

That night the Comanches showed the desperation of horse-riding Indians when deprived of their mounts. McKenzie's Tonkawa scouts had been allowed to pick the finest racing horses from the captured herd for their own. During the night the Comanches returned and, violating their usual customs, made a night attack. There was not much fighting, but the hostiles captured back all their lost ponies and the entire herd of the Tonkawas as well. It was a chagrined bunch of Indian scouts which faced McKenzie next morning, on foot, with a solitary and forlorn burro as their only remaining animal.

McKenzie returned to Fort Concho and a commission was appointed to treat with the tribes. When they met with the Kiowas, the Indians' one and only cry was "Give us back Satanta and Big Tree." Finally the government made the concession. The prisoners were to be released but not pardoned. It was a sort of a parole, dependent on the good behavior of the tribe and the chiefs.

Lawrie Tatum, agent at Fort Sill, opposed very strenuously the release of Satanta. He said that "the effect on the Kiowas of the release of Satanta—a daring and treacherous chief—was like a dark rolling cloud on the western horizon." When his protests were overruled, he resigned, March 31st, 1873.

Satanta and Big Tree were brought to the guard house at Fort Sill where they were kept until the terms of their release were accepted. It was not until October 6th that Satanta walked out of his cell, with the gyves struck from his wrists.

Agent Tatum spoke the truth. Two years of prison life had made a different man of Satanta. Gone was the ofttimes jovial, urbane chief. In his place was a surly, morose, defiant savage, living for one object alone—revenge. Two years of prison had aged him ten years. He seemed an old man although he was only forty-three.

At first Satanta stayed around the agency. But the old warrior was incorrigible. The Indians began to grow restless. The agents believed Satanta was the trouble maker.

Early next spring Satanta suddenly disappeared altogether. At practically the same time both the Kiowas and Comanches, with some of the Cheyennes, took the war path. Spreading over the plains, they carried death and terror over five states.[4] And Satanta was the heart and soul of the uprising.

[4] A partial list of the murders, nowhere near complete, shows 190 settlers killed. These totals are as follows: In New Mexico, 40; in Colorado, 60; Lone Wolf's raid into Texas, 7; Big Bow's raid into Texas, 4; between Camp Supply and Dodge, buffalo hunters, 5; Adobe Walls, 3; southwest from Camp Supply, buffalo hunters, 3; near Medicine Lodge and Sun City, 12; on Crooked Creek, 2; on trail north from Cheyenne Agency, 5; on Santa Fé railroad, 4; Washita and Ft. Sill Agencies, 14; Dr. Holloway's son, Cheyenne Agency, 1; killed in other raids in Texas, 30. Total 190. This list does not contain the casualties of soldiers in any of the Indian battles.

CHAPTER X

BEFORE THE ADOBE WALLS

THE PASSING OF THE GREAT HERD

IN THE spring of 1874 the lean hunters of the plains rode from their teepees in the Indian Territory day after day in vain search for the great herd of buffalo. They were Kiowas and Comanches; Cheyennes and Arapahoes; and all the lesser tribes as well; and they forgot their ancient enmities in a common dread. From the tops of the highest promontories they scanned with keen eyes the farthest horizons for the familiar dark masses which would tell them that the great herd, supplier of nearly every Indian necessity, was come at last.

But the great herd did not come to the Indian country that spring. A scattering of small herds there was, and far to the west on the Staked Plains far-riding scouts reported the presence of buffalo, but the tremendous opaque masses which the red men had known for generations, were not.

In the medicine lodges, the wizards thumped and whirled in the mazy figures of the buffalo dance. The warriors sent skyward, in ever-increasing volume, the quavering hunter's song. And still no answer came. Despair began to lay its hand on the red people of the plains.

The absence of the herds primarily meant starvation. But every portion of the bison was useful to the Indian. The skin, dressed, furnished the covering for his lodge, his robes, his bed, even the shield with which he warded off the weapons of his enemy. Buffalo hides, stretched on frames of willow withe, formed bull boats to carry the people across rivers. Saddles and halters, hair for ornaments, belts, pouches and parfleche bags—the uses for the buffalo's skin were endless.

Every part of the flesh was consumed. The hump ribs were the finest meat the plains afforded, but the Indian did not scorn the less choice portions. He ate even the intestines. Such parts of the carcass as could not be devoured on the spot were "jerked" by drying in thin strips in the sun, or put up as pemmican, to serve as reserve supplies during the long winter months. Even the dried dung of the buffalo was invaluable in the treeless plains. Pioneers still live who can tell how they gathered "buffalo chips" for hot, satisfactory fires with which to cook and warm themselves.

Food, clothing, weapons, shelter, warmth—the five great essentials—all were supplied by the buffalo. Small wonder that when the great herd failed to appear the Indians grew desperate. They blamed the white men for this failure, thinking the herds had been frightened away. The Indians were wrong. The white men had not frightened the herds—they had exterminated them.

The building of the Santa Fé, Union Pacific and other railroad lines across the plains suddenly created a new sort of a market—a market for buffalo hides and meat, which were in demand in the eastern cities. There followed the most disgraceful slaughter of animals the world has ever seen. The hide hunter set forth, pitiless, unscrupulous, absolutely fearless, and as picturesque a figure as the continent ever produced. Each hunter had his corps of skinners and his transport system. Skillful hunters could keep a force of skinners steadily busy.

The favorite weapon was the old Sharps' .50 caliber rifle, shooting 125 grains of powder and 600 grains of

lead. In western parlance this weapon was known as the
"Buffalo Gun," and so it is still called by the old timers.
The hunters acquired an almost miraculous skill with this
heavy, large-bore rifle.[1]

In doing his killing the hunter worked his way to a
hiding place on top of a bluff or perhaps in one of the
buffalo's own wallows. With his cartridges in his hat beside him or spread conveniently on the ground, he method-
ically shot the herd down, one by one. Buffalo have very
dim sight and rely on their noses to warn them of danger.
So far away that his scent could not be carried, the hunter
killed at his ease. The reports of the gun seldom frightened the quarry. Nor would they flee when one of their
number was stricken. Stupidly sensing that something
was wrong, they would paw the ground, bellow and snort,
but remain to be killed.

It was nothing for a hunter to kill one hundred and
fifty to two hundred animals in a day. And there were
thousands of hunters working all the time.[2] Old timers say

[1] The late W. S. (Scott) Rubert of Wichita, an old plainsman, has told me of
witnessing the killing of prairie chickens a long way off without breaking their
skin. The hunters deliberately shot so close to their heads that the recoil of the
air stunned the birds. This sounds unbelievable, but so does Billy Dixon's mile
shot, and plenty of witnesses corroborated the latter.

[2] The following statistics show the rise and decline of the buffalo hunting
industry:

Year	A.T.S.F. Hides	OTHER ROADS Hides	TOTALS Hides
1872	165,721	331,342	497,063
1873	251,443	502,886	754,329
1874	42,289	84,578	126,867
Totals	459,453	918,806	1,378,259

Year	Meat lbs.	Meat lbs.	Meat lbs.
1872	....	....	....
1873	1,617,600	3,235,200	4,852,800
1874	632,800	1,265,600	1,898,400
Totals	2,250,400	4,500,800	6,751,200

In 1875 the business had fallen so low that no figures were kept. The above
table is from E. A. Brininstool's "Fighting Red Cloud's Warriors," by the permission of the publishers, Hunter-Trader-Trapper Co.

Buffalo hunter, killed and scalped by Indians near Dodge City in the early seventies.

Left: Se-tangya (Satank), war chief of the Kiowas. Killed in 1871 by Sergeant J. B. Charlton. Right: Satanta (Se-tain-te), chief of the Kiowas in the border wars of 1864-75.

A Pawnee village, showing the earth lodges peculiar to this people. A council is being held.

the shooting on a clear morning sounded like a sizable battle going on, so many rifles were at work. After the hunter came the skinners. Two skinners worked with a team of horses. A knife would split the skin down the belly and up the legs. Hitched to one edge of the hide the horses would pull it off. The hides were baled and carried to shipping points. Hams and tongues were also shipped to eastern packers. At one time there were forty thousand buffalo hides stacked in Dodge City and so rapid was the destruction that prices dwindled from four dollars and five dollars a hide to as low as a dollar.

THE OUTPOST IN THE WILDERNESS

By the Medicine Lodge Treaty of 1867, the government established the boundary line between Kansas and the Indian Territory. South of that line the Indians were to be sole masters. White men were not to hunt there and the Indians were not to cross to the north. As in so many other cases, however, the government found it could not keep this treaty. Irresponsible persons violated it and the buffalo hunters were the worst offenders.

By the fall of 1873 the buffalo were practically gone from north of the line. Then little bands of white men began stealing across and poaching in the Territory.

In the Texas Panhandle, close to where Bent Creek runs into the Canadian River, stood the ruins of an old, abandoned fort, one of the Bent and St. Vrain trading posts. Built of adobe, or mud-brick, it fell into disrepair and the rains washed the walls until they all but crumbled away. The place was known as Adobe Walls.

Because it was in the heart of a practically untouched buffalo country, a group of Dodge City men, in the spring of 1874, built a trading post and fort there. It was a simple, typical frontier post. At one corner was Myers & Leonard's log store. In another was a sod house, Hanrahan's saloon. Rath & Wright's store formed a third corner, while the fourth was the mess house, built of logs. Myers & Leonard and Rath & Wright were buffalo hide dealers of Dodge City, who helped "grub stake" the enterprise.

Their fort built, the hunters scattered to kill, bringing their hides to the Adobe Walls, constantly coming and going. For a time all went well although some of the men reported Indian signs.

Then, about the middle of June, Joe Plummer took a load of hides to the fort. When he returned to camp he found the bloody corpses of his partners, Dudley and Wallace. Both were scalped and butchered. One was pinned to the ground by a stake through his breast. Plummer almost killed a horse riding back to the Adobe Walls with the news.

Two other hunters were killed on the Salt Fork of the Red River—Cheyenne Jack Jones and Blue Billy, a German. Their camp was destroyed and all their stock run off. A big Indian camp was reported in the headwaters of the Sweetwater and the Washita. Every day saw new parties of the far-ranging hunters hurrying in to the protection of the fort.

The night of June 26th was sultry and the people at the Adobe Walls sat with open doors. Outside, the blackness of the night was only dimly lit by brilliant stars. Heat lightning played on the horizon. Horses, picketed to graze, could be heard stamping and moving about. There was another sound which the buffalo hunters, with all their experience, failed to interpret. In the timber along the creek owls hooted. The eery hooting from the woods was answered from the other side of the fort. Back and forth the owls talked, a sinister, goblin colloquy. It was noticed but the hunters thought nothing of it.

Twenty-eight men and one woman slept at Adobe Walls that night. The woman was Mrs. William Olds, wife of the restaurant man in the rear of Rath & Wright's. It was hot; the hunters spread their blankets out of doors to sleep. The stock seemed nervous. Occasionally a horse snorted or stamped. But no particular disturbance occurred until about two o'clock in the morning.

Hanrahan's saloon was a "soddy," with walls and roof of thick slabs of prairie sod, a favorite primitive building material in the early West. The slabs were laid on top of each other horizontally to form the wall. The roof was also covered with the heavy chunks. A cottonwood ridge pole, which supported the roof, proved too weak. The time it selected to break was two o'clock on that morning of June 27th. At the loud crack everybody awoke. The roof did not fall but it hung dangerously and all hands turned out to repair it. Had that ridge pole broken at any other time—say at noon, or the evening before—twenty-eight men and a woman would have been slaughtered in the Adobe Walls. It cracked just in time to awaken everybody so that there was no more sleep before dawn and thus forestalled the surprise attack the Indians had planned.

The east was pink when the repairs were completed. Billy Dixon [3] started out of the corral early to get his saddle pony. As he reached the spot where it was picketed he glanced toward the dark woods beyond. There was a movement. He strained his eyes through the morning gloom.

[3] The biography of this remarkable plains figure is told in "The Life of Billy Dixon," by his widow, Mrs. Olive K. Dixon, of Amarillo, Texas. Mrs. Dixon is a prominent member of the Panhandle-Plains Historical Society. For many incidents in this and the next chapter I am indebted to her.

Feathered war bonnets and painted ponies—it was a huge band of Indians.

The savages yelled as they saw themselves discovered and Dixon raced for life. Leaping on the back of his pony, he fired his gun and dashed for the stockade. At the shot every hunter seized his rifle. In an instant Adobe Walls was ready for defense.

THE BUFFALO HUNTERS' FIGHT

Everyone expected the Indians to follow their usual tactics—sweep around the buildings, kill anyone they found outside and run off the stock. But these warriors were on no mere horse-stealing raid. Straight as a lance-thrust they drove for the buildings themselves. Plumes tossed and the vivid war paint splashed their bodies with all the colors of the spectrum. Scalps fluttered from shield rims and horses' bridles; rifles and lances waved and ornaments of bead and silver gleamed. It was a splendid, barbaric—and terrifying—sight.

Two hunters failed to make it to the enclosure. The Shadler brothers had slept in their wagon outside the stockade. The Indians caught and killed them. Into the stockade itself the red warriors charged, filling the space around the buildings in which the whites were penned. Nine hunters were in Hanrahan's saloon, where there was plenty of whiskey but very little ammunition. Eleven sure shots, well armed and well supplied with cartridges, were in Myers & Leonard's store. The remainder, six old hands, with Mrs. Olds, were in Rath & Wright's.

Straight up to the doors rode the Indians. Every glass window pane was broken by bullets. The fierce warriors hammered on the doors with the butts of their rifles trying to break a way in. From the windows the hunters never for a second ceased shooting. Indians dropped fast. The wounded crawled painfully out of the stockade. Suddenly all were gone as quickly as they came.

For a time the hostiles busied themselves in carrying off their dead and wounded. Then they began a long-range duel with the fort. But at this game the hunters held all the top cards. They were the finest marksmen in the world. Their huge, heavy guns carried farther than the Indian rifles. The red sharpshooters grew discouraged.

The unusual boldness of the hostiles' first charge was due to the fact that a Comanche medicine man, I-sa-tai, had convinced them that he had an infallible charm which would prevent their enemies' bullets from touching them. They rushed into the battle with full confidence and were amazed and enraged to see their warriors dropping.

During the duel the whites suffered their third casualty. Billy Tyler and Fred Leonard recklessly stepped out into the stockade to get a better shot. A Comanche bullet ripped through Tyler's lungs. Leonard dragged him indoors and he died half an hour later.

Soon after Tyler was hit the Indians made a second rush. The murderous buffalo guns shattered the charge. Then some of the boldest hostiles hid behind stacks of robes, from which they tried to pick off the white men.

At one place in the fort the ammunition question was vexing. Some of the rifles in Hanrahan's saloon were useless because there were no cartridges to fit them. A hundred feet away stood Rath & Wright's. Hanrahan's door flew open. Racing across the courtyard went two men— Billy Dixon and James Hanrahan. At their appearance the Indians opened with every rifle within range. The ground around the feet of the two runners was churned and ripped by bullets. Bounding, zig-zagging, running their best, they reached the store and tumbled inside. By some miracle neither had been touched.

The purpose of the dash now appeared. Dixon and Hanrahan had come for ammunition. Rath & Wright had plenty of cartridges, but it also had the fewest defenders and the added responsibility of the only woman in the fort. The men begged Dixon to remain and help defend the building. He was known to be one of the greatest shots in the Southwest. Dixon consented. Hanrahan elected to carry back the ammunition. Filling a sack with cartridges, he waited a favorable opportunity and dashed back toward his saloon. Once more he drew the hail of bullets. But again he reached his destination safe.

About two o'clock the Indian fire slackened and at four it ceased entirely. After a time a venturesome hunter stepped out of his shelter. Others followed. The Indians were gone. In their first exploration around the stockade the hunters saw what terrible havoc had been wrought. In spite of every effort by the hostiles to carry off the dead, thirteen savages lay near the buildings, too close to be removed. Fifty-six dead horses were counted in the vicinity. There were great splashes of blood here and there in the grass. Nobody knows how many Indians were killed. The defenders estimated one hundred dead and wounded. The Indians subsequently said six Cheyennes and three Comanches were killed, a total of nine. As has been seen, however, thirteen dead bodies were found on the field after the battle.

All the horses were gone at the fort, but next day a hunter brought in some. There were still Indians in the vicinity, but Henry Lease offered to go to Dodge for help. He rode out of the fort the second night and eventually reached Dodge City safely.

Across the creek, east of Adobe Walls was a high bluff.

The third afternoon following the fight a band of about fifteen Indians appeared on this bluff, gazing at the fort. They were almost a mile away, but Dixon reached for his big buffalo gun. The other hunters, among whom he had a wonderful reputation as a marksman, urged him to try a long shot. Carefully he adjusted his sights. Twice he took aim before he fired. So distant was the target that the report of the gun died completely away before there was a movement on the bluff. Everybody thought Dixon had missed. Then one of the tiny figures whirled suddenly out of his saddle. The hunter had struck his mark at nearly a mile!

The buffalo hunters were used to wonderful shooting. But they were simply dumbfounded by this exploit. The Indians scurried for cover. In a few minutes two of them crept forward and dragged their fellow to concealment. Years later a surveyor measured the distance from where Dixon fired to where the Indian was seen to fall. It was exactly 1,538 yards, just 182 yards short of a full mile. Dixon always modestly said it was a "scratch" shot. But it remains a wonder story of the West.

On the sixth day William Olds, whose wife was the only woman at the fort, accidentally killed himself by discharging his rifle while he was climbing down a ladder. His was the fourth death at the fort. Two days later the relief column from Dodge City, under Tom Nixon and Henry Lease, arrived.

CHAPTER XI

THE ARMY TAKES THE FIELD

AFTER THE ADOBE WALLS FIGHT

THE buffalo guns won a bloody victory for white hunters at the Adobe Walls, but the echoes of their thunderous reports were still to be heard on many a distant horizon. The allied tribes—Comanches, Kiowas, Cheyennes, and Arapahoes—scattered in every direction looking for revenge.

Kiowas, prowling northeast, ambushed Pat Hennessey's wagon train, freighting supplies from Wichita, Kansas, to Anadarko, Indian Territory. Every man in the train was killed. Hennessey was tortured to death.[1] Soon after a dozen men were killed by Comanches near Medicine Lodge, Kansas. Both Comanches and Kiowas raided deep into Texas. There was not a road in western Kansas, eastern Colorado, the Texas Panhandle, or the Indian Territory which was safe. About two hundred settlers were killed.

The frontier yelled for the army. General Nelson A. Miles, commanding the department, promptly marched from Fort Dodge on August 14th. Lieutenant Colonel J. W. (Black Jack) Davidson started west from Fort Sill. And Colonel Ranald S. McKenzie advanced northeast from Fort Clark. The plan was to catch the hostile bands between the three columns and thus crush them.

[1] The present city of Hennessey, Okla., which stands on the spot where this massacre occurred, derives its name from this tragic incident.

A cheering bit of news came to Miles on the march. Davidson and his 10th Cavalry "buffalo soldiers" [2] had fought a brisk engagement with Kiowas and Comanches at the Wichita agency at Anadarko. The losses were slight but an important result was the capture of Satanta, regarded as the ring-leader in the uprising.

Meantime Miles had some fighting on his own hands. On the morning of August 30th Lieutenant Frank D. Baldwin, with fifty white and Delaware scouts was suddenly "jumped" by two hundred hostiles as he followed a trail up the Sweetwater Valley. Badly outnumbered, Baldwin's men scattered among the rocks and underbrush and held the enemy off until Major Compton and Major Biddle arrived to extricate them from their danger.

The cavalry wasted no time. Wheeling their men into line, Compton and Biddle charged. Captain A. R. Chaffee led the advance, merrily joking with his men.

"Forward!" he cried. "If any man is killed I will make him a corporal!"

The veterans rode forward laughing, scarcely noticing the bullets which came skipping about them. The Indians mounted and "skedaddled." After following them twenty-five miles over the roughest kind of country, the troops found themselves in a desert without water of any kind. Some of the men suffered so they even opened the veins in their own arms to moisten their lips with the blood.

Miles' command limped at last back to the Sweetwater. September 10th found them camped on McClellan Creek. They were short of rations. Miles' wagon train had been attacked the day before and four men killed or wounded. The general wrote a message to Camp Supply and dispatched it by a small party consisting of two celebrated

[2] Negro soldiers. So called by the Indians because their kinky hair looked like buffalo wool.

scouts, Billy Dixon [3] and Amos Chapman, and four veteran 6th Cavalry troopers, commanded by Sergeant Z. T. Woodhull.

The detail, purposely small to escape notice in the hostile country, travelled unmolested for two nights, hiding by day. The second morning, however, it was discovered by a large Kiowa war party.

TWENTY-FIVE TO ONE

The Kiowas wasted no time. They charged, yelling, at the dead gallop, shooting as they came. The first volley hit four of the white men. Private George W. Smith, holding the horses, fell flat on his face, a bullet through his body. The horses stampeded with all the extra ammunition. A bullet broke Chapman's leg. Private John Harrington was wounded and so was Woodhull.

Somehow, by accurate shooting, they stopped that first Indian rush. Dixon, still unhurt, looked keenly around for cover. The only depression anywhere near them was a buffalo wallow, a few inches deep and ten to twelve feet in diameter. But it was their sole hope.

"Come on, boys," the scout called. "Let's fight it out here."

Woodhull and Harrington, with Private Peter Rath, the only unwounded soldier, followed. But neither Chapman nor Smith moved.

"Come on, Amos," yelled Dixon to Chapman.

"I can't," groaned the reply. "My leg's broken."

There were at least a hundred Kiowas in sight, and every one of their rifles was kicking up the dirt around the

---

[3] The hero of the Adobe Walls fight. He joined the army scouts after that battle. Amos Chapman was a "squaw man." He returned to live with the Cheyennes after the war and died among them in 1926.

wallow. For a few minutes the four men in it worked desperately deepening the hole with their knives.

At the first breathing spell Dixon again looked over the flat. Chapman and Smith were still there, but Chapman was painfully pulling himself along with his hands, inch by inch, toward his comrades. The sight was too much for Dixon. Heedless of warnings, he jumped up and dashed for the wounded man. Bent double to present as small a target as possible, with bullets singing in his ears, he reached Chapman untouched. At his command, Amos climbed on his back, and although Dixon was the smaller man, he carried him to the wallow in safety. As usual the Indian shooting was wretchedly poor.[4]

Dixon's exploit provoked the Kiowas to another attack. This time they swept right up to the buffalo wallow. But the veteran defenders shot deliberately, with careful aim, making every bullet count. Two of the surest rifles in Miles' army were in that wallow. The Kiowas retreated quickly to a safer distance.

It was very hot. By noon every man was suffering from thirst, made more intolerable now that all were wounded, including Rath and Dixon. Yet with the utmost coolness they aimed over the rim of the wallow pulling the trigger every time an Indian came close enough for a good target. A growing clutter of dead horses and accoutrements where stricken warriors had been dragged away, showed how they had taken their toll.

Hour after hour dragged along. Under the torture of thirst some of the wounded grew delirious. But now a

[4] Chapman was quoted by General Richard I. Dodge in his "Thirty-one Years Among Our Wild Indians" as saying that he carried the body of Smith to the wallow in spite of the fact that his own leg was broken off at the ankle and the foot was dragging. This story was disproved by the testimony of the other men at the fight as well as of Dixon himself. The poor shooting of the Indians in nearly all the battles is explained by the fact that they were always so short of ammunition that they had no cartridges to spare for the target practice so essential to good marksmanship.

great black thunder cloud gathered in the southwest. The lightning began to play while the deep reverberations of the thunder gave promise of one of the violent storms which are characteristic of the prairie country. It came quickly. In blinding sheets the rain fell, blotting out the landscape, the hostile Indians, the body of poor Smith, and drenching them to the skin. But though they were wet through, the rain was welcome. The air was cooled and rivulets of water caught in the rim of the wallow to gather in a pool at the bottom. Muddy it was, and bloody too, from their own clotted wounds, but the men lay on their stomachs and drank and drank.

Ammunition was at a premium. When the rain let up somebody noticed the cartridge belt on Smith's body. The Indians had repeatedly tried to reach him but were driven away by unerring riflery. Now, their ardor cooled by the sudden drenching, they sat on the prairie out of range, holding a council while their horses grazed at the end of their lariats.

Rath went after Smith's ammunition. As he stooped to detach the cartridge belt he was surprised to see his comrade twitch. Without stopping to investigate, he lifted the still form and carried it to the buffalo wallow. Smith was still alive but with a bullet through his lungs. A few hours later he died. His comrades propped up his body so the head showed over the edge of the wallow, to make the Indians think he was still able to fight.

At nightfall Rath volunteered to go for help to Camp Supply. He and Dixon were the only ones able to move. He started east but returned in a couple of hours, unable to find the trail. He had seen no Indians. Dixon started at sun-up. He found the trail and later met a detachment of troops under Major Price whose approach had caused the Indians to withdraw. The scout led the way to the buffalo wallow where the men's wounds were dressed and Smith's body buried in the very hole where his comrades had fought for their lives.[5] Then the wounded were taken to Camp Supply and the dispatches delivered.

PALO DURO, CANYON OF DEATH

Lone Wolf, the most active of the confederated Indian leaders, stepped into Satanta's moccasins when that chief was imprisoned. He had his camp in Palo Duro Canyon, in Northern Texas, a splendid base of operation from which war parties went in every direction. The canyon, a deep cleft in the flat prairie, was so naturally advantageous that there were big Cheyenne, Arapaho and Comanche camps there also.

Hoping to locate this camp, Colonel McKenzie, with his 4th Cavalry, four companies of infantry, and a detail of Seminole, Tonkawa and white scouts, marched from Fort Concho the middle of September. Blanco Canyon was supposed to be the hostile rendezvous. He reached it September 27th but no Indians were there. Disappointed, McKenzie left his heavy supply train behind and struck boldly north.

The Tule and Palo Duro Rivers lay in his path, winding through deep canyons. Indian signs indicated the hostiles might be in one or both of these valleys. With a screen of scouts and skirmishers ahead, the command was half-way to the Tule Canyon by noon of the 28th.

A sharp crackle of fire, far in advance, electrified them. "Indians!" was the exclamation on every tongue. The troops pressed forward eagerly but were disappointed. A small band of hostile scouts had exchanged some long

[5] On recommendation of General Miles, Congress later awarded the Congressional Medal of Honor by special vote to all five survivors of this celebrated border fight.

range shots with the advance and drawn off as the main body approached.

It was the first sight of hostile Indians. They camped that night in the Tule Canyon, with a double guard. Just at moon-rise, the expected happened. Silhouetted against the pale, star-lit sky, appeared a mass of Indians. Down toward the camp they swept. But the sentries were alert. At the first alarm shots, the troopers were ready. Two or three white-hot volleys flashed out into the gloom. There were some unearthly war whoops and the Indians drew off. But they did not leave the vicinity. All night long there was skirmishing between the outposts and prowling warriors who crept close to take pot-shots at the men near the camp fires. By morning everyone was thoroughly angry and in the mood for real fighting. The Indians, however, refused to accommodate them. Having kept the troops awake all night, they drew off shortly before sun-rise.[6]

After breakfast, McKenzie assigned Sergeant J. B. Charlton [7] with two Tonkawa scouts, Job and Johnson, to locate the village. It was easy to follow the Indian trail.

[6] Just at dawn occurred a grimly humorous incident. A solitary Comanche rode into range and Henry, a Tonkawa scout, killed his horse with a lucky, long-distance shot. Thinking he had also killed the rider, the Tonkawa rode to the spot. But the Comanche was only stunned. At Henry's approach he leaped to his feet and pulled the "Tonk" out of his saddle. Then began a strange combat. Henry's rifle was in its scabbard on his horse. His blanket so encumbered him that he could not reach his revolver. The Comanche could not get a lethal weapon either but his unstrung bow was in his hand, so seizing his enemy by the hair, he began giving him the trouncing of his life. At every cut of the bow, Henry jumped about three feet in the air, and yelled at the approaching troopers, "Why you no shoot? Why you no shoot?" The soldiers were all roaring with laughter but finally someone shot the Comanche and the discomfited Henry took his scalp with great satisfaction.

[7] The same man who shot and killed Satank in 1871. To Captain R. G. Carter, U. S. A., Retired, of the Army and Navy Club, Washington, D. C., I am under obligations for considerable of the information concerning McKenzie's movements in this campaign. Capt. Carter's book "The Old Sergeant's Story," a compilation of the letters of Sergeant Charlton is worth the attention of any student of plains history. He is author of numerous other works on western Indian campaigns.

For several miles the scouts rode rapidly; then they began to notice other trails converging with the one they were following. At last they were convinced they were almost on a great camp.

But where was it? For miles, as far as the eye could reach, the country stretched bare and level as a table. They were morally certain from the signs which multiplied at every step that they were very close to a monster Indian village. By rights, hundreds of teepees should stretch in every direction; the plain should be populous with grazing pony herds; a myriad flea-bitten dogs should be running hither and yon in joyous canine abandon, while their masters should be visible in scores, mounted and on foot, lazing in the shade or going about their duties.

Yet there was not a sign of life in any direction. It was creepy. The superstitious Tonkawas began to look uneasily over their shoulders as if they expected at any minute to see a full-blown camp of their enemies materialize from the air.

Quite without warning the whole mystery was explained. The scouts were forced to rein their horses to a stop. At their feet yawned one of the colossal crevices which sometimes break the monotony of the plains of North Texas. It was the Palo Duro Canyon, slashed deep into the flat face of the prairie. While Job held the horses, Charlton and Johnson crept to the edge of the abyss. With awe they gazed into its depths. Straight down, the walls dropped sheer for hundreds of feet. Half-way between the men and the bottom of the canyon soared an eagle, looking a mere speck. Far down a small stream of water trickled. Flecks of valley land were visible, with here and there dark masses of cedar trees casting gloomy shadows and making the scene almost nocturnal although the sun shone brightly on the plains above.

But something else riveted the attention of the scouts. In the valley were hundreds of grazing horses. Viewed from the immense height they looked no bigger than prairie dogs. And conical white teepees thickly dotted the banks of the stream as far down the canyon as the eye could see. They were gazing down at Lone Wolf's stronghold.

"Heap Injun!" grunted the Tonkawa in Charlton's ear.

"You bet your life, old scout, and some canyon too," whispered the sergeant as they snaked their way back to the horses.

They did the twenty-five miles back to the command in record time. McKenzie's men were in the saddle almost before the sergeant's words were out of his mouth. It was nightfall but they were spoiling for a fight. All night the troopers rode, reaching their destination just at sun-up.

INTO THE CANYON

At their feet was the canyon, but how should they descend into it? Like hounds the scouts scattered up and down the edge. There must be some easy way down but no time to look for it now. Presently a trail was reported and McKenzie went to inspect.

It could hardly be called a trail unless by that name one can describe a crooked, zig-zag scratch in the face of the mighty cliffs down which antelope, or deer, or perhaps mountain sheep had found precarious footing to the water. But McKenzie did not hesitate.

"Mr. Thompson, take your men down and open the fight," he said.

In a moment the scouts were over the edge of the cliff, starting down the precipitous route. Down, down they went, followed by the whole command. They were descending well above the camp and they hoped to reach the bottom before the Indians were warned. They knew what the hostiles might do to them if they caught them plastered against the sides of the canyon.

Lieutenant W. A. Thompson tested every foot of the way. Sometimes the path was so narrow that the men went along with their faces to the cliff, their arms outspread and their bodies flattened against the rocky wall as they "cooned" across. For a time there was scarcely a sound. But a big body of men cannot go down a route like that without making some noise. Somebody dislodged a small boulder. Down the side of the cliff it bounded, thudding against the wall, carrying with it a miniature avalanche of dirt and gravel which gathered volume and racket as it descended.

Instantly the canyon rang with a war whoop. An Indian down the valley had heard the noise.[8] By the time the first scouts reached the bottom the hostiles were coming up the gorge to meet them. For a time it was a question whether the little group of white men could hold back the Indians long enough to permit their comrades to land. The Kiowas took shelter behind rocks and in the thick cedar trees. The scouts were under heavy fire.

Down the canyon was a ledge, partly hidden by the tree tops, where lay half a dozen Kiowa sharpshooters. Their bullets chipped the rocks all around McKenzie's soldiers, who were in a tight place against the face of the cliff, unable to defend themselves. Two of the scouts ran toward the ledge, threw themselves on their stomachs and under a storm of bullets began a duel with the sharpshooters. White man's marksmanship won. Down from the niche

[8] This man, Red Warbonnet, a Kiowa, had a herd of white horses of which he was very proud. He had gone out to look at these horses in the early morning when he heard the soldiers and gave the alarm. He was instantly shot down by the Scouts.

pitched one warrior after another. In a short time the hole was cleaned out.

By this time the soldiers were nearly all safely down. Powder smoke made a gray cloud, giving the scene a hazy aspect. In the midst of this McKenzie could be heard shouting orders.

Along the canyon went the soldiers. The hostiles retreated. A pony herd, frightened by the uproar, charged back and forth across the bottom of the canyon, adding to the confusion. They were cornered at last in a blind gulch and kept there to the end of the fight.

It was a long way to the hostile village and the Indians were determined to hold McKenzie back until their camp could be evacuated. When sunset came, the troops were still five miles from the pass where the squaws and children were leaving the canyon. By the time the command reached it and climbed to the plain, the canyon was dark— Lone Wolf and his people had disappeared.

McKenzie returned to the gorge. Bodies of four Kiowa braves were found but they knew they had hit many more.[9] Only a hundred teepees were captured but of these they made a huge bonfire. In the morning McKenzie started back to Blanca Canyon, driving before him fourteen hundred captured horses and mules. These he killed in the Tule Valley and their bones whiten that part of the country to this day.

THE END OF THE UPRISING

The Battle of Palo Duro Canyon completely discouraged the Kiowas, not so much because of their losses, but because there now seemed no place they could retreat to in

---

[9] The Comanches say that a number of women and children were killed in this fight.

safety. There were still many Indians out on the Staked Plains, but hundreds surrendered.

It is extremely difficult to follow all the movements of troops and Indians in the succeeding months, so disconnected were they. Everywhere were detachments of soldiers hunting scattered bands of hostiles. There were a number of small fights but only a brief summary of this "cleaning up" phase of the campaign can be given.

Colonel Buell and the 11th Infantry destroyed a Kiowa camp on October 9th on the Salt Fork, killing one warrior and putting the rest to flight. Several hundred lodges were burned. Captain Chaffee, with Troop I, 6th Cavalry, surprised and destroyed another Indian camp October 17th. A large Comanche village surrendered to Major G. W. Schofield at Elk Creek on October 24th. Colonel Davidson brought in ninety-one captured warriors, with three hundred women and children on October 28th. The Indians were on the run everywhere, seeking a place to hide, or some way to surrender without being shot down.

A Tennessee family named German [10] was surprised September 9th by Cheyennes. The father and mother, the eldest son and the eldest daughter were killed. The four younger girls, Catherine, 17; Sophia, 15; Julia, 10; and Adelaide, 5, were carried off as captives. The Cheyennes were from the villages of Gray Beard and Stone Calf. The two older girls went with Stone Calf's band to the Staked Plains while their sisters were taken with Gray Beard's people to McClellan Creek.

Scouts told Miles that the Indians held four white girls. He took immediate steps to recover them. Lieutenant Baldwin was given a separate command and told to find Gray Beard's village and rescue the girls. Baldwin had a

[10] Miles and others spelled this name "Germaine" but the correct spelling is "German." The massacre of the family occurred on the Smoky Hill River in Kansas.

troop of cavalry, a company of infantry, a howitzer and a train of wagons. He discovered the hostile village November 8th. One of the quickest fights in the war followed. Putting his infantry in the wagons and telling the teamsters to stick close to the cavalry, Baldwin charged, as the saying goes, "horse, foot and dragoons." Down into the village galloped the cavalry with the wagons full of infantrymen bouncing and clattering right behind. The Indians, completely baffled by the strange maneuver, did not even stop to kill their prisoners. The children were found in Gray Beard's abandoned teepee, their little bodies scarred and bruised, and half starved. Dr. James L. Powell, the medical officer, took them to Fort Leavenworth where they were lodged with a family named Carney.

Thus two of the girls were saved, but the recovery of their sisters was more difficult. Stone Calf was far out on the Staked Plains. The girls lived lives of terror and ill-treatment. The recent reverses had made the Indians ugly. Their prisoners feared every day they would be murdered—and did not care much if they were.

But early in January Miles sent some of Stone Calf's people who had surrendered, with a message to the chief. A faithful Indian scout accompanied them, carrying a photograph of the two younger girls, taken after their recapture, with this message in the general's own hand:

"To the Misses Germaine: Your little sisters are well and in the hands of friends. Do not be discouraged. Every effort is being made for your welfare.
"NELSON A. MILES, COL., FIFTH INFANTRY."

To Stone Calf went the ultimatum that unless he surrendered the girls uninjured, Miles would hunt him down without mercy, while he would receive amnesty if he did surrender them and came in to the reservation. Stone Calf accepted the terms—he was tired of this profitless fighting. His first act was to take the sisters away from their owners of the moment and lodge them in a teepee close to his own. Late in January he surrendered at Darlington. The girls afterward identified seventy-five Indians who were involved in the murder of their family and other offenses and these were ordered arrested. The sisters were sent to Leavenworth where they joined the little girls whom they had given up as lost.[11]

Practically all the warring Indians had now surrendered. In arresting the men pointed out by the German girls, one resisted and tried to escape. He was shot and some of the bullets flew into the Cheyenne prison camp, causing a panic. The Indians fled to a nearby hill. In the sharp fight which followed eleven Cheyennes were killed and nineteen men of Lieutenant Colonel T. H. Neill's command were hit in trying to take the hill. Later most of the Cheyennes moved quietly to the agency and mingled among their people already there. The worst offenders were sent to St. Augustine, Florida.

Peace reigned once more in the Southwest, but there still remained to be played out the tragic sequel of the Indian war. Satanta, the Kiowa chief, was in prison for his part in the uprising. There was no proof of his guilt but he had violated his parole by leaving the reservation so he was sent to the penitentiary at Huntsville, Texas, for life.

That was the end of everything for Satanta. With downcast head he entered the prison. Nothing was said but the very guards knew he would not live long. A year passed—two years—three. One day he appeared at the prison dispensary.

"My heart is bad," he said and asked for medicine. He

[11] All four of the German girls are still alive at this writing. All married and reared families. Two live in California, one in Nebraska and the fourth in Kansas.

was placed in a second story ward of the prison hospital. Shortly afterward a weird sound was heard; with many a minor chord and long-drawn wail, it descended from the air—the Kiowa death song. Then the guards saw the old warrior at the window. With one last look at the blue sky under which he had so often roamed free as a bird, Satanta folded his arms and plunged headlong. He was dashed to death on the stony ground below.

V.

THE STRUGGLE WITH THE SIOUX
1875–1877

CHAPTER XII

THE DIPLOMAT AND THE WARRIOR

CUSTER'S BLACK HILLS EXPEDITION

SCARCELY was the uprising quelled in the Indian Territory when the hard-worked soldiers of the frontier army were called to face a far more dangerous enemy a thousand miles to the north.

Frantic messages from agents in the Dakotas said that the whole Teton Sioux Nation was on the verge of an outbreak. There were more than thirty-five thousand Sioux in the country and they could muster around seven thousand fighting men. Moreover, from earliest times they had borne a reputation for ferocity and prowess. As a matter of fact, only a part of the Sioux went on the war path, but even so, the army officers were justified in looking grave at the reports.

If ever any people was goaded into war, it was the Sioux in 1876. And if the World Court of today had sat in that period, the United States would have been ruled an "aggressor nation." The Sioux war of 1876 was fought because the government could not make its own citizens abide by its treaties. For eight years after Red Cloud's campaign of 1868 there was peace of a sort, although the encroachments of the white men caused constant trouble, with frequent killings. The treaty which ended that war expressly stipulated: "The country north of the North Platte and east of the summits of the Big Horn Mountains shall be held and considered to be unceded Indian territory," and further agreed: "No white person or persons shall be permitted to settle upon or occupy any portion of the same; or without the consent of the Indians, first had and obtained, to pass through the same." The land described in this article—which closes with the agreement that the Bozeman Trail and all the posts along it shall be abandoned—is the Powder River Country.

At its eastern border lay the frowning Black Hills, sacred to the Sioux and among their best hunting grounds. In 1874, despite treaty stipulations, on the pretext of making a survey for military purposes, General George A. Custer, with the 7th Cavalry, was sent into the gloomy fastnesses of these hills. When he returned he broadcast the news that there was gold there. As if to reassure itself of this fact, the government sent a second expedition under Professor Jenney, which came out of the Black Hills with such indubitable proofs of gold that a stampede of prospectors followed.[1]

Now that the government had started all the trouble it tried to halt the rush of gold miners. Troops were thrown about the mountains and expeditions were sent into them to round up trespassers and bring them back. These, however, were speedily acquitted by the local civil courts. Through the lines drifted miners by hundreds, with the constant news of fresh "strikes" adding fuel to their excitement. The Black Hills were full of them. Deadwood, Custer City and a score of other mining towns sprang up. The Sioux were furious.

Red Cloud saw the handwriting on the wall and sent some of his braves to see how many buffalo were on the

[1] "If this fact [Jenney's expedition] does not lift the thin disguise of military necessity from the first [Custer's] expedition, one could hardly imagine what would."—Dunn, "Massacres in the Mountains," p. 587.

plains. They reported that the buffalo were few; they could not be depended upon for any length of time. Red Cloud knew he could not fight without supplies. He kept peace through the troubles which followed.

Confessing by its act its inability to keep its citizens out of the forbidden territory, the government next tried to buy the Black Hills. A commission did its best in June, 1875, to secure from the Sioux the right of mining there. The reservation part of the Indians agreed to a sale, but at prices ranging from $20,000,000 to $50,000,000. The government's offer of $6,000,000 was rejected with scorn. But the non-reservation Sioux simply refused to sell under any consideration and with deadly seriousness warned all white men to keep out. The commission returned, frustrated, to Washington.

That fall the wild Sioux moved out into the wilderness far from the agencies. The reservation Sioux grew restless. Everyone knew war was inevitable. Two names were on every tongue—names destined to become household words—Sitting Bull and Crazy Horse.

THE LEADERS OF THE SIOUX

No man ever had a more important influence upon the destiny of the frontier than Sitting Bull, the famous Unkpapa chief. To the average reader his picturesque name conjures up a novel-inspired vision of a ferocious savage, careering over a corpse-strewn field, shaking a bloody tomahawk and suffering from a perennial thirst for human gore. A study of the great Indian's character, however, fails to justify this picture.

Sitting Bull was in all respects a remarkable man. He was a natural-born fighter and therefore had enemies all his life, not only among the white people but among his own followers. As a result there has been much traducing of his character.

It is pretty clear, however, that Sitting Bull was no coward. He was not cruel; he was not even particularly bloodthirsty. On the other hand, he was a real patriot, a great organizer and a wily politician. And he was intelligent above all his fellows for "he alone of all his people could see through the curious wiles of the white men, who were as strange and incomprehensible to the Indians as if they were men from Mars." [2]

He was a famous warrior while still in his twenties, going on his first war path at the age of fourteen. He is credited by some authorities with leading the attack on Fort Buford in 1866. Sitting Bull's now famous pictograph autobiography contains pictures showing his participation in twenty-three battles with Indians or whites, and twelve horse-taking raids. It has been charged [3] that Sitting Bull was not present at the Little Big Horn fight. But his ablest biographer, Stanley Vestal, has accumulated plenty of eye-witness evidence that he was not only there but that he fought in the front ranks. After the Miles campaign in 1877 Gall is said to have accused him of cowardice. It was an undeserved stigma. First to last, Sitting Bull's career shows not only high physical courage, but even higher moral courage. He remained the white man's enemy to the end, when everyone else had given up, even though it eventually led him to a dishonored grave.

It was not as a fighter, however, but as a diplomat and organizer that Sitting Bull rendered his chief service to the Sioux. He used his political ability to keep his people together and ready to fight. Vestal says he was elected

[2] Vestal, "Sitting Bull," p. 75.
[3] Notably by Rain-in-the-Face and Major McLaughlin.

Sitting Bull (Tatanka Yotanka), head chief of the allied Sioux tribes against the white men in 1876.

Young Sioux brave undergoing the Sun dance torture. The rawhide ropes attached to spindles thrust beneath raised strips of flesh on his chest, may be seen. Blood is running down his legs. He is wearing his shield, with cover. The young man must dance until he tears out the strips of flesh on his chest and releases himself from the rawhide ropes. Photograph by W. Rau. (From Hutchinson's *Living Races of Mankind*, courtesy of Dodd, Mead and Co.)

head chief of all the Sioux bands in 1851, but the army records credit him with but small influence as late as 1875, when "he was not a chief but a head man, whose immediate following did not exceed thirty or forty lodges." [4]

In his way he was a humanitarian. He secured the release of a white woman, Fanny Kelly, in 1864. At another time he saved the life of an Assiniboine boy, whom he later adopted into his family. There are other instances of Sitting Bull's mercy.

John F. Finerty, a newspaper correspondent, who saw him in British Columbia in 1879, thus described his appearance:

"An Indian mounted on a cream-colored pony, and holding in his hand an eagle's wing which did duty as a fan, spurred in back of the chiefs and stared stolidly, for a minute or so, at me. His hair, parted in the ordinary Sioux fashion, was without a plume. His broad face, with a prominent hooked nose and wide jaws, was destitute of paint. His fierce, half-bloodshot eyes gleamed from under brows which displayed large perceptive organs, and, as he sat there on his horse, regarding me with a look which seemed blended of curiosity and insolence, I did not need to be told that he was Sitting Bull.

". . . After a little, the noted savage dismounted and led his horse partly into the shade. I noticed that he was an inch or two over the medium height, broadly built, rather bow-legged I thought, and he limped slightly as though from an old wound. He sat upon the ground, and was soon engirdled by a crowd of young warriors with whom he was an especial favorite as representing the unquenchable hostility of the aboriginal savage to the hated Palefaces." [5]

So much for Sitting Bull, the most famous Indian who

[4] "Record of Engagements," p. 49.
[5] John F. Finerty, "War-path and Bivouac," p. 360.

ever lived and the real leader of the Sioux War of 1875–1877.

If Sitting Bull was the greatest organizer and diplomat the Sioux ever had, Crazy Horse was one of their all-time preeminent warriors.[6] One of the most tragic and heroic figures of modern history, he combined in his own character most of the virtues of his people. Crazy Horse was an enemy of all the white men but even hard-bitten Indian fighters like Crook and Miles and Bourke yielded him ungrudging admiration.

He was born in 1844 and from his boyhood up was a warrior. At the age of sixteen he had won distinction against the Gros Ventres. When the Fort Phil Kearney war broke out he was just twenty-one years old but such was his fighting ability that he was already a recognized war leader. In both the Fetterman and Wagon Box affairs he was one of the Sioux strategists and a central figure. Although an Ogalalla, he won the admiration and loyalty of the Cheyennes and sometimes there were more of the latter in his camp than of his own tribe. When the trouble started in 1876 he was outstanding among the Ogalallas and rivaled only by Sitting Bull in the whole Sioux Nation. We are fortunate in having an eye-witness description of Crazy Horse, written by Captain John G. Bourke, who saw him in 1877, right after his surrender:

"I saw before me a man who looked quite young, not over thirty years old,[7] five feet eight inches high, lithe and sinewy, with a scar on the face. The expression of his countenance was one of quiet dignity, but morose, dogged, tenacious and melancholy. He behaved with stolidity like

---

[6] The wrong connotation is given this name in translation. Dr. Charles Eastman, a Sioux who has risen to eminence in medicine and writing, says that Tashunka Witko (Crazy Horse) means an unbroken or untamed horse, rather than an "insane horse." The interpreter who first translated it boggled the job and we have the wrong sense of the word as a result.

[7] At this time he was thirty-three years old.

a man who realized that he had to give in to Fate, but would do so as sullenly as possible. While talking to Frank (Grouard) his countenance lit up with genuine pleasure, but to all others he was . . . gloomy and reserved. All Indians gave him a high reputation for courage and generosity. In advancing upon an enemy, none of his warriors were allowed to pass him. He had made hundreds of friends by his charity to the poor, as it was a point of honor with him never to keep anything for himself except weapons of war. I never heard an Indian mention his name, save in terms of respect." [8]

Crazy Horse rarely spoke in council, but when he did, his words carried weight. Generous and brave, of few words and great deeds, it is not an overstatement to say that he was to the Sioux what the great Robert E. Lee was to that other lost cause—the Confederacy.

FIRST BLOOD

By the early winter of 1875 the belief of the non-reservation Sioux that the white man would never let them alone was confirmed. Late in December runners came to all their camps, commanding them to come in to the reservations. This was an obvious impossibility. In cold weather —and the winter of '75 was one of the worst in history— no camp could be moved without serious suffering, particularly for the women, children and infirm.

Not that the Sioux had any intention of complying. When word came from General Alfred Terry to Sitting Bull, naming January 1st, 1876 as the deadline, and threatening to come looking for the Sioux if they did not obey, the chief sent a haughty reply, inviting him to come on.

[8] Captain John G. Bourke, "On the Border With Crook," pp. 414-415.

"You won't need to bring any guides," he ended. "You can find me easily. I won't run away." [9]

Promptly on the expiration of the deadline the army moved. Three expeditions were to strike the Indians in early spring while their ponies were thin and it was too cold to travel. General George Crook was to march north from Fort Fetterman. General George A. Custer was to push west from Fort A. Lincoln. And General John Gibbon was to strike east from Fort Ellis. As it turned out weather conditions prevented the march of Custer and Gibbon. But Crook started early in March, with General Joseph J. Reynolds and ten troops of cavalry out in advance of his main body.

The weather was extremely severe, the thermometer sometimes showing forty degrees below zero, but when an Indian trail was struck in the Powder River Valley, the night of March 16th, Reynolds' men pushed forward eagerly. The following dawn Frank Grouard, a scout, located a village among the cliffs along the Clear Creek branch of the Powder. They had stumbled upon the camp of Crazy Horse himself [10] and the Sioux were still asleep.

Reynolds, following the usual tactics, sent one battalion to cut off the pony herd, a second to charge the village, and a third to cut off the retreat of the Indians. As they took their positions Indian herd boys began to drive the ponies to water. The village was awakening.

One battalion ran plump into a fifteen-year-old Sioux youth. Not ten feet away he confronted their advance guard in a gully. Captain John G. Bourke leveled his revolver. The youngster "wrapped his blanket about him

[9] Dunn, "Massacres in the Mountains," p. 596.
[10] It has been disputed that this was Crazy Horse's village, but Grouard, the chief scout, positively said it was, and moreover yelled to Crazy Horse as the charge began. He should have known it as it was the one in which he lived for months as a friend of the chief. The Cheyennes in it are said to have been led by Two Moons.

and stood like a statue of bronze, waiting for the fatal bullet; his features were as immobile as cut stone." But Bourke did not shoot. They wished to get closer to the village. Then the boy, knowing death would follow, suddenly uttered a war whoop. The village startled to wakefulness just as the first of the troopers thundered down into it.

It was the old story. Indians, when surprised, give way to inexplicable panics. This case was no exception. Leaping from their teepees the Sioux ran for the rocky bluffs which overlooked the valley. Some of the more resolute retreated slowly, shooting. Bullets began to thud among the troopers, killing horses and causing some confusion, but the line galloped forward.

By now the pony herd was rounded up. The Indians were afoot. Captain Egan's troop took possession of the village. So far the attack was a complete success. But the Sioux and Cheyennes recovered from their first shameful panic and Reynolds found he had caught a Tartar. Crazy Horse gathered his warriors and presently they came back up the valley, occupying all the points of vantage and opening a plunging fire on the white men.

Captain Anson Mills' battalion began to set fire to the teepees and the stores. The flames, the frequent explosions of the powder kegs in the lodges and the constant zipping of the Sioux bullets made the village anything but healthy. The troopers, moreover, had discarded their heavy clothing during the charge and suffered from the cold. Four men were dead or dying; others were wounded. The Sioux were becoming more dangerous every minute. There was danger of being cut off.

Reynolds suddenly ordered a retreat and the troops withdrew so rapidly that they left their dead in the Indians' hands.[11] They retreated several miles with Crazy Horse hanging on their rear. That night as they camped, the Sioux swooped suddenly and recaptured nearly all the ponies they had lost in the attack.

Four of Reynolds' men were dead and six wounded as well as sixty-six men badly frozen. Crook came up and saved the cavalry from further punishment. He was deeply chagrined when he heard the outcome of the fight —victory for the Sioux. The aftermath of the disgraceful affair was a series of court martials and several officers resigned their commissions.

[11] There have been charges that at least one wounded man was abandoned in this retreat. If so it is almost certain that the poor wretch suffered the most horrible fate possible—death by Indian torture.

Chapter XIII

ON THE BANKS OF THE ROSEBUD

INTO THE INDIAN COUNTRY AGAIN

MARCH passed and April. It was an unseasonably late spring and the snows had only just cleared away to allow the prairie wild roses to show their buds when, on May 26th, Crook again started north over the trail he had followed when Reynolds was beaten.

Crook had wide experience and considerable prestige, due to his campaigns against the Apaches in Arizona. He had twelve hundred men, not including his pack and wagon trains. He thought he could whip any number of Indians he might meet.

Crazy Horse knew about Crook's march. Before that officer left his base he received a warning from the gallant Sioux not to cross the Tongue River, on pain of being attacked.[1] But Crook marched straight to the Tongue and camped on its banks the evening of June 9th. As he did so, a sudden row of flashes lit up the tops of the bluffs across the river. The whistling of bullets sounded overhead. Crazy Horse was making good his word.

Crook was not the man to leave the gauge of battle lying. Orders began to fly. Three companies of infantry doubled forward to engage the Indians in long-range firing. Captain Anson Mills' battalion of cavalry splashed across the stream in a charge. There was not much of a

[1] Bourke, "On the Border With Crook," p. 296.

fight. Having shown Crook they meant business, the Indians withdrew, content to choose a more favorable battle ground. Two soldiers were wounded. It is not known if any Indians were hurt.[2]

For four days Crook camped on the Tongue, his outposts constantly seeing Indians. On the 15th he was joined by nearly three hundred Crow and Shoshone scouts, the Crows under Alligator-Stands-Up and the Shoshones under Washakie. They were brought by Frank Grouard.

Crook at once left his wagon train under a guard of infantry, mounted the rest of his foot soldiers on mules from the train, and with the scouts, these mule-riding doughboys, and his cavalry, some fourteen hundred men, crossed the Tongue early on the 16th and reached the Rosebud that evening.

Long before dawn on the 17th the troops were on the march and by eight o'clock they reached a widening of the valley where the stream ran across a level flat with high bluffs all around. At the lower end of the valley the river plunged into a gloomy gorge known as Dead Canyon. They halted in the bottoms and dismounted while the Crows and Shoshones went scurrying across the country to see what they could find.

It did not take them long to find something. Crazy Horse's scouts were watching Crook's approach and the chief was slipping up to the attack. Four Crows climbed a hill to look around. All at once they were "jumped" by four hostiles. Their sputtering shots were the first guns of the battle.

Crazy Horse's warriors came out of their canyons and rode toward where the white men were still hidden in the valley. Ahead of them streamed the Shoshones and Crows,

<hr>

[2] Grinnell says the Indians who made the attack were Cheyennes from Crazy Horse's village on the Rosebud. "Fighting Cheyennes," p. 316.

riding for life. Rifle fire crackled. Some of the Crows were hit, but their friends carried them along.

Down the steep bluffs plunged the scouts. They raced toward Crook yelling at the top of their lungs: "Sioux! Sioux! Heap Sioux!" Then the same bluffs suddenly bristled with hostile Indians, mounted and in full war regalia. Sharp, spiteful reports cut the balmy morning air. The fight was on.

CRAZY HORSE'S ATTACK

So many Indians were in sight that Crook knew he was dealing with Crazy Horse's main force. An officer galloped to rally the demoralized scouts. The soldiers wheeled into battle line and their front plumed out in smoke. Captain Mills' battalion detached itself and charged across the valley toward a broad bluff where thick swarms of Sioux had gathered. A moment later Major Royall, on the left, was in motion also. Two pretty cavalry charges were under way at the same time, while the troops remaining in line carried on their duel with the Indians over the heads of their comrades.

With guidons streaming and horses at full speed, Mills thundered across the flat, through some marshy ground and to the foot of the bluffs, eight hundred yards away. The Sioux were shooting right in their faces, but the cavalry mounted the bluffs and drove the hostiles back a quarter of a mile to the high ground in the rear. Royall's charge was as brilliant. He quickly cleared the Indians from the bluffs in front. But as they advanced both Mills and Royall found the going harder and harder. The Indians increased in numbers every minute. Presently Mills sent a courier to Crook asking for assistance and got Captain Noyes' battalion as reinforcement. Even with this addition Mills had all he could handle.

Every man in Crook's force was now engaged. Even the mule packers were in action. Yet with everybody fighting, Crazy Horse was still in the field, undefeated.

The fight was two hours old. Fresh warriors led by Little Hawk of the Cheyennes and American Horse, had arrived. Unexpectedly the Sioux took the offensive. Major Royall's position was far advanced and badly exposed. On his extreme left was Captain Guy V. Henry's command, augmented by a cloud of Crow and Shoshone scouts.

Crazy Horse, the tactician, saw the weakness of this position. Full at its exposed flank, he sent a fiery charge of his warriors. Yelping like a pack of wolves, they rode right into the trooper line. Horses and soldiers went under as the Sioux clubbed them down. The whole mass, Indians and white men, went down the hill in a welter of dust and smoke, confusedly mixed together.

Only Captain Vroom's troop held its position, and they were speedily surrounded. Vroom might have been annihilated, but the full attention of the Sioux was not directed against him at first. His men formed a circle and drove back the first rush. By the time Crazy Horse could swing any considerable number of warriors against them, they had been rescued.

Captain Henry led the counter-charge which reached the lost troop. It cut its way through a desperately fighting mass of red men. Never had the soldiers found the Indians so willing to give blow for blow, so ready to stand up and fight, so apparently reckless of death. When Vroom was rescued, a retreat began to a less advanced position.

Hard upon the heels of the retiring troopers pressed the Sioux. War cry, rifle shot and lance thrust; scowling,

painted, savage faces; tossing war bonnets; rearing, kicking ponies; mounting clouds of dust and smoke—the soldiers knew fear for the first time. But Henry, riding at the
very rear, called out encouragement and his coolness stead-
ied them. He winced once, but his face was turned toward
the enemy. The troopers were too busy fighting to notice
what had happened. They beat the charge off. Then the
captain turned to them a countenance so ghastly that it
chilled them through. A bullet had struck him full in the
face, practically tearing the whole visage out under both
eyes. His mangled features were covered by a great surge
of blood. He was swaying with the shock. For a time he
sat his horse, but the vertigo of wound sickness overcame
him soon. He fell.

The Sioux instantly sensed that a leader was down.
With the same valor they had displayed all afternoon
they charged. Back, back they drove the troops. The ponies of their warriors plunged over the very spot where
Henry lay. His end seemed certain.

But from a quarter utterly unexpected came help. The
Shoshones and Crows had fought hard but futilely. The
Sioux drove them back and they had been rather out of
the fight for the last few minutes. Now they saw the fall
of Henry as soon as their foes did.

Every old plainsman knows how the Indian warrior
shows his greatest daring in rescuing dead or wounded
comrades from the enemy. The scouts knew the Sioux
would be on the ground about Henry in a minute, scalping him, counting "coup." Here was something they understood. With their war cries echoing from the farthest
bluffs, they plunged headlong into the thick of the hostile array. Old Washakie of the Shoshones was there. So
was Luishaw. Of the Crows, Alligator-Stands-Up and
Plenty Coups were foremost.

Rearing, snorting horses, kicking up a dust cloud so dense the riders could hardly see—knife thrust and tomahawk blow—the Sioux ranks opened. Washakie, Alligator-Stands-Up and their warriors stood over Henry's limp body.

The hostiles fought desperately with the scouts. It created a diversion which stopped the Indian advance at its height. Royall and Vroom had time to catch their breath. Now they came back up the hill, driving Crazy Horse's warriors, reoccupying the ground held so heroically by a handful of savage scouts, and getting possession of the captain's unconscious body.

But there was no possibility of holding the position. Fighting as they went, the soldiers and their Indian allies retreated, taking the wounded officer with them. Henry subsequently recovered and eventually rose to the rank of brigadier general. The fight around his body was the fiercest mêlée of the battle. Both sides suffered severely.

DOWN DEAD CANYON

Crook believed Crazy Horse's village lay down the gloomy and precipitous canyon which ran northeast from the wide valley where they were fighting. Mills had temporarily checked the Sioux on the high ground back of the bluffs and Crook ordered him to swing his men out of the fight and take them down the gulch.

Mills' movement was unopposed by the Indians. His sudden change of front apparently caused the Sioux to draw off from the whole line and probably had much to do with saving Vroom's command.

Down the canyon trotted Mills' men, in column of twos, looking for the village which they expected to find at every turn. A clatter of hoofs behind them, a call, and Captain Nickerson and his orderly rode up—with orders to retrace their steps. It was hard to obey that order. Some of the officers, believing the Indian camp almost at hand, actually urged Mills to disobey. But Mills was a soldier; orders were orders and he complied.

Had he failed to obey that order at once, had he gone even a quarter of a mile farther, he and his men might never have come out of that canyon alive. The gorge with the significant name of Dead Canyon, was a natural trap. Only a little way from where Mills halted was a natural obstruction of fallen trees, brush and rocks, washed up by some flood in the past. It formed a great dam across the valley, through which the waters of the river trickled and was a barrier no cavalry could have passed.

There is reason to believe that here Crazy Horse planned an ambush. With this natural abattis he could resist any attempt to move down the valley, while from the tops of the unscalable canyon walls his riflemen could deal untold damage to the horsemen below. This may be why Crazy Horse, fiercely contesting every other move, did not oppose Mills' march. A little farther and the troops would have turned the last bend. A tremendous fire from the abattis; a steady stream of lead from the canyon walls; a short, desperate struggle to get through the tangle at the Indians—then it would have been over. Another great disaster like the Custer fight would have been written.[3]

Crook's order to retreat was not based on any knowledge of this situation. He had been badly mauled and had

[3] Grinnell denies that such a trap was planned ("The Fighting Cheyennes," p. 317) but both Mills and Bourke ("On the Border With Crook," p. 315) speak of it. So does Finerty ("War-path and Bivouac," p. 133). I believe in the face of this testimony by men who were on the spot at the time, the theory of Crazy Horse's trap can be accepted. Grinnell visited the spot many years later.

many wounded.[4] He could not support Mills so he recalled him.

Crook camped that night on the battle field. Next day
he retreated to his base of supplies. Crazy Horse was the
victor. He had checked Crook, forced him to retreat and
thus disposed of one more enemy.[5]

[4] Crook lost eight killed and twenty-three wounded; the Crows had one dead
and six wounded; and the Shoshones one killed and five wounded, a total of ten
dead and thirty-four wounded. The Sioux loss is unknown, but the Crows secured
ten scalps and the Shoshones three.

[5] Sitting Bull took part in this fight, but merely as a warrior, according to
Vestal ("Sitting Bull," p. 156). Crazy Horse commanded. According to Indian
testimony less than half their warriors in this fight were armed with guns. The
others had to be content with bows and arrows. Under these circumstances the
Sioux victory is all the more remarkable.

CHAPTER XIV

THE GREATEST VICTORY

THE CAMP ON THE LITTLE BIG HORN

AFTER the fight on the Rosebud, Crazy Horse and Sitting Bull moved their people across the divide into the Little Big Horn Valley. The long file of travois-laden ponies, with their mounted escort and the huge herd of extra animals, began the trip on June 19th. At a place where the valley widened into a beautiful, smiling meadow, half a mile wide and five or six miles long, the teepees were put up. Sitting Bull looked over the ground and of course picked out the choice site for his Unkpapas, at a bend of the river, in a grove of fine trees, almost exactly in the center of the valley. A couple of small creeks ran into the river from the south. Around these the rest of the Indians camped, the Sans Arcs, Minneconjous and Ogalallas taking one, and the Brulés and Cheyennes the other.

Estimates vary as to their numbers. The Indians themselves say it was one of the greatest villages they ever got together. There must have been ten or twelve thousand people there with, say, two or three thousand warriors. Here all Sitting Bull's well-known tact, diplomacy and organizing ability were necessary. As usual where such a huge camp was located the game soon disappeared, killed off or driven away. The Indians wanted to hunt but Sitting Bull, by strenuous effort, managed to keep them together.

Toward this pleasant encampment, a famous officer and a famous body of men marched on the night of the 24th— Custer and his 7th Cavalry. Custer was under the displeasure of President Grant through his political activities, and it was only through the intercession of Sheridan and Terry, his superiors, that he was allowed to accompany the expedition at all. Terry commanded the column to which the 7th was attached. From a temporary camp at the junction of the Powder and the Yellowstone, Major Marcus A. Reno, with part of the 7th, went scouting and returned to tell of striking a big trail on the Rosebud. This was the trail of the main Indian camp as it moved over into the Little Big Horn.

The report confirmed Terry's belief that the Sioux were concentrated somewhere between the Rosebud and the Big Horn—probably at the Little Big Horn. He decided to move in that direction at once. To the famous 7th and its equally famous leader, Custer, he gave the post of honor—the advance. They were ordered to strike for the point where Reno had found the Indian trail. At the same time Gibbon, who had joined Terry after Crook's defeat, followed with a force equal to Custer's. Definite orders were given to Custer that if the trail led to the Little Big Horn he was to pass it and turn south long enough to let Gibbon come up to the mouth of the stream. The inference was that the two columns should then converge, catching the Indians between them. These are the instructions upon which half a century of controversy over Custer's subsequent actions have hinged. In parting, however, Terry, one of the finest officers in the army, but inexperienced in Indian fighting compared to his fiery subordinate, gave some verbal instructions which permitted Custer a far greater leeway:

"Use your own judgment, and do what you think best

War Department

War Department

Bureau of American Ethnology

Bureau of American Ethnology

Upper left: Gen. George Crook, commander in the Powder River and Rosebud campaigns. Upper right: Gen. George A. Custer, killed with his five troops of the 7th Cavalry, at the Battle of the Little Big Horn. Lower left: Rain-in-the-Face, Unkpapa sub-chief under Sitting Bull. Lower right: Gall (Pizi), one of Sitting Bull's lieutenants, and a leader in the Little Big Horn fight.

War Department

This picture, taken on a picnic shortly before General Custer set out on his last campaign, contains the faces of eight persons killed in the Battle of the Little Big Horn. Reading from left to right they are: Lieut. James Calhoun (killed); Mr. Swett (son of Leonard Swett of Chicago); Capt. Stephen Baker; Boston Custer (killed); Lieut. W. S. Edgerly; Miss Watson (with fan); Capt. Myles Keogh (killed); Dr. H. O. Paulding (on ground); Mrs. A. E. Smith; Dr. G. E. Lord (killed); Capt. T. B. Weir (seated); Lieut. W. W. Cooke (killed); Lieut. R. E. Thompson; the two Misses Wadsworth; Capt. Thomas W. Custer (killed); Lieut. A. E. Smith (killed) if you strike the trail; and whatever you do, Custer, hold on to your wounded." [1]

And so, with general instructions, but with specific permission to use his own best judgment if conditions arose to warrant it, Custer rode out for his fatal rendezvous with the foe.

He found an Indian trail half a mile wide, on the second day, and followed it twenty-eight miles up the Rosebud before he camped. His scouts reported ever-increasing Indian signs. It was apparent that the trail crossed the divide. Custer held a council of war and announced he would go over into the Little Big Horn Valley "to avoid detection by the Indians." His decision was at least a technical disobedience of his written orders. Two hours later the regiment was on the march again, stopping at two A.M. near the top when the scouts reported the pass could not be crossed at night.

Custer crossed the divide at dawn. Shortly afterward he knew his trail was discovered. A party of packers who went back to pick up a box of hard-tack, dropped on the trail, saw and fired at a couple of young Sioux, killing one.[2] The other escaped to bear the news. Under the circumstances, orders or no orders, the general decided to go after the Indians and make the most of his opportunity. Had he not been smarting under what he felt was unjust censure at Washington, he might not have taken the risk. But Custer felt poignantly the need for something to win back Grant's favor. A spectacular Indian victory like the Washita would do it.

As the column topped the divide, they saw in the rays

[1] Quoted from General Nelson A. Miles, "Personal Recollections," pp. 204-205.
[2] Strangely, although this occurred at eight o'clock in the morning the surviving Indian did not bring word of it to the village until after noon. By that time the troops were almost within view. In fact, Sitting Bull saw them shortly after the news was brought to him. Vestal, "Sitting Bull," p. 164.

of the early sunlight a low-lying fog far down in the valley. It was the smoke of an immense Sioux village. With never a premonition of defeat, Custer made his plans to crush it. Following the usual Indian fighting tactics of the day, he divided his command into four detachments.[3] Major Benteen, with three troops, was sent far to the left to circle the southern end of the valley. Captain McDougall, with one troop, was told off to follow with the pack train. Custer and Reno continued their march together but as they reached the valley they separated, Custer going on northwest with five troops, while Reno and three troops, together with most of the Arickaree scouts, rode straight on down.

Custer was sure of victory. As he approached the valley he assumed once more the old, jaunty air he had lost since his trouble with Grant. The thought of action always served him as a stimulant and he was the jovial Custer of yore as he parted with Reno.[4]

THE VALLEY OF THE SHADOW

Down into the valley rode Reno. As his men entered the gulch of a small stream which would take them out onto the bottoms, they had a last glimpse of Custer alive. He sat his horse on a high hill. As they looked back, he snatched his hat from his head and waved it—the beloved

[3] Custer has been much criticized for "dividing his force in the face of the enemy," but such criticism is unwarranted. No matter how axiomatic that rule is in ordinary war, the expedient of dividing and attacking a village from several sides had repeatedly proved successful in Indian campaigns. Chivington at Sand Creek, Reynolds at Powder River, McKenzie at McClellan Creek and Custer himself at the Washita all used these tactics.

[4] To show how confident of victory Custer was, Trumpeter John Martin, last man to see him alive, told Benteen to whom he carried dispatches that when the general saw the camp, he slapped his thigh with his hat and exclaimed: "Custer's luck! We've got them this time!"

gesture of boyish exuberance which they knew so well. A few yards farther and the bluffs shut him from view.

Reno was supposed to strike the head of the village near the mouth of the creek while Custer crossed the high ground to the right and attacked the lower end. But when Reno rode out of the defile he knew that plans had miscarried—he was not within two miles of his objective. Turning to the right he led his men at a fast trot down the valley. Indians on horseback began to appear before him. Then he saw teepees. Off toward the flats his Arickaree scouts were dashing forward in an attempt to drive away some Sioux ponies which were grazing there. Rifles began to flash in the woods ahead while swarms of warriors came riding toward him. Reno halted. The rippling crash of his first volley sounded. The whole valley in front was filled with a yelling mass of savages.

It was the power and might of the Sioux and Cheyenne Nations. Sitting Bull was there and so was Crazy Horse. Dull Knife, Two Moons and Little Wolf of the Cheyennes led their people. Of the Sioux Pizi (Gall), American Horse, Hump and White Bull, Sitting Bull's daredevil nephew, were encouraging their warriors to fight. Without warning the Indians charged. As the howling, shooting horde bore down upon Reno's men the horses of two troopers became unmanageable and bolted right into the Sioux array. The hostile line simply opened and then closed, swallowing them. They were never seen again, dead or alive. At the same moment the Arickarees on the left flank gave way. Oppressed by their hereditary fear of the terrible Sioux some of the Rees did not stop running until they reached Terry's camp. Reno had to execute a rapid pivot movement until his back was against the river with both flanks resting on it. An old "ox bow" loop of the stream-bed in a point of woods formed a natural breast-work behind which the men took refuge.

The troopers dismounted, every fourth man holding the horses. In a solid line, at long rifle shot, the Sioux rode up and down with their chiefs galloping among them, making their dispositions. The rifles roared a crescendo of sound. With men falling left and right, Reno rode over to his senior captain, French.

"What do you think of this?" he shouted.

"I think we'd better get out of here," replied French.

Reno gave the order to mount. In the terrific noise he was not heard. Added to the concussions of gunfire were the constant whooping of the savages and the yelling of the soldiers. Some of the nearer troopers at last understood and began to mount. The others followed their example. With no attempt at order, seeking only safety, the survivors of the detachment started for the ford.

It was a rout. The Indians rode a race with the flying soldiers and death overtook many. There were deeds of heroism too. With the Sioux right on top of them, troopers reined in their horses and helped dismounted comrades to climb up behind them. Lieutenant MacIntosh was killed on the river bank. Lieutenant Hodgson's leg was broken by a bullet which killed his horse as they leaped into the river. A stirrup was thrust out by Trumpeter Henry Fisher. Hodgson seized it and was dragged to the other bank. An instant later a second bullet ended his life. Scout Charley Reynolds, Custer's right-hand man, sacrificed himself trying to hold back the savages so that his comrades might escape. And many another fell in that mad scramble across the Little Big Horn.

Struggling across, the remaining officers and men reached the bluffs on the other side. Reno had left three officers and twenty-nine men and scouts behind him in the valley, dead. Seven men were wounded seriously. And Lieutenant De Rudio and fifteen men were missing.[5] That was a total of fifty-five out of one hundred and twelve— fifty percent of the command.

Benteen came over the rise from the east. He had seen no Indians but an hour before received an urgent message from Custer, carried by Trumpeter John Martin [6] as follows:

"Benteen. Come on. Big village. Be quick. Bring packs.
"P.S. Bring packs."

The language of the note and the repetition of the last instructions showed that Custer was in contact with the Indians and needed ammunition. But where was Custer? Benteen and Reno were at a loss. They supposed he had struck the hostiles higher up and pursued them.

At present they were more concerned with their own fate than Custer's. Dense masses of Indians around their bluffs kept up a heavy fire. The position was poor for defense, being commanded by higher hills from which Sioux sharpshooters kept picking off men.

About three o'clock in the afternoon a strange thing happened. As if at a signal most of the savages surrounding them suddenly galloped off toward the northwest. Within a few minutes a terrific burst of firing was heard in that direction. It kept up, increasing in volume and varying little in position.

Custer was engaged at last.

[5] Most of the missing men later rejoined Reno on the bluff. De Rudio and Thomas O'Neill, a private, hid in the bushes when their horses were shot. After almost unbelievable adventures during which they were more than once discovered by the hostiles they managed at last to cross the river and join their comrades. On one occasion they were so close to the Sioux camp they saw what they believed was the torture of some of their captured comrades.

[6] Martin, who died in Brooklyn in 1922, was the last to see Custer.

WHAT HAPPENED TO CUSTER

Most of the Indians in the great village had gone to the upper end to fight Reno with no thought that they would be attacked from any other direction. Sitting Bull alone thought of that possibility and said so.[7] Some old men in the Cheyenne camp seem to have known of Custer's division and went about the circle haranguing that soldiers were coming from the lower end of the village also.[8] But the bulk of the Indians swarmed around Reno, shooting and riding.

The situation was ideal—just made to order for Custer. But that officer had much farther to go than Reno. He had to make a circuit of nearly ten miles. Then, instead of striking the lower end of the village, he came down opposite the center at a shallow ford. By the time he appeared Reno had been beaten and driven across the stream as has been noted.

Custer's five troops were seen from the Indian camp when they reached the bluffs at the edge of the valley. There were only a few men in the village at the time— chiefly warriors who had not been on hand when the fight started, but had just come hurrying in from hunting or scouting at the sound of the battle. A charge by the troops at that moment would have completely changed the result of the battle. The Indians themselves have said that if Custer had gone through the village then, the fight would have been over.

Small things sometimes alter history. As Custer's men trotted down the slope across the river toward the ford,

[7] This is the story Stanley Vestal got from relatives and friends of Sitting Bull ("Sitting Bull," p. 168). Mr. Vestal went to the Sioux themselves for his material and his book contains much information never before available to students of western history.

[8] Grinnell, "The Fighting Cheyennes," p. 336.

there was a panic among the squaws and old men in the camp. In a frightened mob they rushed away from the soldiers, out on the prairie where they huddled, helpless and scared.

Four Cheyenne warriors remained. They saw the menacing line of blue and knew the soldiers would soon be at the ford. The main body of fighting men was far up the valley fighting Reno. Those four Cheyennes turned their horses and rode across the river to fight Custer all by themselves—four against two hundred.

The names of three members of that dauntless quartet are fortunately preserved and deserve to go down in history just as surely as Horatius the Roman or Leonidas the Greek. They were Bobtail Horse, Calf and Roan Bear. The fourth man is not remembered.

As they crossed the river, two more Cheyennes, White Shield and Mad Wolf, joined them. They were both famous fighters, but Mad Wolf thought the determination of the four to fight two hundred soldiers was insane. He argued with them: "No one must charge on the soldiers now; they are too many." When he saw that Bobtail Horse and his friends had their grim faces set toward the troops, he turned off down the river with White Shield, out of the direct line of march.

The four Cheyennes kept on. Creeping behind a low ridge, they waited for the soldiers to come close. They knew they could not stop the white men's charge, but they were warriors—what little they could do must be done. If ever men looked death in the eye, unafraid, these men did.

Down the slope trotted Custer. Four or five scurrying Sioux were running before him. Seeing that Custer was headed for the ford, they swung off to one side, knowing the soldiers would not follow them. They were right; Custer did not deviate from his direct line of march.

Suddenly rifles began to crack in front of him. Bobtail Horse's tiny band had opened. A trooper was killed. The soldiers halted and dismounted. The halt was in line with good tactics. They had no way of knowing how many Indians were over that ridge. The very audacity of the challenge of that volley worked in favor of the Cheyennes. The presumption was that no mere handful would dare to oppose a force like Custer's. There must be more Indians ahead than could be seen.

But the hesitation proved fatal. While the soldiers remained on the hill, word reached Sitting Bull and Crazy Horse as they faced Reno. That was what caused the sudden change of front which had so puzzled the soldiers on the bluff.

Part of the Sioux galloped down the left bank of the river and dashed across the ford in front of the village in a smother of spray. Another big division rode up a dry coulee which ran close by the hill where Custer had halted. Still others must have gone around behind the bluffs to the east where they cut off the white men from retreat later in the battle.

Custer's men had mounted and started again for the ford when the first of the swarm of fighting Sioux, probably headed by Crazy Horse, appeared there. The soldiers began at once to retreat. But it was too late. The Indians swirled up the hill and around them. Gall was on one side; Crazy Horse on the other. And they were followed by a fighting mad horde of Sioux and Cheyennes. Pushed back by the mass of savages, Custer crossed a deep gulch and climbed a hill on the other side which looked like a good place for defense. The line of his retreat can be traced today by the stone markers which were placed at the spots where the cluttering bodies of his men were later found.

Custer evidently thought that if he could reach the round knob on top of the hill—where the monuments now stand—he could fight off the Indians. But he never got to the top. Something stopped him when he was still a hundred yards down the slope. Very likely it was a wave of savages which came over the knob, down upon him— the Sioux who had ridden behind the bluffs to the east. Custer and many of his officers and men died there on the slope.[9]

But Custer's death was by no means the end of the fight, or rather the retreat. Headed off from the north, the survivors of his command apparently struggled southeast, at an angle of almost forty-five degrees from their former direction. The line can be clearly traced today. It headed over the ridge and down the other side, back in the direction from which Custer had originally come. Lieutenant James B. Calhoun, whose body was found almost at the end of the bloody trail far to the southeast of where Custer lay dead, was probably the last officer killed. With him were found a few straggling bodies—the last of Custer's command.

Throughout that agonizing retreat the white men fought with desperate valor. But the hill, which superficially looked like a good defensive position, proved just the opposite. Its sides were scarred by deep gullies, ideal places for Sioux riflemen to hide. And there were more of those riflemen all the time. At the beginning of the battle many of the Indians were armed only with bows and arrows but they captured a good many new Sharps carbines from Reno's men and obtained ammunition from

[9] Their bodies were found not where the monuments are, but farther down the slope. The monuments were placed in their present location because it is superior from a view standpoint.

the saddle bags of the dead or captured horses and the cartridge belts of the dead men. To these they constantly added the arms they took from Custer's troopers as they fell.

Within an hour all the white soldiers were down. The Sioux and Cheyennes went about, looking the bodies over, giving an extra shot [10] in the head to those about whose condition there was any question. A few wounded survivors were clubbed to death.

The great tragedy was ended.

RENO'S FIGHT ON THE BLUFFS

To return to Reno: The noise of Custer's battle at first cheered his men, but the feeling changed to apprehension as that sinister roar rose to a climax, then hung on the air, a terrific tumult of sound. Officers and men gazed with concern toward the northwest. Instead of a sudden, sharp attack, Custer must have a real battle on his hands. More likely—they could no longer conceal it from themselves —he must be fighting for his very life.

Although most of the Indians had gone and everybody expected Reno to move to Custer's support, he remained where he was, a bandanna handkerchief tied about his head, bewildered and indecisive. Some of the officers over-

[10] The theory that Custer committed suicide has pretty well been exploded. Best proof of this is that at least three Cheyennes counted coup on his body. The third of these, Medicine Bear, is still living. The Indians never counted coup on the body of a suicide. T. J. Gatchell, of Buffalo, Wyoming, says that he has proof that Custer's slayer was a Cheyenne, but has promised to withhold the name until the deaths of interested parties. On the other hand, William J. Bordeaux, federal Indian interpreter of Sioux Falls, quotes Foolish Elk, a Brule, as naming Spotted Calf, a Santee of Inkpaduta's band as the slayer. Custer's horse fell into the hands of Sounds-the-Ground-As-He-Walks, another Santee. Evidence in the form of a bullet hole through the head that Custer killed himself is discounted by David Cummings, still living near Buffalo, who helped bury the dead after the battle. Cummings, who examined the general's body, says Custer was shot twice, once through the body and once through the head. The body shot killed him. The head shot was merely a "coup de grâce" given after the fight was over.

stepped their authority to urge him to join Custer. But he refused to move. At length Captain Weir with Troop D, reconnoitred down the line of bluffs without orders. At the farthest bluffs he could see, a mile and a half away, immense numbers of Indians. The firing was still heavy but he could see no soldiers. The Sioux turned toward him and he had to repulse an attack. Then Reno cautiously followed. By the time he arrived the heavy firing was over. With field glasses they could still see clouds of Indians but no troops.

There was some conjecture as to what had happened. Nobody dreamed of the real catastrophe even when they saw the Sioux coming back. Reno did not wait for them. He returned to his first position and entrenched.

The Sioux attacked without delay and there was some desperate fighting on the hill, but the white men continued to hold it. Then the savages posted themselves on the high ground and deluged the troops with bullets. In the three hours before darkness, eighteen men were killed and forty-three wounded on that bloody bluff.

Night brought a cessation of fighting. A detail of soldiers got down to water and replenished the canteens. They could hear much racket from the Indian camp [11] and were constantly annoyed by sniping from the bluffs. At dawn the battle reopened. For hours the long-range pot shooting continued, and the Indian rifles in some cases outranged the troopers' carbines. At nine o'clock a charge swept down the slope from the north. The hostiles almost carried the entrenchments. One daring Sioux, Long Robe, actually got within the lines and counted coup on a soldier

[11] Frank Grouard, one of Crook's scouts, was actually on the battlefield that night. Not knowing there had been a fight, he stumbled on to some of the bodies of Custer's men in the darkness. A few minutes later he was discovered by some Indians and forced to ride for his life. This was about eleven o'clock at night. He did not know then that Reno's men were besieged on the bluff. (Joe De Barthe, "Life and Adventures of Frank Grouard," pp. 136-139.)

before he was killed. But eventually the Sioux were driven back. After that they contented themselves with long-range shooting. Toward evening the whole village packed up and the Indians left the valley.

Another night passed. In the morning a large dust cloud was seen coming up the valley. "The Indians are returning" was the first thought, but the blue of uniforms was soon seen. They knew now why the Sioux left. Terry and Gibbon were approaching.

"What has happened to Custer?" was the question on every tongue. Terry naturally thought he was with Reno. Reno thought he had joined Terry. Gibbon went to reconnoitre the now deserted village site. Far out across the river, a mile or two to the east was Lieutenant James Bradley, his chief of scouts. A dead horse attracted Bradley's attention. Riding in that direction he saw some curious white objects which at first he could not understand. As he drew nearer, the truth burst upon him. They were the naked bodies of Custer's dead.

Bradley's hurried search discovered one hundred and ninety-seven bodies. Later nine more were found, a total of two hundred and six. Custer was found, stripped but not mutilated—not even scalped. Most of the others were butchered in some manner.

Gibbon and Terry gave what burial they were able to the dead. This was of the sketchiest nature—only three spades could be found in the entire pack train which was equipped only for rapid movements in the Indian country. The men used their tin cups, axes, canteen halves, even tin spoons and sticks, to scratch earth over the bodies.[12]

[12] Following are the losses in the Battle of the Little Big Horn:

Custer's command	Killed
Commissioned officers	13
Enlisted men	191
Citizens and guides	4
	208

Then the expedition sadly began its trip back to the Yellowstone, carrying the wounded to where the steamboat "Far West" waited to convey them to a hospital down the river. The red man had scored his greatest triumph in history over his white enemy.

Reno's command	Killed	Wounded
Commissioned officers	3	
Enlisted men	48	52
Scouts and interpreters	6	
	57	52

Total killed, 265. Total wounded, 52. Total loss, 317.

Officers killed: Gen. George A. Custer; Captains T. W. Custer, Miles W. Keough, G. W. Yates; Lieutenants W. W. Cook, A. E. Smith, Donald MacIntosh, James Calhoun, J. E. Porter, B. H. Hodgson, J. G. Sturgis, W. Van W. Reilly, J. J. Crittenden, H. M. Harrington; Assistant Surgeons, C. E. Lord, J. M. DeWolf; Civilians, Boston Custer (brother of the general), Armstrong Reed (Custer's nephew), Mark Kellogg, (newspaper correspondent), Charlie Reynolds (chief scout), Frank C. Mann, Isaiah Dorman (Negro interpreter), Mitch Bouyer (half breed scout); Indian scouts, Bloody Knife, Bob Tail, Stab.

The bodies of Lieutenants Harrington, Porter and Sturgis and Dr. Lord and two enlisted men were never found. They may have been captured and tortured, although the Indians have denied they tortured anybody in this affair.

Chapter XV

WANING OF THE RED STAR

THE DEATH OF AMERICAN HORSE

AFTER the Little Big Horn the Sioux scattered. Sitting Bull had held them together as long as he could—they had to hunt or starve during the coming winter. The Sioux had no further desire to fight. They had used up nearly all their ammunition beating Crook and Custer; they never had enough cartridges after the Little Big Horn fight for a major battle.[1]

A couple of trifling advantages were gained by the soldiers in July. General Wesley Merritt surprised a band of Cheyennes on the 17th, killed one young warrior, and chased them back to the reservation. At about the same time a scouting party under Lieutenant Frederick W. Sibley fought and defeated a Cheyenne war party, killing their leader, White Antelope. Otherwise the troops hunted fruitlessly through the Bad Lands for the Indians.

---

[1] Dr. Thomas S. Williamson, who lived among the Sioux for decades and knew them as few white men have ever known them is authority for this statement. In an article written March 15, 1877, he says:

"Since the fall of Custer, Sitting Bull and his associates never had enough ammunition for a regular battle, and have avoided fighting whenever it was possible. To supply their urgent needs they have captured supply trains and sometimes ranches, driving off the horses and cattle." (Minnesota Historical Society Collections, Vol. III, p. 292.)

This explains the unwillingness of the Sioux to fight pitched battles from the Custer engagement on. They did not have a chance with the well-equipped troops and they knew it. In spite of this circumstance Crazy Horse still was to offer battle at least once to Miles, a fight he might have won had it not been for Miles' hidden artillery.

American Horse, one of the great old Sioux fighters, had camped on Rabbit Creek, near Slim Buttes. He was one of Crazy Horse's most trusted lieutenants and closest friends. Captain Anson Mills, escorting a wagon train to Deadwood for supplies for Crook, discovered this village by accident. His surprise attack, delivered the morning of September 8th, as usual sent the panic-stricken Indians scrambling up the bluffs which rose behind the camp site.

But Mills penned up American Horse and four warriors, with about fifteen women and children in a cave at the end of a blind gorge. The old chief held the soldiers off nearly all day. He repulsed two charges, killed a scout, "Buffalo Chip" Charley, and a trooper, and wounded nine men, including Lieutenant Von Luettwitz, whose leg was so shattered by a bullet that it had to be amputated. Then Crook arrived, brought by an urgent message from Mills. He took charge at once.

Frank Grouard crept up under cover and told the Indians to surrender. "Come and get us!" was American Horse's scornful yell.

Crook directed a concentrated fire of two hundred rifles into the mouth of the cave. They could not silence the five Sioux rifles which fought back. Again the interpreter offered the Indians a chance to surrender. This time, after some hesitation, the squaws and children came out.

"Crazy Horse will rub you out!" American Horse taunted. Crook knew he was hoping for rescue. What was done must be done quickly.

The bombardment began again with redoubled fury. For two hours it raged. Gradually the Sioux fire dwindled, stopped altogether. Grouard crept forward again and yelled a summons to give up. A young warrior stepped into view. The offer was repeated. "Washte helo," (Very good) murmured the Indian and disappeared into the cave.

There was a brief wait. Then the youth reappeared with another brave. Between them they supported American Horse, pale with the agony of a terrible wound. He was shot through the bowels. A piece of his intestine protruded from the hole. Between his teeth was a flat piece of wood on which he bit hard to keep from showing the pain. Yet he was every inch the chief as he handed his gun to Crook.

Too late Crazy Horse and Sitting Bull came riding from their camp a few miles away, to help their friend. They retired as Crook swung into battle line, knowing American Horse was finished.

That night gallant old American Horse died, as stoically and silently as he had lived. Two other warriors and a woman and child were also dead. A handful of wretched Indians were prisoners. It was a small victory. But the white man made the most of it—his successes had been so few.

MILES AND SITTING BULL

General Nelson A. Miles was summoned from the south to the Platte region and at once proposed a winter campaign. In spite of the advice of veterans of the country he went about his plans. With him were the troops who had campaigned in the Southwest in a winter when the temperature went as low as twenty-eight degrees below zero. But in this country it fell to sixty or even sixty-six below. To use his own phrase, "I equipped my command as if they were going to the arctic regions." They had abundance of woolens and fur clothing, even masks for the face—and it was well, for the winter of 1876–77 was very severe.

Sitting Bull and Crazy Horse separated to make hunting easier. Crazy Horse camped in the headwaters of the

Tongue and Rosebud. Sitting Bull was north in the valley of the Big Dry. Miles set out to attack Sitting Bull.

Miles' approach was soon discovered. One night daring Indian riders attacked the soldier camp and Miles came within inches of death. They swooped down like the wind —a mere handful of them—to stampede the horses. Finding the animals too well picketed, they fired a fusillade into the camp and rode away, yelling. Two bullets whistled through the general's tent, cutting holes in the canvas a few inches above his cot, but he was not harmed.

Next morning, October 18th, Sitting Bull attacked Miles' supply train with a large force of warriors. Colonel E. S. Otis, in command of the train, formed his men as a guard on each side and ordered the wagons to keep moving. The Indians rode around and fired long-distance shots. During one of the lulls in the fighting a warrior galloped to the brow of a hill directly in the line of march but out of range, dismounted and left something, then rode away. It was a note from Sitting Bull himself. This curious missive is worth quoting. It sums up the Indian arguments and gives an idea of the imperious attitude of the great chief:

"Yellowstone.

"I want to know what you are doing travelling on this road. You scare all the buffalo away. I want to hunt in this place. I want you to turn back from here. If you don't I will fight you again. I want you to leave what you have got here and turn back from here.

"I am your friend,

"SITTING BULL.

"I mean all the rations you have got and some powder. Wish you would write me as soon as you can." [2]

---

[2] "Big Leggins" Brughiere, a half-breed with a smattering of education, wrote the note at Sitting Bull's dictation. The document is still preserved.

Colonel Otis replied that he would go wherever he wished and if Sitting Bull wanted a fight he would have no trouble in finding it. There was some additional skirmishing but the wagon train got through.

On the 21st a group of Indians carrying a white flag approached the army lines. Most of them stopped at a distance. The flag bearer, a warrior named Long Feather, came forward to present a message from Sitting Bull, who was in the group, asking for a conference. Miles invited the chief to come within the lines, but the canny Unkpapa, no doubt remembering the fate of some other Indians who had trusted the white man, refused. He sent three emissaries instead. Nothing came of the conference.

Next day Sitting Bull again asked to talk with Miles. This time a conference was agreed upon, to be held between the lines. Sitting Bull, accompanied by six warriors and a sub-chief, White Bull, met Miles, with an officer and six troopers. They were midway between the Indian array and the soldiers.

There are varying accounts of that interview. The Indians say that Miles opened up by accusing Sitting Bull of being an enemy to the whites and scolding like an old woman. To this the chief mildly replied that he was not an enemy to the whites as long as they let him alone. There was uneasiness on the part of both leaders, each fearing treachery. They soon separated.

The following day they met again in the same place, escorted as before. This time both Miles and Sitting Bull quickly grew angry. Miles says in his memoirs that "Sitting Bull looked like a conqueror and spoke like one"—as indeed he had a right to do. His demands were just and reasonable from the Indian standpoint, or from any neutral standpoint, for that matter. He had fought no war of aggression and was willing to stop fighting now if the troops were withdrawn from his country and their posts abandoned. But if the chief really expected the land-grabbing white man to accede to so simple and equitable an arrangement, he soon learned his error. Miles told him such a peace was impossible; that only the unconditional surrender of the Indians would be accepted.

Then the chief flew into a towering rage, according to Miles' story. Sitting Bull looked "more like . . . a wild beast than a human being; his face assumed a ferocious expression; his jaws were closed tightly . . . and you could see his eyes glistening with the fire of savage hatred."

At last he fairly shouted his defiance: "Almighty God made me an Indian—but not an agency Indian!"

That is the story as told by Miles, one of the participants, but some of the Indians who were near have denied that Sitting Bull ever made the statement quoted.[8]

Miles and Sitting Bull rode back to their lines. Within fifteen minutes the soldiers charged. The Sioux fired the prairie but the grass was short and the flames did not hinder the cavalry which dashed right through the smoke. Sitting Bull's people fled. The troops captured their camp but the Sioux disappeared in the distance.

That autumn the soldiers twice struck Sitting Bull's band which was searching through the Bad Lands for Crazy Horse's village. But each time the chief evaded them. Pursued and hectored all the way, he at last reached the Canadian border.

There in the north, among the black pines of Canada, the Unkpapas found refuge. But Sitting Bull, scowling in the dark recesses of his teepee, took no satisfaction from that fact. He was a king without a kingdom; an emperor whose empire was broken.

[8] Vestal, "Sitting Bull," pp. 204-205.

THE AWFUL NIGHT

After the hostile Indian camp broke up, the Cheyennes went into the Powder River Valley where they made a snug camp deep in the canyon of the Crazy Woman fork. They spent the cold months in safety and comfort there while Miles was chasing Sitting Bull to Canada, and the troops were surrounding and intimidating the friendly villages of Swift Bear and Red Cloud, who knew too much to go to war.

A Cheyenne youth, Beaver Dam, travelling across the winter landscape, was seen by Arapaho government scouts, and captured November 20th. Taken to Fort Reno, he was questioned by General Ranald S. McKenzie, Crook's cavalry commander. The youth said his camp was on the Upper Powder and that Crazy Horse was on the Rosebud.

Two days later McKenzie moved his eleven hundred soldiers and scouts over to the Crazy Woman. On the morning of the 24th, he set out to seek and crush Crazy Horse's village.

It had snowed and they picked up an Indian trail. By evening the Arapaho scouts, riding far ahead, said there was a big village down the canyon. It was not Crazy Horse, but McKenzie got ready to attack anyhow. He hoped to surprise the Indians. The Cheyennes in the camp, however, had known of his proximity for some time. In fact they almost moved, and would have done so but for the obstinacy of Lost Bull, one of their chiefs, who insisted on staying where he was, to fight it out.

The ground was deep in snow and the weather was arctic. As the men worked their way through the gorge, between whose rocky sides a wild, icy mountain stream splashed its way, they began to hear ahead the sounds of an Indian camp. Drumming and singing could be heard as the Cheyennes celebrated a recent successful foray against the Shoshones in retaliation for the part Washakie and his braves had played in the Battle of the Rosebud.

Near the camp the soldiers halted. The night hours slowly passed, the village slept. Before dawn the ghostly blue masses of men in the canyon began a cautious advance. Just as the first rays of the sun touched the topmost crags of the canyon walls, the notes of a bugle sounded the charge. The famous brothers, Frank and Luther North, and their wild Pawnees led. Almost before the Cheyennes were awake, McKenzie's men were among the teepees.

A few warriors, caught in their lodges, died fighting. But most of the Cheyennes scurried up the sides of the canyon. Many of them had no time to dress, and were naked except for the breech clout. Undaunted, however, they rallied at the head of the gorge and their rifles were soon blazing.

Some of the Cheyennes at the upper end had time to catch up horses and mount. A few of these mounted warriors charged right at the front of the oncoming troops. It was only a bluff at a charge, to stop the soldiers long enough to let the women and children from the lower part of the village get away.

Helped by this brief check, the Indians on foot fell back rapidly and some of them, under Yellow Nose, who had distinguished himself at the Custer fight, took up a position on a low rocky eminence which commanded the field. It was the key to the battle ground and McKenzie sent Lieutenant McKinney with his troop to capture it.

McKinney charged the knoll. Yellow Nose's braves began to shoot as fast as they could work the levers of their guns. McKinney fell. His men dropped back out of sight in a deep gulch which ran across the valley there, and three Cheyennes ran forward to "count coup" on the fallen officer.

From the knoll Yellow Nose could see the brave Little Wolf herding a big bunch of women and children to safety up a canyon which led to a pass over the cliffs. Several warriors with Little Wolf had already been knocked over by the white men's fire, but the chief stood upright at one side, directing the helpless ones up the gorge, a target for hundreds of rifles. He never left that post of greatest danger until the last of the people were safe.

Two troops of cavalry started up the gulch after the women and children. But Little Wolf had not left it unprotected. As the soldiers entered the gulch mouth, shots rang out. A trooper fell from his horse. The others drew back.

Then the cavalry dismounted and began firing volleys up the gorge. Before long a few Cheyennes jumped out of it and ran across to another cut bank. They were what was left of Little Wolf's rear guard. Nine dead Cheyenne warriors were found in that gulch after the battle. But the women escaped.

Only a few braves were now left in the valley. Five of them had been cut off on a knoll near the center of the amphitheater formed by the hills. There they kept up a grim defense but it seemed certain that they would be lost. The Cheyennes made many efforts to reach these men and save them, but all failed. Then Yellow Nose appeared on the scene. In some manner he had secured a horse, and with him were about twenty or thirty mounted warriors. All wore gorgeous war bonnets.

Yellow Nose charged toward the hill to reach his beleaguered friends. Behind him came the other warriors, yelling and shooting. They made a colorful sight as they galloped hard toward where their comrades lay, hugging the rocky ground. The troops turned their guns on the charging Cheyennes. In a minute the air was full of lead. Yellow Nose raised his arm and pulled his horse back on its haunches. The whole band rode off at right angles, and swept around back to safety. The charge had been halted —but its object was accomplished. During the excitement, the men on the knoll had escaped and rejoined their friends.

Little Wolf and Dull Knife shortly had their warriors swarming along the upper ledges of the canyon where they blazed away at the troopers until their ammunition was all gone. But it was useless. McKenzie's men had the village and in spite of the bullets whining among them, they destroyed every one of the one hundred and seventy-three lodges and all ammunition and supplies. Several troopers [4] were hit but the others went stolidly about their work of destruction, which included the slaughter of the captured herd of one hundred and fifty ponies.

Night came on, bitter cold. The heroic Yellow Nose was shot through the breast. Many other warriors were dead or badly wounded. But the terrible cold was more deadly than bullets. Some of the Indians had fought naked all day. Accustomed though they were to hardship, the killing temperatures were too much for the Cheyennes, unblanketed and unprotected. Twelve babies froze to death that night and several old or sick people died. Many others were saved only by a horrible expedient. Some of the few remaining horses were slaughtered. Their bodies were disemboweled and into these bloody cavities the little children were thrust by their mothers, that the warmth

---

[4] McKenzie lost five killed, including Lieutenant McKinney, and twenty-five wounded. Twenty-five dead Cheyennes were left on the battle-field. Others may have been killed and carried away.

and protection of the walls of flesh might save them. Some of the aged were allowed to thrust their hands and feet in and thus preserve circulation and life.

They camped six miles up the valley, without shelter, clothes or food. McKenzie retired down the gulch to rejoin Crook. Next day the Cheyennes wandered off seeking Crazy Horse. Scouts who crossed their trail later said it was red with blood and that tiny footprints showed where even little children tramped through the snow with their tortured feet bleeding.

In three days the Cheyennes reached the camp of Crazy Horse. They were not disappointed in their hope of succor. The Sioux had little, but what there was they divided with the Cheyennes. Many of them stayed right with the Sioux. But many others filed away into the snowy mountains and a few days later surrendered at an Indian agency, conquered by the ruthless elements in one week, when ten years of fighting had failed to bow their heads.

THE LAST OF THE HOSTILES

Crazy Horse's situation was desperate. With the Cheyennes gone and Sitting Bull gone, less than a third of the forces which beat Custer and Crook remained. Moreover those who did remain had very little ammunition left. In the next two months Crazy Horse played hide and seek with Miles. Poorly equipped for winter campaigning, and trailing the women and children with him, he kept the soldiers on the jump until January, when Miles finally caught up.

The general had two regiments of infantry and a couple of howitzers camouflaged under wagon bows and canvas to look like wagons. On Tongue River, January 3rd, he fought a sharp skirmish with a party of Sioux. There was another brush two days later. Crazy Horse's people were tired out. They could not pull away any longer.

On the morning of the 7th, Miles' Crow scouts captured a small party of Cheyenne women and children. These people were not Sioux, but Crazy Horse turned back to rescue them just the same. A desperate raid that night, trying to recapture the prisoners, showed Miles he was on the verge of a big fight.

Early the following morning, while the soldiers were eating breakfast in the shadow of Wolf Mountain, the battle began. Sioux appeared on the cliffs. The crackle of rifle fire stung the air. Taunts and yells of defiance from the gaunt Indians added to the noise. The situation looked bad for the troops.

But Miles had a trump card. The canvas covers were torn from the two cannon and the frosty morning air shook at the thundering reports of the guns and the screeching of the shells as they soared across the valley to explode in the Indian positions. At the first outburst from the "wagon guns," the Sioux ducked behind their rocks. Shell-fire was the thing they dreaded most. It took all of Crazy Horse's leadership to keep them in the battle. Still, they kept a very annoying fire plunging down into the valley.

About the middle of the morning Major Casey was ordered to charge a high cliff where about fifty Sioux had climbed. Struggling across the snowy flats, the men fought their way up to the crags. Big Crow, a famous warrior of outstanding courage, led the Indians. During the charge, although his war bonnet was a target for every rifle in the attacking column, he ran back and forth across the front in full view, to draw the soldiers' fire and encourage his own braves. For a time he was not hit. But presently he fell. The Sioux then retreated and the troops occupied the bluff.

In the meantime the cannon had been spreading consternation wherever they turned their black muzzles. Besides, the Indians were almost out of cartridges. So taking advantage of a blinding snow storm which began to fall, Crazy Horse drew off his people.

Miles did not capture his band at that time but on February 1st, Big Leggins Brughiere, the half-breed who wrote Sitting Bull's note to Otis, and who had deserted to the soldiers, came to the Sioux camp carrying a summons to surrender. He found the Indians camped in the snow, nearly frozen, with most of their horses dead. Two Moons and Little Chief surrendered three hundred Cheyennes on April 22nd. A few days later, Crazy Horse, discouraged and seeing the uselessness of resistance, brought his two thousand followers to Red Cloud Agency.

One hostile band remained—that of Lame Deer, a Minneconjou, who had been with Crazy Horse and refused to accompany him to the agency. Miles started after this band of bitter-enders on May 2nd. They reached and charged the village at dawn five days later. Of course there was not much of a fight. The Sioux were in no position to give battle. A soldier or two and several Indians, including one old woman, were killed; then Lame Deer waved a white rag as a flag of truce.

Everything was apparently over, but tragedy was still to follow. Lame Deer's son refused to lay down his gun. It chanced that the old woman who was killed was the youth's grandmother. He was wild with grief and rage. "I am a soldier on my own land," he kept explaining. An officer and one of the scouts rode up to him and seized his gun to disarm him. The weapon was discharged.

Nobody was hurt. But Lame Deer, hearing the report, believed he was going to be treacherously murdered. He had already laid down his rifle. Now he snatched it up and aimed a shot full at Miles. Straight back the general reared his horse. The bullet passed through the thin air where he had been a minute before and killed his orderly.

In an instant all the soldiers were shooting in retaliation. Several more Indians were killed—a needless sacrifice. A total of fourteen Sioux died in this fight, including Lame Deer and his son, Big Ankle. Four soldiers also lost their lives. The band was soon rounded up and brought to the reservation.

THE END OF A GREAT FIGHTER

The day he surrendered was the saddest in Crazy Horse's life. In the succeeding months his enemies constantly circulated rumors that he was plotting another uprising, and kept him under the suspicion and in the bad graces of the military. It is unlikely that Crazy Horse ever thought seriously of going on the war path again. He had not surrendered until it was impossible to fight longer and he knew well enough that he would be even worse equipped if he took the field now.

Crazy Horse never grew to love the white man. He simply recognized the futility of resistance. Hectored and spied on, he did his best to settle down to life as a virtual prisoner on the reservation.

The chief was still a young man and that spring he fell in love with the daughter of a half-breed interpreter, Louis Richard, at the Red Cloud Agency. The girl, three parts Sioux, reciprocated the love of the renowned warrior, and in spite of Richard's opposition, they married according to the Indian custom. For some months Crazy Horse lived peacefully and apparently happily with his bride. Then the girl sickened and the chief saw with concern that she was growing very weak.

One of the reports circulated by Crazy Horse's enemies was that he planned to murder General Crook. "Only cowards are murderers," the chief scornfully said when he was told of the rumor, and the matter dropped. But with the new stories going the rounds, Agent J. M. Lee grew "jumpy." At this critical time a further misunderstanding was caused, intentionally or unintentionally, by Frank Grouard, the interpreter.

When the Nez Percé war broke out, Crook called a council of the Sioux to enlist a group of scouts. Crazy Horse attended. He was surprised at the request. But according to Louis Bordeaux,[5] he only said: "We are tired of war; we came in for peace, but now that the Great Father asks our help we will go north and fight until there is not a Nez Percé left."

Bordeaux was not the official interpreter. Grouard was, and he rendered this speech: "We will go north and fight until not a white man is left." Whether or not the mistake was intentional [6] it threw the council into tremendous excitement. Crazy Horse, probably very much puzzled at the commotion, not understanding the error, left. Crook's attention was called to the discrepancy between the two translations, but his mind was made up that the chief meant war. Nothing could persuade him differently. From that day Crazy Horse was a marked man.

The famous Ogalalla grew more and more concerned

[5] E. A. Brininstool, "Chief Crazy Horse, His Career and Death," Nebraska History Magazine, December, 1929, pp. 15 and 38. Bordeaux was a reliable interpreter according to Dr. McGillicuddy.

[6] Grouard had plenty of reason to fear Crazy Horse and wish him out of the way. He had long lived among the Sioux before the war, had been a personal friend of Crazy Horse's and had deserted him to scout for Crook in 1876. Grouard was a Kanaka from the Sandwich Islands. Many thought him a half-breed, but this was not the case. At the time the disputed interpretation took place, he was publicly called a liar by Bordeaux. It stands to reason that Crazy Horse, in the power of his enemies, would have made no such remark as was attributed to him by Grouard. It would be rank insanity and Crazy Horse was both sane and intelligent.

about his wife. The girl had tuberculosis. Dr. V. T. Mc-Gillicuddy, stationed at the Spotted Tail Agency, had the confidence of Crazy Horse. As his wife failed the chief asked permission to take her to the doctor. The permission was refused. Somebody suggested he appeal to the President, the "Great Father."

"I am not hunting for any Great Father," he haughtily responded. "My father is with me, and there is no Great Father between me and the Great Spirit."

On the morning of September 4th, with a few companions and his ailing wife, he rode quietly out of Red Cloud Agency, toward Spotted Tail, in spite of orders.

Wild excitement ensued. Agency officials feared Crazy Horse more than the whole Sioux Nation. Word flew to Lieutenant W. P. Clark at Fort Robinson that the chief had broken away. It was, of course, a badly garbled account. Crazy Horse had not "broken away." He was merely taking a sick wife for medical attention. Indian police overtook him, riding slowly along beside the ailing girl. At their demand that he return with them to Red Cloud, he drew himself proudly up.

"I am Crazy Horse! Do not touch me! I am not running away!" he exclaimed.

Before his glare the scouts quailed. Meekly they fell behind and accompanied him to Spotted Tail.

There Crazy Horse tried to explain that he had come merely to have his wife treated. But the rattled agent could not believe it. Here was Crazy Horse, the renowned leader of the Sioux, idol of his people. He must be gotten away and that quickly.

The chief was disappointed when told he must return to Red Cloud, yet agreed with quiet dignity. He expressed misgivings, saying he "was afraid something might happen." Those were well-grounded apprehensions.

Plans were made to imprison him. Fearing resistance, the officers in charge merely asked Crazy Horse to follow them. The Indian unsuspiciously entered the guard house. Not until the bars of the prison struck his eyes did he realize the treachery. There before him stood the grated door of a cell.

Like an animal at bay, he turned, gazing wildly about. No loop hole for escape here. His war cry sounded like the scream of an eagle. A long knife flashed in his hand. Captain Kennington struck at him with a sword.

"Kill him! Kill him!" rang the shouts. The mêlée raged furiously. Alone in his last extremity, Crazy Horse fought like a cornered wolf. Everybody aimed blows at him. Little Big Man, one of his own warriors, tried to seize him. Crazy Horse slashed his arm to the bone. Three Brulés, followers of Spotted Tail who envied and hated him, grabbed him at last by the arms. It took all three to hold him. As they pinioned him, helpless, a soldier ran up behind and plunged a bayonet deep into his side.

Crazy Horse sank to the floor. The uproar was terrific. Even his enemies raged over the murder. From the nearby camp hundreds of excited warriors rushed to the scene. They were with difficulty kept from fighting.

They laid the dying chief on a counter. He grasped the hand of Agent Lee, who had protested against the tactics used, and said between labored gasps: "My friend, I don't blame you for this."

Just before the end he said:

"I was hostile to the white man. . . . We preferred hunting to a life of idleness on our reservations. . . . At times we did not get enough to eat and we were not allowed . . . to hunt. All we wanted was peace and to be left alone. Soldiers . . . in the winter . . . destroyed our villages. Then Long Hair came. . . . They say we massacred him, but he would have done the same to us. . . . Our first impulse was to escape . . . but we were so hemmed in we had to fight. After that I . . . lived in peace; but the government would not let me alone . . . I came back to Red Cloud Agency. Yet I was not allowed to remain quiet. I was tired of fighting. . . . They tried to confine me . . . and a soldier ran his bayonet into me. I have spoken." [7]

A few minutes later the listeners heard the weird sound of the Sioux death song. At last it faded away. Crazy Horse had passed to the land of his fathers.

Dark charges have been made that the whole thing was deliberately planned to "get Crazy Horse out of the way." Years later it was revealed that the government had planned to take the chief from the guard house at night, rush him to prison in the Dry Tortugas, Florida, and there keep him.

His old gray-haired father begged for the body. At daylight on the morning of September 6th, 1877, the old man and his wife followed a travois on which was lashed the body of their dead son to its final resting place on Wounded Knee Creek.

As Captain John G. Bourke, one of the officers who fought hardest against him, has said:

"Crazy Horse was one of the great soldiers of his day and generation. As the grave of Custer marked the high-water mark of Sioux supremacy in the trans-Mississippi region, so the grave of Crazy Horse marked the ebb."

[7] The full text of this remarkable death bed statement is worth reading. It may be found in Col. Homer W. Wheeler's "Buffalo Days," pp. 199-200. The portion quoted here is with the permission of the publishers, the Bobbs-Merrill Co., of Indianapolis.

VI.

THE LONG TRAIL

1877

Chapter XVI

"NEVER SELL THE BONES OF YOUR FATHER"

IN THE NEZ PERCÉ MOUNTAINS

An old man lay dying in an Indian teepee high up among the hills of the Wallowa country. Outside, in the inky blackness of the night, the flat monotony of the tom-toms continued so persistently that those who sat in the ghostly circle of firelight by his pallet heard it no more than they heard the throbbing of the pulse-beats in their own ear drums. Afar in the outskirts of the shadowy village the eery wailing of the squaws rose and fell with skin-prickling quavers and minor chords. The feverish stamp and shuffle of the medicine dance, maintained by the steel-limbed tribal wizards had sounded for a long time now.

The Indian who was gasping out his last was a great man—a father to the wild people of whom he was chief. At any time the death of Old Joseph would have been enough to plunge the Nez Percés into a frenzy of grief, but at this time it was double cause for sorrow. A great crisis faced them. The question at issue was, should they live on as a free people or as conquered prisoners of an alien race. Small wonder that the women wailed and the medicine men stamped and whirled in the unending spirit dance.

The sick man's eyes were glazing fast, but presently he summoned a part of his lost vigor. A thin hand was raised from the buffalo robes. A weak voice spoke.

"Where is my son?"

A young man stepped to the old chief's side. Dead silence reigned in the lodge. This was Old Joseph's own son, In-mut-too-yah-lat-lat (Thunder-traveling-over-the-mountains), but history was destined to immortalize him as Chief Joseph.

Parental pride glowed in the eyes which the old chief turned upon him. This was his boy—his heir! Tall, straight as an arrow, and wonderfully handsome, he was enough to stir pride in any father's heart. The old man spoke and for a time his voice regained those sonorous qualities his tribe had loved to hear.

"My son!" he said, and affection thrilled his voice. Then began that wonderful charge to his heir, the simple oratory of which, coupled with the patriotism it expressed, have so fortunately been preserved for us: [1]

"My son, this old body is returning to my mother earth, and my spirit is going very soon to see the Great Spirit Chief. Give ear to me. When I am gone, think of your country. You are the chief of these people. They look to you to guide them. Always remember that your father never sold his country.

"You must stop your ears whenever you are asked to sign a treaty selling your home. A few years more and white men will be all around you. They have their eyes on this land. My son, never forget my dying words. This country holds your father's body. Never sell the bones of your father and mother."

The old chief sank back. Within an hour the keening of the women announced the passing of one of their tribe's greatest figures.

Young Joseph walked forth from the death lodge the

[1] The words are from Joseph's own story as told to Bishop William H. Hare and published in the North American Review, in 1879.

hereditary leader of his people, with his father's last words resting on his soul. Those words remained the guiding spirit of his life during the strange adventures and battle-filled days which followed.

BIG TROUBLE

What kind of people were the Nez Percés? And what manner of a man was the young chief who found himself so suddenly with all the responsibility for their welfare on his shoulders?

Lewis and Clarke first met the tribe in 1805, occupying what is now Idaho and Washington. They were named from an early habit of piercing the nose for ornaments, long discarded. A peaceful hunting and fishing tribe, they were vicious fighters when aroused to war. They had shown a constant friendship for the white man, notable for half a century.[2]

When Oregon was settled, the Nez Percés ceded all their lands except the Wallowa Valley in Oregon and a large section of Idaho. Here they lived peacefully and happily until gold was found, and the gold hunters, disregarding treaties, swarmed on the reservation. At the Nez Percé protest, another treaty was offered. This time the tribe was to be moved bodily out of its home land into the Lapwai Reservation in Idaho. The Southern Nez Percés refused to sign. They have never signed to this day.

The death of Old Joseph left at their head an Indian who approaches nearer to Cooper's famous Indian heroes than any modern red man. Young Joseph was little known except as a handsome young man and a fine hunter. He had never seen a shot fired in anger. Yet such were his

[2] The Nez Percé boast was that no member of the tribe had ever taken the life of a white man in fifty years. It could not be said that no white man had ever killed a Nez Percé.

natural qualities that before he finished he taught the best soldiers in the United States Army lessons in tactics.

Joseph was fortunate in that the Sioux War on the plains kept the army too busy to bother with the Nez Percés for three years after his father's death. By that time his people had grown to know and trust him. In 1877 the Sioux were beaten, and General O. O. Howard, a fine officer and a sincere friend to the Indian, was ordered to round up the non-agency Nez Percés and put them on the reservation.

Howard called a council with Chief Joseph and his head men at Fort Lapwai. Joseph did not attend. He sent his younger brother Ollicut, a fine, dashing youth, and five other chiefs. Howard insisted that Joseph come and he finally did so. The council lasted all day. Joseph astonished Howard with his dexterous intellectual fencing. Here is a sample of it:

"If we ever owned the land we own it still, for we never sold it. In treaty councils the commissioners have claimed that our country has been sold to the government. Suppose a white man should come to me and say, 'Joseph, I like your horses, and I want to buy them.' I say to him, 'No, my horses suit me, I will not sell them.' Then he goes to some neighbor and says to him, 'Joseph has some good horses. I want to buy them but he refuses to sell.' My neighbor answers, 'Pay me the money and I will sell you the horses.' The white man returns to me and says, 'Joseph, I have bought your horses and you must let me have them.' If we sold our lands to the government, that was the way they were bought."

The logic was all on Joseph's side. Howard's patience became frayed. He got into an argument with Too-hul-hul-sote, a medicine man, and had him arrested. Joseph, Ollicut, White Bird, Hush-hush-cute and Looking Glass left the council at once. The Nez Percés were indignant over the arrest of their high priest. Joseph had difficulty in keeping them quiet.

Five days later, to secure Too-hul's release, Joseph unwillingly promised to go on the reservation. His intentions were honest. He thought he was doing the best thing for his people. But while he was preparing to move them, they took affairs out of his hands.

Among the young warriors were three who wanted blood atonement for past wrongs. One was the son of a man who had been killed by a drunken white. The others were two who had been tied up and whipped by another white. This trio rode out from the camp on June 13th, 1877, and killed an old ranchman named Devine on the Salmon River. Next morning they killed three more whites and in the afternoon a fourth. Then they rode back to the Nez Percé camp, waving their scalps and yelling for war. The blood-thirst of the young braves was aroused. Seventeen of them joined the three. They rode back to the Salmon Valley. Harry Mason, the man who had whipped the two warriors, was living there. The Indians killed him like a rabid wolf. Seven more persons in the vicinity died also. Next morning they attacked Cottonwood House, a ranch, killed three, wounded two others so badly that they died, and hurt others. In two or three days the Nez Percés had taken the lives of eighteen white persons.

Joseph was away at the time. When he returned he found his people in a fighting mood. Already plans were made to send war parties in every direction. Joseph protested. In vain. Either he must go with his people or leave them. The young chieftain must have muttered something equivalent to Stephen Decatur's famous toast, as he made up his mind to stay with his tribe.

WHITE BIRD CANYON

As has been said, Joseph had no war experience. Nobody knew his capacity as a soldier, but they were to find it out without delay. As the first messengers reached Fort Lapwai with news of the Salmon Valley massacre, General Howard sent two troops of the 1st Cavalry under Captains Perry and Trimble to protect the settlers and punish the Indians. Nobody expected much fighting. The Indians had always been peaceful. Two days brought Perry to the deep canyon of White Bird Creek, eighty miles away.

It chanced that the Nez Percés were camped in that very canyon. The White Bird runs through mountainous country, cutting a deep gorge. It is slightly timbered and opens widely into the Salmon River valley. Perry with his one hundred men moved down the canyon looking for hostiles. The village was hidden among the buttes and ravines at the mouth of the gorge, and Nez Percé scouts discovered Perry miles up the canyon. Joseph took command in his first battle as though he were the veteran of a hundred engagements.

He had about two hundred warriors which he divided into two groups. Part of them under White Bird, hid in the brush to one side of the canyon. The others lined the buttes at the opening into the valley.

No West Pointer could have set a neater trap. Perry blundered right into it. Lieutenant Theller with eight troopers rode somewhat in advance of Perry's and Trimble's commands. The buttes ahead suddenly became alive with Indians. The sharp roll of rifle fire broke out. A yelling body of mounted Nez Percés charged across the valley at the startled soldiers. Theller had to run. Then Perry and Trimble galloped up and wheeled into line beside him. The troops formed a line clear across the valley. On the extreme left, on a high bluff, Perry's scouts ensconced themselves where they could make their marksmanship felt.

The firing was heavy for a few minutes. Battle smoke began to fill the valley. Under the close shooting of the soldiers, several Nez Percés were hit. The rest fell back. Perry thought he had the fight won.

At this moment White Bird dealt his blow. A blast of fire which knocked over several troopers was their first knowledge of the flank movement. The howling Nez Percés charged and drove the sharpshooters from their bluff. Trimble was driven back, but Sergeant McCarthy with six men was left behind. They fought off the hostiles until Trimble charged again and brought them off. Two more men were killed. The rearward movement became a retreat.

Up the canyon streamed the soldiers, swiftly becoming panic-stricken. Perry was badly whipped. Leaving gallant Theller with sixteen troopers as a rear guard, he turned his efforts to extricating his command. Grimly Theller held back the rushes of Joseph's victory-mad warriors, until the last of his comrades crossed the top of the divide. Then he followed.

But this remnant was not to escape. Joseph swooped like a hawk. Fighting to the end, Theller and his men, to the last trooper, were killed. The rest of Perry's command was chased clear to Graingeville. It was a stunning disaster. Theller and thirty-six men were dead. The Indian loss was slight as they fought almost entirely from cover.

That evening the Nez Percés moved across the Salmon, forestalling Howard's prompt march with three hundred men. Arriving at the river the general found Joseph where he could retreat in any direction or oppose a crossing as he chose.

"No general could have chosen a safer position or one more likely to puzzle and obstruct a foe," was Howard's admiring comment.

The leaders, red and white, sat down on opposite sides of the turbulent stream, to watch each other.

Chapter XVII

ACROSS THE MOUNTAINS

THE FIGHT ON THE CLEARWATER

It was war to the hilt now, without hope of mercy to the vanquished—and Joseph had only two hundred warriors. Seven hundred soldiers were mustered against him, with more coming.

All day he watched Howard across the river. At noon the general dispatched Major Whipple with two troops of cavalry to intercept Looking Glass's band of Nez Percés which was marching to join Joseph.

It was what the chief was looking for. He pulled his people away after dark, descended the heights and was after Whipple like a cat after a mouse. That officer, sparring with Looking Glass, learned to his dismay that Joseph was almost on top of him. Just in time he threw up defenses at the Cottonwood. The Nez Percés surrounded him. They cut up two scouting forces, killing Lieutenant Rains and eleven men.

It took Howard twenty-four hours to untangle himself from the mountains. When, by forced marches, he followed Joseph to the Cottonwood, the Indians were gone. Looking Glass's reinforcements raised Joseph's fighting total to two hundred and fifty—and incidentally increased his baggage train and non-combatant list in proportion. Joseph was encumbered with four hundred and fifty women, children and aged, and a herd of two thousand ponies. But that did not discourage him.

Like a grim old bulldog Howard hung on the Nez Percé trail. At last, seeing he could not evade pursuit, Joseph deliberately chose a battle field and waited to meet his foe. On the banks of the Clearwater River, far south of the reservation, he threw up rude breastworks. Howard's scouts crept up on the morning of July 10th and drew shots from the Indians. Then the main force came up. The first spattering of shots grew into a steady roar. Joseph was badly outnumbered but he handled his small force with consummate skill. The general later admitted that only the arrival of reinforcements prevented the loss of his supply train. Joseph almost turned Howard's right with a flank movement. There was some violent hand-to-hand fighting. The chief led repeated charges, but the troops managed to hold their ground.

Night fell. The Nez Percés held the only spring and they also controlled the river banks—so the soldiers slept thirsty. At dawn the battle reopened fiercely. The Nez Percés showed the same fighting qualities and deadly marksmanship.[1] But Howard's artillery, a howitzer and two Gatling guns, had at last arrived. The big guns drove Joseph's men back from their trenches. Major Marcus P. Miller led a charge through the Nez Percé left, then crossed the ravine and took Joseph in the rear.

A critical moment. But Joseph called a handful of warriors and threw himself so fiercely at Miller that the troops were driven back. Then he turned on Howard and held him off until he could get his people safely away. There was not one false move. He withdrew in masterly manner and retreated slowly northward. Thirteen soldiers

1 "The Indian fire was terribly accurate and very fatal, the proportion of wounded to killed being about two to one"—Major C. E. S. Wood.

were dead and twenty-seven wounded. The Nez Percé loss was larger, twenty-three dead and forty-six wounded—chiefly because of artillery fire. Joseph had lost no honors.

At Kamiah Falls, Joseph and his chiefs sat in council. Should they stay and fight? Or should they leave their country and try to reach safety elsewhere? Joseph decided on the latter course. The wrench it gave him is shown by his own words:

"I said in my heart that I would give up my country. I would give up my father's grave. I would give up everything rather than have the blood of my people on my hands. . . . I love that land more than all the world. A man who would not love his father's grave is worse than a wild animal." [2]

That was a momentous decision. It involved a retreat of two thousand miles with certainty of pursuit. It meant hard fighting and harder marching. But once they reached the haven of rest, British Columbia, it meant safety. The only alternative was surrender.

THE LO-LO TRAIL

His decision made, Joseph, like Napoleon, called his fighting men before him and made a short, stirring speech.

"Some of you tried to say once that I was afraid of the whites," he ended. "Stay with me now and you shall get your bellies well filled with fighting." [3]

The Nez Percés rallied around their leader in wild enthusiasm. Rifles, knives, spears were tossed on high. They were ready.

Like Moses of old, Joseph struck into the unknown and

[2] Joseph's personal narrative, North American Review, 1879.

[3] From Major C. E. S. Wood's article "Chief Joseph the Nez Perce" in the Century Magazine, 1884, copyright by the Century Co. Major Wood got his information about this incident from one of Joseph's warriors.

barren country, with his flocks and herds, his women and children, his old and weak. But, unlike Moses, he had no Almighty to swallow up the pursuing hosts in an ocean. Joseph had to stand off pursuit by his own unaided effort. Leaving a small rear guard which delayed Howard for a day at Weippe, he started up the Lo-lo Pass.

The Lo-lo trail crosses the Montana mountains at one of their most inaccessible points. It is admittedly one of the most difficult trails in America. With jagged rocks, fallen timber, shoulders hanging over dizzy abysses, torrents and seemingly impassable forests, its natural difficulties were complicated by extremely nasty weather. It rained practically all the time. Every foot of the trail was slippery. So great was the difficulty of crossing this pass, that the troops, unencumbered by camp baggage, averaged a scant sixteen miles a day. Joseph's people with their women, children, herds and camp luggage, pulled steadily away from them.

At the pass which led down to the plains from the Coeur d'Alenes, they found a hastily constructed fort, held by Captain C. C. Rawn and about sixty men. Rawn had been told to stop those Nez Percés. Outnumbered, he bravely prepared to do his best. But he was dealing with a great strategist.

When Rawn refused to let him pass even though he promised to commit no depredations, Joseph made a noisy feint in front of the fort, then quietly led his people through some hitherto unknown mountain trails, around the fort and down into the Bitter Root Valley. The doughty captain retreated hastily to Fort Missoula.

Joseph religiously kept his promise to commit no depredations. The Indians were peaceful, and they amicably traded with the whites in the little towns they passed, buying rifles, food and cartridges. When the military after-

War Department *Bureau of American Ethnology*

Left: Gen. O. O. Howard, the Nemesis of the Nez Percés. Right: Chief Joseph (In-mut-too-yah-lat-lat), the brilliant Nez Percé strategist who gave the best U.S. generals lessons in tactics in the campaign of 1878.

Indian scaffold burials. These burials by the Crow Indians were photographed in 1871 in southern Montana.

Shoshone village in the foothills of the Wind River Mountains, photographed in 1870.

war protested, these frontiersmen replied that the Nez Percés had always been good Indians and they could see no reason for fighting them.

Howard was clear out of the picture for a time. But from Helena, General John Gibbon was straining every nerve to cut the Nez Percés off. The Indians, after their friendly treatment in the valley, supposed the war was over. They camped peacefully, their teepees pitched on a little meadow by the Big Hole River. Willows and underbrush choked the sides of the stream. The high ground was covered with trees. On this unsuspecting village, Gibbon with two hundred men made a stealthy advance, just as day broke on August 9th.

THE BATTLE OF BIG HOLE

A Nez Percé boy, out to look at the horses, saw the moving shadows fording the river in the first gray light. His wild war whoop ended all concealment. Thrashing through the willows, the soldiers swept the camp. The Nez Percés dove into the bushes of the bank and the trees beyond, naked and carrying only their arms and ammunition. Gibbon had captured the village.

But he did not get to keep it long. Joseph had his men in hand in a few minutes. Here and there his chiefs—Ollicut, White Bird, Too-hul-hul-sote, and Looking Glass—were busy rallying their warriors. Back came the Indians; the thickets and woods were full of them. The soldiers heard the chiefs exhorting their braves.

"Why are we retreating?" shouted White Bird. "Since the world was made, brave men have fought for their women and children! Fight! Shoot them down! We can shoot as well as any of these soldiers!" [4]

[4] Quoted from "The Battle of the Big Hole" by G. O. Shields.

Captain Logan's troop penetrated farthest. Now it was beset by a pack of human wolves. A tall warrior leaped at Logan and both fired. The Indian fell dead. From nearby a woman—his sister—sprang forward, tore the still smoking revolver from his dead hand, and shot Logan through the head. Instances of this kind of hand-to-hand fighting were many. The white men were pushed back with heavy losses. During the charge Tap-sis-il and Wal-lit-ze, two of the three youths whose massacre had caused the war, were killed.

Joseph posted sharpshooters in the heights overlooking the valley. These braves, the best Indian marksmen on the continent, deliberately picked off the officers. Gibbon was one of the first to be wounded. Lieutenant Coolidge was shot through both thighs and Lieutenant Woodruff was hit. In spite of his pain, Gibbon formed his men in two lines, back to back, and sent them charging through the woods in opposite directions. The Nez Percés hurled both lines back.

A detachment led by Lieutenant James Bradley [5] was cut off. Bradley was killed. Only by very hard fighting did a few survivors reach Gibbon. The troops could no longer stay where they were and the general ordered a retreat. Carrying their wounded, they went back up the hill to a little rise. As they left the camp the Nez Percés took possession.

The soldiers faced a new difficulty. A height above was occupied by the Indians. Gibbon's men now had to carry the place by assault.

From behind rocks and trees the warriors fought fiercely. One, with a few large rocks piled in front of him, fired through a loophole and picked off man after

[5] Lieutenant Bradley was the officer who discovered the dead bodies of Custer's men after the Battle of the Little Big Horn.

man, secure from the many shots aimed at him from short range. At last a veteran soldier, an expert marksman, sent a bullet into the loophole which struck the rock on one side, glanced and entered the Indian's eye, passing out of the back of his head—a perfect carom shot.

Meantime the Nez Percés swarmed to attack Gibbon's knoll. His men dug rifle pits with their trowel bayonets and settled down to the grimmest defense of their lives. All day the destructive Indian rifles snarled and snapped. Lieutenant English was killed and Captain Williams was wounded twice. Many of the men were hit. Every officer used a rifle now, to augment the fire. Gibbon, despite his wound, handled a hunting rifle with deadly aim.

Gibbon had a howitzer, which had fallen behind during the march. Now its gun squad tried to bring the gun to him. But Joseph had tasted artillery fire at the Clearwater. Thirty mounted Nez Percés burst out of the woods and charged. The gunners had time to fire their piece twice. Then the white men fled. The Indians dismounted the howitzer so it was of no further use in the fight. The same thirty horsemen also captured a packload of two thousand rounds of ammunition.

Late in the afternoon the Nez Percés set fire to the grass. For a time it looked as if the flames would drive Gibbon out. But luckily for him the wind changed, the blaze faltered and died.

As darkness fell the Indians withdrew. Volunteers, covered by a firing party, managed to crawl to the river and fill their canteens. A dead horse formed the soldiers' food. They did not dare build a fire for fear of sharpshooters, so had to eat the horse raw.

During the night Joseph struck his teepees, packed his baggage and moved his people down the valley. A few warriors stayed in the vicinity the next day. Gibbon's crippled command could not pursue. By the night of the 10th the last Nez Percé left and when the 11th dawned there was not an Indian in the country.

Joseph had won again. He had lost eighty-nine dead but of these, fifty were women and children. There were twenty-nine soldiers killed and forty wounded. Joseph's faithful lieutenant, Looking Glass, was among the fallen. Looking Glass' daughter and two of Joseph's wives were also killed.

It was a thankful Gibbon who saw Howard's advance guards pushing down the valley next day. He knew exactly now how Reno had felt that fatal day on the Little Big Horn, months before, when Gibbon was the rescuer.

Chapter XVIII

"FROM WHERE THE SUN NOW STANDS"

CAMAS MEADOWS

SOUTHWARD, ever southward went the Indians. Joseph was getting farther away from the Canadian border with every step but there were to be no more surprises. Nez Percé scouts hung far back on the trail, keeping constant watch on Howard's movements. At last the chief reached his farthest south. Not one step more would he be driven. It was northward or die.

Joseph's scouts brought word that a detachment of soldiers—under Lieutenant Bacon—had been sent away to occupy a pass ahead. This fitted exactly with his plans. On the night of August 20th forty warriors, riding in column of fours, entered Howard's camp. Their formation was so unusual for Indians that they were mistaken in the dark for Bacon's returning force. They were inside the picket lines before the alarm was given.

Among the tents the Nez Percés worked with perfect coordination. Some shot at the soldiers who rushed out of their sleeping places; the rest went to the picket lines and tried to stampede the horses. They got the pack mules loose but the horses were too well tethered.

When things got too hot, the audacious forty rode out of the camp with Howard's troopers in close pursuit. It was a race for a while. Then spurts of flame sprang out from rocks on three sides of a wide ravine into which the

Indians had led the cavalry. They were in a cul-de-sac—
it was sure death to remain.

Out of those jaws of death they galloped—all but Captain Norwood's troop. Cut off, they found a strong position and by sheer cold courage held off the Nez Percés until Howard could return and rescue them. Then the whole command retreated. The night had saved them from being cut to pieces as the Indians could not see to shoot accurately. One man was killed, and seven, including Lieutenant H. M. Benson, were wounded.

The Camas Meadows fight stopped Howard's pursuit. He was without a pack train and with a sizable hospital list. He had to sit down and wait for supplies from Virginia City.

Joseph was free to go where he chose. He moved leisurely eastward through Thatcher's Pass—which had been vacated by Bacon—and into Yellowstone Park. Here two parties of tourists were surprised and captured. The men fought and were killed or wounded. Two women were captured but were released unharmed.[1]

Crossing the park, Joseph burned Baronet's bridge over Clarke Fork of the Yellowstone and turned north. By this time practically every body of troops in Montana was on the move. Lieutenant Gilbert's two troops of cavalry crossed the Nez Percé trail, but such was this tribe's reputation that Gilbert retreated, and at such speed that he failed to make a junction with Howard and finally arrived at Fort Ellis.

The 7th Cavalry tried to trap Joseph in the Yellowstone Valley but the chief laughed at them and slipped through a dense forest northward. Not until next day did

[1] J. P. Dunn says this is the only authentic case on record where white women captured by Indians escaped outrage. "Massacres in the Mountains," p. 427.

Colonel Sturgis learn he had been tricked. He gave chase. With his fresh horses he overtook the Nez Percés at Canyon Creek, on September 13th.

It was a short but very hot battle. Joseph had posted his rear guard to hold back the cavalry while the women and camp equipment escaped. As the 7th galloped after the main body of Indians, seen a mile down the stream, a sudden rattling fire broke out from the ridges on each side. Two saddles were emptied and all thoughts of catching up with the noncombatants departed.

Sturgis dismounted his men and sent them swarming up the slopes. Less than a hundred warriors were there to oppose three hundred and fifty troopers. One by one the 7th drove the Nez Percés from their positions. By night Joseph was again in retreat. But Sturgis, with his wounded to care for, could not pursue.

The Indians lost twenty-one braves killed and wounded in the fight. Sturgis had three dead and twelve wounded, including the veteran Captain French. The most serious loss the Nez Percés suffered was the capture of their herd of nine hundred ponies by the Crow scouts.

MILES AGAIN

Westward and northward rode the Nez Percés. Behind, exhausted or crippled, were three strong bodies of soldiers, each outnumbering them, but beaten and out of the fight. Howard, Gibbon and Sturgis were disposed of, but a new enemy loomed ahead. The enormous advantage of railroad and telegraph was working for the white man.

General Miles with his famous 5th Infantry and five troops of cavalry, two guns and a supply train, was marching at an angle calculated to cut off the Indian retreat.

Joseph, through his peerless scouts, knew every movement of the enemies in his vicinity. But he had no way of knowing distant movements, so was ignorant of Miles' approach.

Past the Snow Mountains and straight toward his long-sought goal he drove his Spartan people at a killing pace. Some instinct told him every minute was precious. At the ford of the Missouri he found a little fort on Cow Island, garrisoned by twelve men. Joseph could easily have destroyed the place. But he contented himself with a single attack in which three of the defenders were killed. During this attack he got his women and children across the river; then he burned all the freight at the station and went on.

On the Mussell River he halted just long enough to brush aside the weak force of Major Ilges, a troop of cavalry and thirty-six civilians. Far ahead loomed the Bear Paw Mountains, with Canada and safety only thirty miles beyond. Could the Nez Percés make it? On and on they marched, with ponies dropping at every mile along their agonized path. Human flesh and blood could not endure the strain. They reached the mountains, but there for a time they halted. That halt was necessary but fatal. One brief day's journey would have taken them to the border. But the people were unspeakably weary. Joseph's humanity caused him to relax his iron purpose—he seemed so very near the goal. The cup, poised to his lips, was dashed to the ground. The prize, almost won, was snatched away.

Miles rode to cross the Indian trail. He had fresh troops, fresh horses, fresh scouts. And he was fresh to the fray and knew the mistakes of his predecessors. In the dead of night he crept up on Joseph's camp, pitched on the northward slope of the mountains, where he could almost see his destination.

Morning of October 3rd dawned, cold and stormy.

With the first light came the opening shot of the final battle. The Indian camp was in a cup-shaped ravine overlooked by high cliffs and bluffs. What sickening despair must have been Joseph's as he saw the troops galloping toward him, spreading out like a mammoth fan. No chance to escape here. The Nez Percé knew his time had come. He was outnumbered four to one. Everything favored the soldiers.

On charged the cavalry, converging from three sides. Captain Hale's troop led. A sudden level sheet of fire cut his men down. Posted on the bluffs, the Nez Percés made every shot count. In two minutes half the troop was hit. By the time the supporting companies under Captains Moylan and Godfrey arrived, Hale's men were almost wiped out. The Nez Percé wolf was at bay at last, but he was going to make his end memorable.

Godfrey and Moylan rode to the right, to the rear of Hale, their horses leaping over the bodies of his fallen. A shot killed Godfrey's horse and he was stunned in the fall. Moylan was hit at almost the same moment. When the soldiers reached him Hale was the only captain left in the battalion.

With a trail of dead and wounded behind them, Hale's men dismounted on the ground which was too steep for their horses and slippery with the blood of their comrades, and began the last stage of their charge on foot. Godfrey revived from his fall and took the head of his men only to be shot down. Lieutenant Biddle dropped with a bullet between his eyes. Under that storm of lead the troopers wilted like autumn leaves. But the survivors kept on.

Up, up they climbed. Over boulders and through underbrush, to come to hand grips with their red foes. Fifty feet remained—thirty-five. And every foot, almost, won by the life of a comrade. Only twenty feet remained to the crest of the bluff and then—a choking gasp. The gallant leader was down—brave, chivalrous Hale, joking in the face of danger—instantly killed.

One officer was left now. All the rest lay somewhere on that bloody slope. Lieutenant Eckestrom led on. The men clenched their teeth, gripped their carbines, and using finger nails as well as toes, made the last grim climb into the very muzzles of the heated Nez Percé rifles.

It was madness. But it was splendid. The impossible was accomplished. The men tumbled over the top of the bluff—the hill was theirs.

But at what a cost. Fifty-three were killed or wounded out of the one hundred and fifteen who began the charge. Hale's troop lost more than sixty percent of its strength.

Meanwhile Joseph, cool headed, seeing everything, set at naught the charge by withdrawing his men at just the right time. The Indians retreated to the ridges behind the camp. But the 5th and the other cavalry had gotten into action. The Indians were surrounded.

THE SURRENDER

Miles found he had an old wolf instead of a stag at bay. But he was not the man to halt for that. The 5th charged directly into the teeth of the Nez Percé fire. Their first lines were mowed down and they reeled back. But not until they had almost captured Joseph himself.

The rush cut the camp in two. The chief was cut off with about seventy of his people, including White Bird. He could have escaped but he put his ten-year-old daughter on a pony, told White Bird to lead her to safety, and turned his own horse to the main camp.

"With a prayer in my mouth to the Great Spirit Chief who rules above, I dashed unarmed through the lines of soldiers," he said afterward. Bullets cut his clothes; his horse was shot; but he was unhurt. At the door of his lodge was his brave wife. "Here's your gun. Fight!" she said. And he turned to meet the foe.

White Bird's group got across the hills to eventual safety. Two days later they joined Sitting Bull's Sioux in British Columbia.

But the fight still raged in the Bear Paws. The cavalry attacked repeatedly. They were beaten back by the deadly Nez Percé rifles. Ollicut was killed. It was like a stab in the heart to Joseph. Between the brothers was the deep affection sometimes seen in men of noble natures. The dash and ardor of Ollicut had turned many a critical situation. After the youth died the heart seemed to go out of Joseph.

When night fell Miles called his troops into besieging lines. Joseph's position was too strong to be taken by direct assault. The white man had two other expedients—artillery and hunger. Next morning the guns were brought up. All day the shells shattered in the Indian lines. All should have been killed, but when a troop of cavalry began a cautious advance, it was driven fiercely back.

That evening General Howard with a few aides, rode into Miles' camp. He had learned that Joseph was at last cornered and, leaving his wearied men behind, rode fast to be "in at the kill".

Early the following morning a white flag was raised by the Indians. The long fight was over. Miles, who had lost a fifth of his force and dreaded the possibility of Sitting Bull's coming down at his back, saw that white banner with a sigh of relief.

At sunset Joseph gave himself up. With him were five of his warriors. The chief was riding, his body bent forward, his head bowed, his hands clasped over the saddle horn. The five with him walked, their faces earnest as they looked at him. Miles and Howard waited on a little hill. As he reached them, Joseph dismounted and handed Miles his rifle, butt first, in token of surrender.

Then he spoke. And the speech remains one of the most pathetic and beautiful Indian utterances ever recorded:

"Tell General Howard that I know his heart. What he told me before—I have it in my heart. I am tired of fighting. Our chiefs are killed. Looking Glass is dead. Too-hul-hul-sote is dead. The old men are all dead. It is the young men who say 'yes' and 'no' (that is, vote in council). He who led the young men (Joseph could not bear to utter the name of his slain brother Ollicut) is dead. It is cold and we have no blankets. The little children are freezing to death. My people—some of them—have run away into the hills, and have no blankets, no food. No one knows where they are (he referred to White Bird's detachment which contained his daughter). Perhaps they are freezing to death. I want to have time to look for my children and see how many of them I can find; maybe I shall find them all among the dead. Hear me, my chiefs, my heart is sick and sad. From where the sun now stands, I will fight no more, forever!"

It was the end. Joseph, who never commanded more than three hundred warriors, had opposed five thousand soldiers, besides hundreds of civilians. He had actually met in battle two thousand troops. Of these he had killed or wounded two hundred and sixty-six. His own loss, including women and children, had been two hundred and thirty-nine killed and wounded. He had defeated the best soldiers of the nation again and again; had marched at least two thousand miles through enemy country without a supply train and carrying his noncombatants; and had come within thirty miles of complete success, in spite of his tremendous handicaps. The history of warfare hardly shows a parallel to this campaign.

The captured Nez Percés, eighty-seven warriors and two hundred and fifty-four women and children, were sent to a reservation in Kansas. Years later, through the influence of General Miles, they were moved to a reservation near their former home, where they resumed the peaceful trend of their lives. And Joseph, adopting the white man's ways in education and industry, lived out his years, and finally died, honored by red man and white.[2]

[2] The losses in the Battle of the Bear Paw Mountains were as follows: The troops suffered twenty-four killed, including Captain O. Hale and Lieutenant J. W. Biddle; and forty-two wounded, including Captains Moylan and Godfrey and Lieutenants Baird and Romeyn—a total of sixty-six officers and men. The Indians lost seventeen killed and forty wounded. "Record of Engagements," p. 74.

VII.

THE BUFFALO HUNTERS' WAR

1877

CHAPTER XIX

WITHOUT BENEFIT OF MILITARY

THE STAKED PLAINS

THE Battle of Adobe Walls, in which a handful of buffalo hunters beat a large body of Kiowa, Cheyenne and Comanche warriors in June, 1874, has been widely celebrated. But the Staked Plains War, a bona fide campaign, conducted without the benefit of military assistance or sanction, against the Comanches in 1877, by a party of those same buffalo hunters, has scarcely been noticed.[1] Yet the Staked Plains War, culminating in the Battle of Pocket Canyon, was far the most daring of the two and its results were more important, since it broke the warlike power of the fierce Comanches.

The feud between the buffalo hunters and the Indians was of long standing. The hunters had practically exterminated the great buffalo herds and the red men bitterly resented this wanton slaughter of their chief source of food. There was no love lost between the two groups.

By the summer of 1876 the buffalo had been so killed off that only in the Texas Panhandle could they be found in sufficient numbers to make hide hunting profitable. The hunters therefore moved to that section. With them went

---

[1] For incidents, names and much of the information in this and the next chapter I am indebted to John R. Cook's valuable little book "The Border and the Buffalo." Use of these facts is made by the kind permission of the copyright owners, Mrs. Alice V. Schmidt, of Houston, Texas, and Charles A. Maddux of Los Angeles.

the traders. Charles Rath of the Dodge City firm of Rath & Wright, whose trading stores had been on every buffalo hunting frontier, established a post on Double Mountain Creek, a tributary of the Brazos.

Far to the east lay the Comanche reservation. The Indians were supposed to be peaceful, but the Comanches had not really felt the brunt of the 1874 war, and many of them were still unconvinced of the white man's power. Besides, the government was slow with its rations. And constant reports came to them of the continued extermination of the buffalo—their buffalo—in the west, contrary to the promises made to them. They grew very restless.

The Comanches were one of the great fighting tribes of the plains. General Richard I. Dodge called them "the most cunning, the most mischievously artful of all the United States Indians." For two centuries they carried on a constant war against Mexico. Their warriors were as familiar with the passes of Chihuahua as with their own Red River country. When Texas became independent, the Comanches extended their hatred to the Texans, and long distinguished between "Texans" and "Americans" with whom they were friendly.[2]

It is not strange that this warlike tribe should chafe under conditions as they existed, nor that, late in December, 1876, a band of Comanches numbering one hundred and seventy warriors, under Black Horse (Tu-ukumah) with their families, should leave Fort Sill and head toward

[2] One of the Comanches' most celebrated exploits was the sacking of Parker's Fort in northern Texas. The Comanches, led by Peta Nokoni (The Wanderer), captured the fort and killed nearly everybody in it. Among the prisoners were two children, one a little girl named Cynthia Ann Parker, granddaughter of Elder John Parker, in whose honor the fort and later the city were named. The girl was thirteen years old. Peta Nokoni later married her. She bore him three children before she was recaptured by the whites. Her eldest son was the famous Quanah Parker, who took his surname, by Comanche custom, from his mother. This chief at last became head chief of all the Comanches, and the town of Quanah, Texas, is named after him.

Comanche squaws butchering cattle at a government beef issue in the early seventies.

Cheyenne village, with jerked meat drying on scaffolds in the foreground.
Indian Territory.

Bureau of American Ethnology

Nez Percé encampment on the Yellowstone River, near the mouth of
Shields River, Montana, photographed in 1871.

the Staked Plains. Two troops of cavalry pursued them but lost their trail when a heavy snow came unexpectedly. That winter Black Horse's band camped in Thompson's Canyon, an opening in the escarpment of the Staked Plains. It was an ideal location, with plentiful game, protection from the elements, and far enough from the nearest buffalo hunters' camps so that nobody suspected the Indians' presence.

BEGINNING OF HOSTILITIES

In the latter part of February, 1877, a few of the young Comanche braves went on the prowl and came on some outlying hunters' camps close at hand.

John F. Cook and Rankin Moore, camped with the Benson outfit south of the Red River, were the first to see the enemy. A solitary Indian sneaked up on Cook and tried to shoot him from ambush. He missed and escaped, but not until he had dodged a perfect spray of bullets from Cook and Moore.

The incident disturbed the buffalo hunters. They remembered Adobe Walls. Warnings were sent around. Late that evening came a report that Marshall Soule [3] whose camp was near the escarpment had been killed. On the same day the camp of Bill Devins was raided. Although his men escaped with their lives and their weapons, the Indians captured all their ammunition and supplies.

That was February 22nd, Washington's Birthday. Rath's store on Double Mountain Creek was the natural gathering place of the hunters, and thither they went as fast as they were warned. A tall, raw-boned Texan, Pat Garrett by name, was largely responsible for carrying the

[3] Or Sewell. The hunters were not very sure how they spelled their own names. The spelling in the text is that of the army records.

word of warning, riding scores of miles to tell outlying camps of their danger. It was this same Pat Garrett, who later as sheriff of Lincoln County, New Mexico, was to put an end to the career of the notorious outlaw, Billy the Kid.

Nearly three hundred hunters gathered at Rath's and a council of war was held. It was voted first to send a party of eighteen volunteers to Soule's camp, to see if he was really dead. The party made the trip and found the scalped and mutilated body of the hunter. They buried him and returned to the post.

Rath's bartender was Limpy Jim Smith. He was an ex-road agent from Montana, had escaped from that country just ahead of the vigilantes who broke up the Plummer gang, and carried a bullet in his leg to his dying day. But he was a man of nerve and courage. He proposed that the hunters organize. At the proposal one Tom Lumpkins cried out that "he hadn't lost any Injuns and didn't propose to hunt any." The remark brought sharp words between Lumpkins and Smith which culminated a month later in a gun fight and the death of Lumpkins.

Most of the hunters favored the sending of a punitive expedition against the Comanches. If anybody had the nerve to suggest an appeal to the army, he was laughed to scorn. The buffalo hunters knew how to handle this case themselves. Forty-five volunteered to go, which was considered a sufficient number.

Among the hunters was Big Hank Campbell, an old Indian fighter. He had been one of the leaders in the Sappa Creek massacre in 1875, when a band of Cheyennes was wiped out by buffalo hunters and soldiers in northern Kansas. He was elected commander. Limpy Jim Smith was also elected one of the leaders. The third was Joe Freed.

The expedition set out the next day. Thirty hunters were mounted. Fifteen went on foot to guard the wagons which carried two hundred and fifty rounds of ammunition for every man, besides bar lead, powder, primers and reloading outfits. They had with them Jose, an English-speaking Mexican, who had scouted for General McKenzie in 1874 and knew the country thoroughly. Ben Jackson as quartermaster, issued grain, and Shorty Woodson, tallest, slimmest man on the range, a former druggist, took charge of the medicine supply. The roster was kept by Powder Face Hudson, with guards detailed in rotation. Most of the men had been soldiers in either the Union or Confederate armies. The whole thing was handled in thoroughly military fashion.

All told, it was one of the best equipped and outfitted expeditions ever to go against the Indians, army expeditions included. The men carried their long range, heavy calibre Sharp's buffalo guns, with which, by continuous practice they had become wonderful judges of distance and could shoot extremely accurately by raising the muzzle, without adjusting the rear graduated sights.

Just before they started, another bunch of hunters came in from Godey's camp. There were fifteen or twenty of them and they carried in one badly wounded man, Spotted Jack, while two or three others were slightly wounded. There were only three horses among them. This was the story they told:

The previous day, while camped on their way to Rath's rendezvous, a band of Comanches, headed by Black Horse himself, had stampeded their entire horse herd, except for three animals. Badly outnumbered—they had counted sixty hostile war bonnets—they opened fire. The buffalo guns did good execution. A couple of Comanches turned flip-flops in the sun as the ounce slugs hit them, and the rest took to cover.

Most of that day, completely surrounded, they fought against odds of more than three to one. Every once in a while they could hear the heavy report of a buffalo gun, whose dull roar formed a contrast to the sharper cracks of the Winchesters most of the Indians carried. This meant the party was the same which had killed Soule and carried off his gun.

In the afternoon Moccasin Jim, one of the hunters, "got a bead" on the Comanche who was using Soule's gun and "drilled him." The Indian crumpled up. Another Comanche snaked through the bushes and got the gun. It was soon busy again.

The hunters were certain they killed at least three of the Comanches, probably more. Three or more of their own number were wounded by this time. Old Godey finally rose and said: "Well, boys, this is no place to be tonight. Let's go back."

In spite of the redoubled fire of the Indians, the stark hunters arose, walked down the trail, and leaving the Comanches behind, joined their fellows at Rath's.

CHAPTER XX

THE BATTLE OF POCKET CANYON

ON THE INDIAN TRAIL

MARSHALL SOULE had been universally respected and liked by the buffalo hunters. John R. Cook, one of them, later wrote:

"My mind wandered back to the lonely apology of a grave (Soule's). He was an educated man, a native of Pennsylvania. He was a man who possessed a useful fund of information. He was not obtrusive, but was courteous and polite; respected others' opinions even when he differed from them. He was not a professed Christian, but believed in the observance of the Golden Rule. . . . Why should he have been taken when such men as Hurricane Bill, Dutch Henry, Squaw Johnny and some others that I had in mind, could roam those prairies, disregarding law and morality, with a price placed on some of their heads?"

The expedition started at last. At the edge of the Staked Plains on the escarpment, they had great difficulty in getting their wagons to the top. This was finally done by passing along its base until they reached a narrow, winding, steep incline, where by doubling their teams they finally reached the upper level.

Here they found an Indian trail, dim it is true, but still a trail. Congratulating themselves on their luck, they started in pursuit. It seems almost incredible to think that this handful of men were actually gleeful as they took the trail of an Indian band containing many times their number of warriors, to carry war to their vastly superior foe. But the buffalo hunters, each a hair's-breadth shot with his heavy rifle, each endowed with a reckless disregard for his own life, were probably, man-for-man, the most formidable individuals who ever trod this continent.

The whole day was spent ferreting out the dim trail. That night they came upon traces of a camp, where they found two burned teepees. This meant two men had died, and they thus were able to determine the extent of the damage done by Godey's outfit.

At midafternoon the next day, Jose, riding ahead with Cook and Louie Keyes, located the hostile camp. Back they went to warn the hunters. That night the audacious white men made their camp within two or three miles of the Indian village, in a gorge which hid their wagons and horses.

As camp was being made, Jose saw an Indian cross the canyon and ride the back trail. If he discovered their track the Comanches would break camp at once and be "hard to catch." To stop him was vital.

Louie Keyes was a half-breed Cherokee. He now daubed his cheeks with red paint and snaked out to intercept the rider. On came the Comanche. Suddenly a rifle rang out. The Indian whirled out of his saddle. The shot had not been fired by Keyes but by an Englishman, a member of poor Soule's outfit. The Indian got up and started to run, zig-zagging. It was useless for him to attempt to escape. The hunters killed him and hid his body among the tall reeds near a water hole.

Hank Campbell now gave his simple orders. The wagons and camp outfit were to be left where they were. Three fighting divisions were named. Campbell commanded half the mounted men; Limpy Jim the other half; and Joe Freed the dismounted men. Old Man Godey with Cook and Jose were to scout the Indians. Smith's men were to charge through the village and run off the pony herd. Then the hunters expected, with supreme self-confidence, to exterminate the whole Comanche outfit, although they were admonished by Campbell not to kill any women or children "if they could help it."

Darkness came and the three scouts, their horses' hoofs muffled with grain sacks, started up the canyon. By lighting a match under a blanket, they were able from time to time to examine the trail. It was perilous in the extreme and nerves were keyed to high tension. The whir of a disturbed bird, a stumble or an involuntary cough or sneeze might mean their deaths. Near morning they discovered the camp. Cook rode back to bring the hunters.

THE FIGHT IN THE CANYON

Broad daylight on March 18th. The three divisions of hunters, approximately fifteen men each, stopped at the head of the pocket canyon where the Comanche village stood. There Campbell arranged the two mounted platoons about two hundred yards apart, with the "infantry" between. Everything was ready.

"All right!" shouted Campbell.

"Go for them!" yelled Limpy Jim, the ex-road agent.

Forward swept the hunters. There were many stalwart fighters in their line. John Cook, a veteran Indian scout; Joe Jackson, an ex-Confederate soldier; Squirrel-eye, another ex-rebel; Lee Grimes, taciturn and dour; Louie Keyes the Cherokee, now beginning his war chant—they were a formidable group. As they began to move Keyes uttered a war whoop and Squirrel-eye gave the old rebel yell. Then, shouting like mad, the hunters charged.

Indian teepees came into view. The Comanches were seen running out to a low hill from which they began shooting rapidly at about two hundred yards. It was death to continue into the teeth of that fire. Hank Campbell, riding like a crazy man, headed the hunters and yelled at them to fall back to the canyon. Before they could obey, Joe Jackson flopped from his saddle and Lee Grimes was down, his horse shot under him and his wrist broken.

Devins and Cook leaped from their horses and ran to Jackson, whom they began dragging to a place of safety. A sharp cry from Devins, and he dropped his hold. A Comanche bullet had shattered his arm.

"For God's sake," gasped the wounded Jackson, "lie down or they'll get you all!" Grimes crept up and the four men, three of them hurt, listened to death whispering above them.

Hank Campbell's men, down in the draw, did not see the new menace slipping up on them. They were so much interested in the fight on their front that the band of more than one hundred warriors, creeping up the gorge toward them on the north, escaped their attention. But Cook and the wounded hunters, forced to lie out in their exposed situation, saw them. Their sudden shooting revealed the move. Campbell's men turned their rifles and the Comanches retreated, dragging six of their number with them.

Cook, Devins and Grimes crawled down from their perilous location, taking the helpless Jackson with them. All chance of capturing the Comanche herd was gone and for the first time the buffalo hunters were beginning to respect the fighting ability of their adversaries.

Now the Comanches mounted and swept about the white men in a wide circle. The latter scattered to places of advantage. Part of them faced clear around to meet the attack from the rear. Whooping and yelling, the Indians flashed across one draw opening after another, the hunters' rifles shooting like mad. Several horses went down. A warrior, his pony shot out from under him, ran for a ravine. He had thirty yards to go and the heavy slugs from the buffalo guns ripped the sod all around him. All at once he was flat on the ground. The hunters turned their rifles elsewhere.

Grizzled Hank Campbell and Limpy Jim Smith held a conference. Then Campbell spoke:

"Boys, we must leave this place. Smith will take horses and wounded men down the side ravine to the long water hole. The rest of us will crawl to that crest and fire at the camp until Joe Freed can get his foot men out of the mess they are in."

The whole aspect of the fight had changed. Instead of a joyful campaign of annihilation, it had become a grim struggle for life with the odds heavily in favor of death. Campbell's sharp shooters crept to the crest. About four hundred yards away was the Comanche camp in plain view with a big bunch of horses behind it; among the tee-pees fifty or sixty ponies with travois were being loaded by the squaws. Off to the left was a tall pole with a red flag flying from it—some Indian signal. To the right was an Indian working his looking glass to flash messages to his comrades. Campbell's hunters fired a couple of long distance volleys at the camp. Then, like a swarm of bees, a fusillade of bullets buzzed over their own heads.

"Let the camp alone and comb the grass at the crest this side of it," ordered Campbell. From end to end that crest was swept with bullets, about three hundred rounds being fired at it. Then the shooting at the camp began again, the cool hunters, with their tobacco quids in their cheeks, deliberately picking special targets to shoot at.

THE ESCAPE OF THE COMANCHES

By this time Joe Freed and his men had returned to the main body. Poor Jose, the Mexican scout, was shot through the shoulder but wore a grin on his face. Jose told them they had picked a hornet's nest indeed. Instead of seventy-five or a hundred Comanches there were nearly three hundred warriors fighting them. Another camp was just around the bend of the canyon with a big band of Plains (Lipan) Apaches, allied with the Comanches for years.[1]

But Campbell, the indomitable Scot, merely laughed. "Mebbe we've bit off more than we can chew," was his only comment.

The Indian fire suddenly died down. Something was up. Black smoke sprang up and advanced down the draw. The Indians had set the prairie grass ablaze.

Right behind the smoke dashed a daring young warrior, wearing a magnificent war bonnet and riding a speedy white horse. Directly across their front he rode, drawing the fire of half the men, some of whom shot the second or third time before the running horse fell. Then under the fusillade from the crest the daring brave quickly crumpled up and was still.

Far down the draw, waving their lances and uttering the demoniac Comanche scream, which once heard is never forgotten, came a band of Indians. They halted at long rifle range. Their purpose was to draw attention from the

---

[1] Some of these Apaches were later shown to be Mescaleros from the Victorio band in northern Mexico.

camp where the real attack was being prepared, but they failed to catch the hunters off their guard.

Suddenly through the grass smoke of the upper draw came a magnificent, swooping rush of the Comanches. The smoke screened their movements until they broke through it. Then the full roar of the buffalo guns crashed out. Many warriors went down. The Indians drew off.

The wounded white men were calling for water now, and during the lull which followed the charge through the smoke screen, Ben Jackson, brother of the wounded Joe, and Cook volunteered to get some water from a hole, fifty yards away. With their comrades shooting over their heads to keep down the Indian fire, they crawled to the spring and came back with their boots filled with the precious liquid. "Shorty," the druggist, had bound up the wounds and given each wounded man a big drink of fourth-proof whiskey.

It was noted that the Indians had disappeared. Cautiously scouts advanced to their first position. Then came the surprise. The wily Comanches had tricked them. The whole camp was gone. The Indians had escaped.

The buffalo hunters did not try to pursue. They were burdened by wounded, but more than that they were devoutly thankful to be alive after their attack. They craved no further experiences of the kind. Poor Jackson was in particularly bad shape. The bullet which had struck him in the groin was from Soule's buffalo gun, which the Indians used throughout the fight. Jackson lived until he got to camp but died a little later.

Weeks later they found out the extent of the damage they had done. Captain P. L. Lee, with a troop of the 10th Cavalry, rounded up the Comanches near Lake Quemado, after a brief fight in which he killed four of them. Both Black Horse and his wife were among the dead he reported.[2] The Indians were very ready to surrender.

Lee learned that the hunters had killed thirty-one Indians in the fight, mortally wounded four more, and seriously wounded twenty-two. Fifteen pack horses were killed in the camp during the battle. Lee also found out something else: the Soule gun was a hoodoo to the Comanches. Everyone who used it had been killed or wounded. The first Indian who used it was killed, the second badly wounded. Then Black Horse's son took it and he too died with the gun in his hands. Five Feathers used it until near the close of the fight when he, too, was killed. After that the Indians would not use it. They left it wrapped in a blanket with the two scalp locks they had taken from Soule's head. It was found by Lee's men.

The Comanches never went on the war path after that campaign. It was planned, carried out and fought by buffalo hunters, but it could not have been more effective had it been executed by the best trained of soldiers.

[2] This report was in error. Black Horse, also known as Pako-Riah (Colt) and Ta-Peka (Sun Rays) lived for many years afterward and died at Cache, Oklahoma, about 1900. The leader killed at Lake Quemado was Ek-a-wak-a-ne (Red Young Man), who was not a chief, but is remembered by the old Comanches as an extremely fearless and reckless warrior who absolutely refused to surrender and never went on the reservation.

VIII.

THE ODYSSEY OF THE CHEYENNES
1878

CHAPTER XXI

LITTLE WOLF'S RAID

THE FAITH OF THE WHITE MAN

Two years had passed since McKenzie wiped out Dull Knife's village in the Crazy Woman canyon. Not long after that the Cheyennes surrendered—as fine a body of Indians as the continent contained.

"Tsi-tsis-tsa" [1] they called themselves, which means "*The* People" with a large, black accent-mark over "The." Proud, well-dressed, handsome, fearless, famed for their horses, the beauty of their women and the prowess of their warriors, such were the Northern Cheyennes when they surrendered in the spring of 1877.

One would scarcely have recognized them as the same people two years later. September 8, 1878, found them famished and dying of fever in the Indian Territory, nearly a thousand miles south, penned on a reservation so unhealthy that their extinction was only a matter of time. The white man had promised them a reservation on their northern plains, with supplies, protection and other rewards for making peace. Thus had the white man kept his faith.

Almost without arms, almost horseless, squalid, in rags,

[1] The Bureau of American Ethnology gives another spelling as Dzi-tsii-tsa. Literally "Our People" or "The People." The word Cheyenne is from the Sioux "Sha-hi-yena" or "Shai-ena," meaning "people of alien speech", and is the French corruption. The word has no relation to the French "Chien", meaning dog, as has been claimed by Custer and others.

with the ribs of their children standing out, and with patched teepees, the Tsi-tsis-tsa begged to be allowed to return to their own country. It was Little Wolf, tall, high-shouldered, gaunt with fever, who spoke for his people, every word carrying intense meaning. The agent, looking at his pock-marked face, with its tremendous breadth through the cheek bones and its lines of chiselled granite, may very well have remembered that here was the greatest warrior in the Cheyenne Nation.

It was Little Wolf who, in 1857, refused to give up his horse which was claimed by some white man. They offered to pay him a "reward" for "finding" the animal, but the Cheyenne, already a famous man, coldly refused. There followed the treacherous arrest of a Cheyenne and the killing of another near the Platte Bridge. That was the genesis of the Cheyenne troubles with the white men.[2]

Little Wolf was one of the ten warriors chosen to decoy Fetterman's command into the trap near Fort Phil Kearney in 1866. Eighty-one men died as that trap closed.

He fought at the Rosebud and the Little Big Horn. In the attack by McKenzie on Dull Knife's village in 1876, it was Little Wolf who led the helpless women and children to a place of safety and stood on a high rock while the bullets sprayed around him until every one was hidden. And it was he who led the Cheyennes later when they desperately tried to recapture their camp.

Many other brave deeds were attributed to this man. The agent may well have listened with more respect than he showed.

"Why did you send for me?" asked Little Wolf.

---

[2] It was a matter of principle with Little Wolf. Four horses had been lost and three picked up by the Cheyennes. The white owners claimed the three and identified one of Little Wolf's string as the fourth. This particular animal had been in his possession for a long time and they had no claim on it. Hence his refusal, in spite of threats, to give it up.

Bureau of American Ethnology

Bureau of American Ethnology

Left: Little Wolf (O-kum-ha-ket), the real leader of the Cheyennes in the Dull Knife war of 1878. Right: Dull Knife Ta-me-la-pash-me), Cheyenne chief in the outbreak of 1878.

Upper: These are the warriors who survived the extermination of Dull Knife's band of Cheyennes in 1879, taken on the courthouse steps at Dodge City, where they were brought for trial for murder. In the picture are, left to right, front row: Wild Hog, George Reynolds (interpreter), Old Man, and Blacksmith; second row, Frizzly Head, Left Hand, Crow, and Porcupine. The white man seated behind the group is not identified. Lower: Gen. Wesley Merritt, who saved Thornburgh's men from the Utes.

"Three of your young men have run off. Now I want you to give me ten of your young men to hold here as prisoners until I get back the three that have gone," replied the agent. Wild Hog and Crow, who had come with Little Wolf, stirred uneasily as they heard this insane request. They knew before it was spoken what the answer would be.

"I will not do what you ask," said Little Wolf. "If you follow those three men, you cannot find them. Three men travelling over the country can hide so that they cannot be found. You never could get them back and you would always keep my men in prison."

It was simple justice. Why should ten young Cheyennes be imprisoned because three others had grown home sick and started back to their own country in the north? Little Wolf did not blame them.

"If you do not give me these men, I will cut off your rations," threatened the agent.

As Little Wolf bleakly continued to refuse the ten hostages, the agent grew more and more insistent. At last the chief turned away. As he did so, he shook hands with the agent and the army officers present. There was something in his cold manner which made them stare. Then out of a clear sky, the Indian hurled this ultimatum:

"I am going to my camp. I don't wish the ground about this agency to be made bloody, so listen: I am going to leave here. I am going to my north country. If you are going to send soldiers after me, let me get a little distance from the agency. I do not want to see blood spilt about it. If you want a fight, I will fight you and we can make the ground bloody at that place." [3]

There was no dispute with his decision when he an-

[3] The man who interpreted this conversation, Ed Guerrier, was still living in Oklahoma up to within the last few years. This conversation is quoted by Grinnell. "Fighting Cheyennes," pp. 387-88.

nounced it to his people in their camp, about twenty miles above on the Canadian River. Every Cheyenne knew that in two years their fighting men had been reduced in numbers from two hundred and thirty-five to seventy-nine, and their women and children in proportion. It was time to fight, and fight hard. With silent speed the ragged tee-pees were struck. The few thin ponies were gathered in, the worn belongings loaded on travois, all as quietly as if by shadows. The littlest child knew better than to whim-per. By dawn the Cheyennes were on the march—a march which will always live as a tradition of the West.

Five great military barriers were opposed to their north-ward flight. Along the Santa Fe trail were General Pope's forces. General Crook lay along the Union-Pacific in Nebraska. The banks of the Niobrara were watched by General Bradley. A fourth line stretched east from the Black Hills; and a fifth, under General Gibbon, guarded the Yellowstone. Thirteen thousand soldiers, with additional thousands of civilians, cowboys, miners, and ranchers; forts, artillery, railroads and the telegraph were pitted against the tiny handful of starving Indians.

THE RAID ACROSS KANSAS

Little Wolf's first necessities were mounts and arms. To get them he scattered his foragers over a thirty-mile front. Here and there they swooped down upon herds of horses in corrals and pastures; here and there they picked up guns or ammunition. Before they crossed the Kansas border they were well supplied with horses and fairly well with rifles.

Their escape was discovered early the following day. Telegraph keys rattled; troops were mustered; the war jig was on. A hard-riding troop of cavalry caught up with the Indians on the Little Medicine Lodge River. Little Wolf rode out alone to meet and talk with them. He exchanged a few words with an Arapaho interpreter, when the soldiers began shooting at him. The chief rode back to his lines under fire and the fight began. It was a long-range battle. Nobody was killed. The troops retreated and the Cheyennes went on.

Two nights later they were again overtaken near the Cimarron River. This time the Indians were ready. They built some fortifications on a hill. The soldiers advanced on foot. When they were very close, the Cheyennes gave them a volley which hit several men and drove the rest back. Three soldiers were killed. No Cheyenne was hit.

They were unmolested the next day. That was the last time the troops overtook the Indians. Henceforth the Cheyennes fought—many, many times—but their battles from that hour were with foes on their front, not in the rear. No cavalry could keep the killing pace they set, sometimes seventy miles a day.

The Indians traveled most of the time at a steady lope. Far in front and on each side rode their scouts, nosing here, listening there, prowling and searching, alert, wild, seeking news of danger for their people. Sometimes these scouts were miles from the main body. The women and children and the camp travois kept bunched well together. Dull Knife was the nominal chief of the band, but the grim Little Wolf was the real leader.

They crossed the Kansas border, eluded a detachment from Larned and turned west toward Dodge City. As they rode, they gobbled up the ranches, killing a few cowmen and hunters who tried to fight, and taking every horse, gun and cartridge.

Colonel William H. Lewis and two hundred and fifty men waited at Fort Dodge for word of the Indians. Be-

fore he knew it, they were past him and gone. Some Cheyenne scouts were seen within four miles of Dodge City on
the evening of the 19th. The following morning, just
before daybreak, a shadowy mass which drifted across the
prairie like smoke in the vagueness of the night, reached
the Arkansas River. It was the main Cheyenne body. A
few miles west lay the little cattle town of Pierceville, but
not a soul in the sleeping hamlet knew it, as the Indians,
travelling at the steady Cheyenne lope, rode down to the
river, splashed across, and disappeared into the dim distance.

Next morning Lewis learned that Little Wolf's people
had crossed. Taking an angle calculated to cut off the fugitives, he rode after them. The Cheyennes stopped for a
day or so to rest on the Punished Woman fork of the
Smoky Hill. There Lewis' scouts located them about five
o'clock on the evening of the 28th. The cavalry, vastly
superior in numbers, charged at once. In an angry clatter
the Cheyenne rifles spoke in the dusk. Lewis spun out of
his saddle. Three more of his men dropped. The charge
halted. There was a cloud of dust and the Indians were
gone. Lewis was dead.

Straight north Little Wolf rode while the soldiers bore
the colonel's body back to Fort Dodge. The Cheyennes had
one great, vital need—horses, ever more horses. When
they found them they ruthlessly took them. If the white
owners fought, they were killed. But the Indians never
went out of their way to kill white men—except once.

On the night of September 29th the band crossed the
North Fork of the Solomon River. They had just had the
sharp fight with Lewis. Troops were flocking behind in
great numbers. At such a time it would seem that the Indians should have made all speed out of Kansas. But they
had one inviolable law. "An eye for an eye, a tooth for a

tooth," the Old Testament teaching, was also the red man's teaching.

Three years before, April 23, 1875, a company of soldiers under Lieutenant A. Henely, and some buffalo hunters led by Hank Campbell,[4] surrounded Bull Hump's village of Cheyennes, some seventy men, women and children, camped on Sappa Creek in northwestern Kansas. The Indians had taken some horses from nearby ranchers and looted the hunters' camp. In the fight which followed, twenty-seven were cut off from their main body which escaped. When the smoke cleared away, twenty-two of them were dead, including Bull Hump. Only two soldiers were killed.

The Cheyennes neared Sappa Creek on the morning of September 30th. With a single mind they turned aside and visited a terrible vengeance upon the place. Down on the peaceful community which had sprung up in the intervening years, they swept like a whirlwind. The white men had given Bull Hump's people no chance, and the Cheyennes gave the white people no chance. Women screamed, guns thudded, and tumbling clouds of smoke rose from burning homes.

When the Indians rode on they left eighteen corpses behind to pay for the lives of the Cheyennes taken three years before.[5] Thus far they had taken forty white lives and lost less than ten braves. But they were approaching the Union Pacific Railroad and Crook. It was wise to take

[4] This was the redoubtable Hank Campbell who later commanded the buffalo hunters in the Staked Plains war against the Comanches in 1877.

[5] The following were killed on Sappa Creek: William Laing, John Laing, Freeman Laing, William Laing, Jr., J. D. Smith, Frederick Hamper, E. P. Humphrey, John Humphrey, Moses Abernathy, John C. Hutson, George F. Walters, Marcellus Felt, Ed Miskelley, Ferdinand Westphaled and son, Mr. Wright, Mr. Lull and Mr. Irwin.

H. D. Colvin and his brave wife barricaded their cabin and successfully defended their lives. The Cheyennes left the settlement a smoking ruin. No women were killed but some were outraged it is claimed. This was the only deliberate massacre on the whole journey.

precautions. In small parties, scattered over a wide front, they slipped across the Kansas line into Nebraska.

The pace was beginning to tell. Some of the weaker ones in the tribe died under the awful strain of the march. The constant skirmishing had reduced the number of warriors until there were hardly enough left for scouting. Each day's journey was shorter now. But at last the Cheyennes crossed the South Platte and entered the comparative safety of the Niobrara Hills.

Here the leaders disagreed at last. Dull Knife, old and beloved, wanted to wait and rest. Little Wolf, hard and fierce, insisted on continuing the march. Their arguments were characteristic.

"This is our own country. Nothing bad ever happened to us here. Let us rest. The soldiers will leave us alone, for lo, we are in our own land," said Dull Knife with the simplicity of a child.

"You can go that way if you wish, but I intend to work my way up into the Powder River country. I think it would be better for us all if the party were not divided," responded Little Wolf.[6]

The upshot was that the band divided. During the night Dull Knife's retainers moved their teepees a few yards away from Little Wolf's. We have no record of the words that passed between the two chiefs in parting, but between these men was a deep affection and respect.

Next morning Little Wolf's band was gone.

[6] This incident and conversation were given to George Bird Grinnell years later by Little Wolf himself. "Fighting Cheyennes," p. 395.

CHAPTER XXII

DULL KNIFE'S LAST FIGHT

CAPTURED

DULL KNIFE hoped the white men would leave him alone. Like a child trying to reassure himself, he went about the camp next day saying: "Now we have reached our own ground, and from this time forth we will no more fight any white people." On almost the last horse able to trot, a messenger rode to Red Cloud's camp, while the rest of the Cheyennes scattered to avoid discovery. A few days later they reassembled to hear the answer to their message. It fell like lead on their hearts. Red Cloud's sad reply to their plea for protection was that it was hopeless to resist the President's will. The time had come to meet the white man face to face with no chance of escape.

That was a piteous assemblage. In rags, nearly out of ammunition, with scarcely a single horse, suffering from cold, they were in no condition to resist. And they were mostly old men and women.

Colonel J. B. Johnson, with two troops of the 3rd Cavalry, discovered them in the sandhills on October 23rd, and received Dull Knife's surrender. The soldiers were astonished at the plight of the fugitives. A few stalwart warriors were there, including Wild Hog, a young chief, and Buffalo Hump, Dull Knife's own son. There was a scattering of young women. But haggard, old men; ancient withered squaws; a few thin-faced little children—these constituted the bulk of the "capture."

"There can be no resistance here, surely," thought the soldiers. They were mistaken. Dull Knife and his chiefs talked to Johnson and told him they would rather die than return to the Indian Territory. They wished to go to the Sioux agency. Two days later they were told they must go to Fort Robinson. This was toward the hated southland and the Indians grew bleak and sullen as they listened.

A heavy snowstorm set in. The Cheyennes were told to camp in the brush along the deep valley of Chadron Creek, while the soldiers retired to the upper levels. That night, in the bitter cold, old men and women worked through the dark hours digging rifle pits in the bushes. In the morning the soldiers saw a fight looming. Persuasion was vain. Only when two pieces of artillery came up did the Indians submit.

Again Dull Knife's people, weaker than ever, were prisoners. Sullenly they marched to Fort Robinson. They had been searched for arms, but in some manner managed to retain five guns and about eleven revolvers, with some ammunition. During the search the men were deprived of their firearms but allowed to keep their bows. The women were not searched. One of them later said that throughout the search she had a carbine hanging down her back. Other guns were taken to pieces and concealed by the squaws and children—a piece of stock on this one, a lock there, a barrel yonder. Some of the children wore springs and locks as ornaments around their necks, where they were not noticed. When they reached the fort they were confined in long wooden barracks. The first thing they did was to reassemble the guns and pistols and hide them under the floors of the prison.

Winter came down with extreme rigor. One day Dull Knife was told that the Interior Department had ordered him and his people sent back to the Indian Territory. Surprised and angered, he refused to obey. After that the Indians' small measure of liberty was taken away and guards were set over them in the barracks.

In December a group of Sioux chiefs was brought over to talk with them. Red Cloud, American Horse the Second, Red Dog and No Flesh sat in the council which was also attended by army officers, including Captains Wessells and Vroom. Red Cloud counselled submission. He reminded the Cheyennes of his friendship but called attention to the power of the government, and to the fact that snow was on the ground, ponies thin, and resistance madness.

"So listen to Red Cloud, your old friend, and do without complaint what the Great Father tells you," he concluded.[1]

Then Dull Knife, the grand old leader, stepped forth. His sixty-odd years seemed to slip from him. Grim faced, he looked every inch the chief in spite of his shabby blanket and worn canvas moccasins. His speech was terse but eloquent:

"All we ask is to be allowed to live, and live in peace. . . . We bowed to the will of the Great Father and went south. . . . There we found a Cheyenne cannot live. . . . So we came home. Better it was, we thought, to die fighting than to perish of sickness."

Turning to Wessells he pleaded that his people be allowed to remain in their northern home.

"Tell the Great Father if he tries to send us back we

[1] The description and quotations from this council are from E. B. Bronson's book "Reminiscences of a Ranchman."

will butcher each other with our knives rather than go!" he concluded.

Silent as graven images sat the Cheyennes, except that the powerful figure of Buffalo Hump, the chief's son, unable to restrain his feelings, arose and paced the floor behind the council circle, hate burning in his eyes.

Captain Wessells could only promise to send the message to the Great Father. That was all. The fruitless council adjourned.

TREACHERY

With the 1st of January a blizzard covered the ground deep with snow and sent the mercury far below zero. It was weather for staying close indoors. Yet on January 5th Wessells received as a reply to his message containing Dull Knife's plea, a peremptory order to march the captives, without delay and with proper escort, to Fort Reno, far to the south, over the same trail they had travelled with such pain coming north.

Wessells saw the terrible mistake. The swivel-chair bureaucrats in the Indian Department could not. But duty was duty. He had the three chiefs, Dull Knife, Wild Hog and Crow, brought to him and explained the order. Dead silence greeted his words. Only the wild beast glare in their eyes told the suppressed passion which was making infernos of their hearts. It took Dull Knife minutes to control himself so he could speak with a steady voice. His reply, quiet and cold, was:

"It is death to us. If the Great Father wishes us to die —very well. We will die where we are. If necessary by our own hands."

But Wessells could only obey orders. He gave his ultimatum: Unless they agreed, he would cut off all their fuel, food and water. In stony silence the chiefs heard their sentence; then went back to their people.

.   .   .   .

Days passed—five days of bitter cold and hunger in the wooden barracks where shivered the half-clad Cheyennes. Day and night their despairing death songs sounded, with even the little children joining their weak treble voices in the chants. The Indians had made up their minds to die of cold and hunger rather than submit.

At last Wessells sent again for the chiefs. But this time the people would not let Dull Knife go. Strong Left Hand took his place.

For an hour the Cheyennes paced the floor of their barracks, straining their ears. Then they heard a sudden wild, desperate war whoop. It was Wild Hog's voice and it told its own story. Strong Left Hand ran in. The two others had been seized and put in irons. Wild Hog had defied Wessells. And he had stabbed and all but killed a guard before he was overpowered. That wild, ringing cry was his warning and farewell to his people.

From the prison barracks rose the yells of the Cheyenne men, the cries of women and even the shrieks of little children. Wild Hog knew his people had heard and were ready.

Doors and windows were barricaded. From under the floor were taken the five rifles and the revolvers which had been smuggled in. Floors and iron stoves were broken up to make clubs. Every man who had a gun gave his knife to another who had no weapon. The Cheyennes expected an immediate attack, but none came. Night came on, still and frightfully cold.

Just as the last tremulous notes of "Taps" sounded, a shot rang from the barracks, startlingly clear and sharp.

A sentry pitched forward in the snow. Three more shots in a rapid rat-tat-tat. Two more guards were down. Then from the doors and windows of the barracks poured the heroic last fragment of the Dull Knife band.

Starved, despairing, they nevertheless acted with coolness and clear judgment. The dead sentries, Corporal Pulver and Privates Hulz and Tommeny, were stripped of their arms. While the few braves with guns formed a rear guard, the Indians ran out of the fort and started across the snow-clad plain.

Out of the barracks poured the troops, half-clad but shooting. Under the heavy fire the gallant Cheyenne rear guard melted fast. But the main body was well on its way to the hills, where a high, precipitous divide separated Soldier Creek from White River, three miles from the fort.

That was a forlorn hope if ever there was one. Within the first half mile of the awful running fight, more than half the Cheyenne fighting men were shot. But as the warriors fell, their weapons were seized by half-grown boys, tottering old men, even women. Often the advance guard of the soldiers and the rear guard of the Indians fought hand-to-hand. The women fell as thickly as the men.

A mile from the fort the troops, many of them badly frozen, were called back to get their clothing and horses. Across the frozen river and up the steep hill toiled the Indians. The cavalry caught up again as the ascent was being made. At the foot of the bluffs the shattered rear guard drew up for a last resistance. The cavalry charged. Back it was hurled. Dull Knife's daughter, known as the "Princess," fighting in the front rank, was killed. So were several others. But the precious minutes gained allowed the rest of the people to climb the cliff.

Further pursuit ended for the night. On the way back

to the fort the soldiers marked the line of retreat by the huddled bodies in the snow. Buffalo Hump, the chief's son, was one of the dead.[2]

As the soldiers returned to their warm quarters, the surviving Cheyennes struggled on through the bitter night. For seventeen miles they travelled without a halt. Even well-fed, well-clothed troops would have considered it a wonderful march under the circumstances. Yet it was made by women, children, old men and wounded men, half clad and weak from five days' starvation.

The limit of even a Cheyenne's endurance finally came. They camped back of a knoll and prepared an ambush— fighters to the very last. In the morning Captain Vroom's pursuing troop stumbled right into the trap. The spiteful crackle of fire emptied three saddles. The cavalry retreated, dismounted and surrounded the knoll. All that day they fought a long range battle. As night fell the troops built decoy fires around the knoll and marched back to the warmth of the fort.

But Dull Knife's scouts were not "decoyed." They laughed grimly at the white man's transparent trickery and walked over the decoy fires to continue their retreat.

THE FINISH

Thirty-seven Cheyennes were dead and fifty-two, mostly wounded, were captured by the night of January

[2] His dying gesture was splendid. "He lay on his back with arms extended and face upturned. In his right hand he held a small knife, a knife worn by years and years of use from the useful proportions of a butcher knife until the blade was no more than a quarter of an inch wide at the hilt, a knife descended to domestic use by the squaws as an awl for sewing moccasins, and yet, the only weapon this magnificent fighter could command in this, his last fight for freedom! As I sat . . . believing him dead . . . he rose to a sitting posture and aimed a fierce blow at my leg with his knife. Instinctively . . . I jerked my pistol, but . . . he fell back and lay still . . . dead. So died Buffalo Hump, a warrior capable, with half a chance, of making martial history worthy even of his doughty old father."—E. B. Bronson, "Reminiscences of a Ranchman."

10th. Next day the remnant was brought to bay in a difficult position to attack, far up Soldier Creek. During the fighting that day a troop horse was killed. At night the Indians sneaked out and from the carcass of that horse the poor wretches got the first mouthfuls of food they had eaten in seven days. The troops withdrew, so taking what little flesh was left on the dead horse, the Cheyennes slipped away for six miles more and entrenched themselves in the bluffs, dogged and defiant.[3]

Wessells brought a twelve-pounder Napoleon gun from the fort that day. It arrived at noon and all afternoon its sullen boom was the dominant sound in the snowy wastes. Forty rounds of shell were thrown into the Cheyenne position. The Indians could not reply. Yet Wessells failed to dislodge them. Flattening themselves in the shallow depressions they dug in the frozen ground, they endured as well as they could the concussions of the bursting shells.

Toward evening Wessells sent James Rowland, an interpreter, close to the lines, to tell them to surrender. Here was something the Cheyennes could reach with their guns. Rowland was glad to get back to his own lines with his life. No surrender yet.

Wessells was growing worried. The Indians were working toward the cattle country where they could find food and horses. He doubled the guard around their position. But on the morning of the 14th the Cheyennes were gone as usual. Somehow they had slipped through the cordon once more and gone up Hat Creek.

---

[3] During the second day's pursuit the troops ran into unexpected opposition. A single old man, unable to keep up longer because of frozen feet, remained behind with a loaded carbine to do what he could as a rear guard of one. As the soldiers came up he opened fire. Sixty men concentrated their rifles upon him. But the old Cheyenne continued to shoot his carbine as long as he could. Toward the last he was seen to fire three times with his left hand, resting the barrel of his gun along the edge of the washout where he lay, his right arm hanging useless. Then he dropped lifeless in the washout. He had been hit five times, the bullet which killed him passing through the top of his head. Corporal Everett was killed and a private wounded by this old man before they got him.

It is wearisome to repeat the details. For six days it continued. Day after day the Cheyennes fought. Night after night they used their matchless skill to slip away from the encircling lines of soldiers. Each day their numbers grew smaller.

The inevitable came at last. The Cheyennes made their last stand in the Hat Creek Bluffs, forty-four miles southwest of Fort Robinson, on the morning of January 21st, 1879. Worn out, most of them wounded, practically all suffering from frozen hands and feet, they lay in a washout, shoulder deep, on the edge of the bluffs.

A last summons to surrender. It was answered by three scattering shots from the washout. Those three shots were the last cartridges the Cheyennes had. Forward rushed the soldiers, up to the very edge of the washout. Not a shot was fired by the Indians. Into the huddled mass the troops poured a single crashing blast of flame. Without waiting to see the execution done, they leaped back to reload.

And now they saw a strange, uncanny apparition. Over the edge of the washout clambered three awful figures. Smeared with blood they were, their starvation-pinched features looking like living skulls. One carried an empty pistol. Two had worn knives. Tottering on their weak limbs, they poised for a moment on the edge of the grave of their people—the last three warriors of the unconquerable Cheyennes. Then with quavering war cries they madly charged, right into the muzzles of three hundred rifles.

With a shattering roar the fire leaped from those muzzles. The three warriors collapsed, literally shot to bits. They were the last fighters of their people. The Odyssey of the Cheyennes was ended.

WHAT HAPPENED AFTERWARD

The washout was heaped with bloody bodies, twenty-two dead and nine desperately wounded. All but six of the Indians who had fled the fort were accounted for, and one of them was Dull Knife himself. As fate would have it, the old chief had become separated from his people and did not even have the satisfaction of dying with them. With five others he found refuge in the teepees of the Sioux, where he lived, embittered, brooding, hating the white man with his last breath.

But what of Little Wolf and his half of the tribe?

They went north after leaving Dull Knife. Near Fort Robinson they carried out a bold coup. A mile from the fort was the cavalry remount depot. One night Little Wolf led his raiders right under the muzzles of the cannon in the fort. There was a flurry of shooting; two ranchers were killed and another wounded. The Indians, without a warrior lost, rode away with horses for the whole band.

The cavalry mounted in hot haste and pursued for hours that night. Morning found them near Crow Butte where they found the vestiges of an Indian camp—but the Indians were gone. The trail was plain, but what cavalry could follow its makers?

In the wilderness of Montana, far from the settlements, the Cheyennes spent the winter. Spring came and on March 25th, Little Wolf met Lieutenant W. P. Clark —"White Hat" to the Indians whom he had always befriended.

"I have prayed to God that I might find my friend Little Wolf," said Clark. "And now I have done so." Sincere joy was in his voice. The Indians knew White Hat would allow no massacre of their women and children.

"It is well; we will go with you wherever you say," replied Little Wolf.

This part of the Cheyennes, with few exceptions, was allowed to remain in the north. There Little Wolf and his warriors, enlisting as scouts, did valuable work for the government in helping to run down the few outlaw bands of hostile Sioux who, in spite of the peace made by their chiefs, still remained on the war path.

IX.

MURDER IN THE MOUNTAINS
1879

Chapter XXIII

TIIE MEEKFR MASSACRE

MOUNTAIN FIGHTERS

From the time the first white trappers entered the Rocky Mountains, the Utes were known by them—and respected. Those early mountain men knew the Utes for natural warriors, great wanderers, and "bad medicine" generally speaking.

By preference they made the high ranges their home. But they often went hundreds of miles out of their way, into strange country, for the sheer joy of fighting with the plains Indians. Thus, the reports of the Indian Service from 1862 to 1865 are full of references to the trouble given to settlers by Utes travelling through the passes near Denver and Pueblo, in their raids against the Cheyennes and Arapahoes, and the return raids against the Utes by those tribes. A large war party of Arapahoes in 1859 camped in the heart of what is today Denver. They left their women and children there and crossed the mountains to steal horses from the Utes. Shortly they came pell-mell back over the mountains, with the Utes close behind. The whites in Denver feared that the fierce warriors from back of the ranges might seek reprisals on them for allowing the Arapahoes to camp there. In 1863, a Ute war party ran off a herd of Cheyenne ponies under the noses of their owners, and within sight of Fort Lyon, Colorado.

These incidents are mentioned merely to show what

manner of warriors these Utes were. Surprisingly, outside of occasional fights with the early trappers and miners, they avoided warfare with the white men, even when the latter began coming in increasing numbers, elbowing the Indians for room in their own domain.

The Utes signed a peace treaty in 1859. During the next few decades they suffered the usual fate of Indians. They were shunted around here and there, each time the white man discovered that their latest habitation was valuable.

All this the Utes bore with great patience. Ouray, their chief, knew they must remain friendly. He was an Indian of exceptional wisdom and force of character. His name signified "The Arrow" and he was all that the name implies—keen, straight, direct and swift. Over the Utes he had tremendous influence. He was recognized as head chief by the Uncomphagre, White River, Unintah and other Ute bands, but not by the Cimarron or Southern Utes, whose chief was the great Ignacio.

Placer miners had long dug for gold in the mountains. But one day in the northwestern part of Colorado, deep in Ute territory, a peculiar heavy substance resembling clay was found, and an enterprising miner, annoyed by its clogging of his rockers, had it analyzed. It was carbonate of lead, rich in silver. Followed the famous Leadville mining excitement, which filled the mountains with prospectors. The rush was a typical mining stampede. Every little stream was defiled; every mountain canyon, no matter how inaccessible and wild, soon had it claims staked out. The country was ruined for game.

The Utes naturally viewed the horde of earth-grubbing white men with horror and alarm. The boundaries of their country were recognized by government treaty. Yet these men invaded with impunity those boundaries. The powder was all set for an explosion.

Horace Greeley, of the New York Tribune, was patron of a colony in Colorado named after him—Greeley. The leader of this colony was N. C. Meeker, an honest, upright man, but overbearing and arrogant. Meeker used his influence with Greeley to get the appointment as agent for the White River Utes in 1878. He had his own ideas about handling Indians and his first act of office was high-handed. He arbitrarily moved the agency to Powell's Valley, on the White River, fifteen miles below the old location, over the protests of every Ute on the reservation. The Indians used the valley as a winter camp, and the presence of the agency buildings ruined it for hunting.

Old Utes still remember "Nick" as they called the agent.

"He was always mad. I think he was sick in his head," is the way Samson Rabbit,[1] a brother-in-law of Colorow, one of the chiefs, describes him. This was the impression his aggressive, dictatorial attitude gave to all the Indians. His erratic actions puzzled them. "We never knew what to do. He was mad all the time."

When the agency was moved, Meeker took his next step. "I shall . . . cut every Indian down to the bare starvation point if he will not work," he wrote Senator Teller soon after he assumed office. One thing which prevented any great interest in work among the Utes was their love of horse racing. They had a race track in the valley. Meeker ordered the building of a school house in such a way that it ruined this track.

[1] Samson Rabbit, now about eighty-five, lives near Durango, Colorado. His brother, Buckskin Charlie, is the present chief of the Southern Utes. His sister married Colorow, one of the leaders in the Meeker uprising. He was a young man in his early twenties when the trouble took place.

Next the agent quarrelled with his Indians over the question of their sending their children to school. According to Rabbit, he summoned Colorow, Douglas and Matagoras, chiefs of the White River Utes, and demanded that they send their youngsters to his school. The Utes were still savages, in the "hunting stage." They were suspicious of this white man's device. "They did not know what it would do to their children." Moreover the school, because of its location, was an object of execration. The chiefs were evasive. "Too hot now. In about a month it will be cooler," they said. This was about September 1st.

Meeker flew into a rage, according to the Indian account, and threatened to call the soldiers. That alarmed the Utes. Meeker took it that they agreed to his proposition. But several days passed and still no children came. He sent for the military this time and some soldiers came and talked with the chiefs. Just who these soldiers were, the old Utes do not know, but they were probably from Fort Fred Steele. The talk accomplished nothing. The troops admonished the Indians and went back to the post.

Seven days passed. Meeker ordered the valley ploughed for cultivation. Again the Utes protested, but as usual the agent refused to listen. As the ploughing began, some Indians appeared with their guns. A shot was fired. Rabbit claims the "farmer" (the ploughman) fired with his six-shooter, but Meeker reported that one of the Indians fired from ambush. At any rate, the ploughing stopped.

By this time the feeling against the agent was murderous. A half-breed named Johnson got into an argument with him. They fought. Meeker was badly thrashed and thrown out of his own house. What authority he may ever have had was completely destroyed. He telegraphed to Fort Fred Steele for help.

At the receipt of the message, Major T. T. Thorn-

Fort Yates, photographed about the time of the Ghost Dance uprising.

Short Bull, one of the chief prophets of the Indian Messiah, whose claims precipitated the death of Sitting Bull.

Left: Big Foot, chief of the Sioux at the Wounded Knee fight. He was killed. Right: Ouray, head chief of the Utes.

burgh, with three troops of cavalry and a company of infantry, about one hundred and fifty men, left the fort, just north of the Wyoming border, and marched rapidly south. Close to the reservation line he was met by a party of five Utes, who protested against his entering the reservation. The Indians were deadly serious. Thornburgh replied that he must go on, but suggested that he would not go to the agency direct, camping near it instead. The Utes disappeared.

At this critical time, Ouray was somewhere in the mountains hunting deer. He was the only one who could have averted the coming tragedy. Rabbit says that the five chiefs after their talk with Thornburgh, dived into the bush and went straight to the Ute camp. There they held a council and the Utes voted to stop Thornburgh from going to the agency. The Indians were "not mad." This is reiterated over and over again. Evidently their decision was perfectly dispassionate and was gone about in the most methodical manner.

THE BATTLE OF RED CANYON

The road which Thornburgh took passed through a deep canyon known as Red Canyon. Its sides are covered thickly with scrub oak and along the ridge on one wall runs an ancient Indian trail. Here Colorow and Jack arranged their warriors, in the shrubbery and behind the boulders. The reason given by Rabbit is that the trail runs through tall bushes. Most of the Indians had no guns. "They had to hide near the road so their arrows would reach."

Thornburgh's command started into Red Canyon. Captain Payne's troop led, with Captain Lawson following, and Lieutenant Paddock, with the wagons, in the rear. But for an accident the whole command would have been wiped out. The wagons were hard to bring over the mountain road and Lieutenant Paddock had fallen back about half a mile. Up the canyon a scout saw a movement and reported Indians. Thornburgh halted and Lieutenant Cherry's advance guard pushed forward to reconnoitre.

The sudden chatter of many guns and a sleet of arrows sent the advance riding hard for their supports. The hills ahead were alive with Indians. Thornburgh threw his cavalry into battle line and signalled Paddock to stop and park his wagons.

Through the rocks and bushes the Utes began to slip, concealing themselves so skillfully that the troops could hardly see them, and keeping up a constant shower of bullets and arrows. From the flanks came the cry that the Indians were stealing around behind. Thornburgh had to retreat at once if he ever hoped to get to the wagons.

"Fall back!" came the order. The troopers executed the dangerous movement with veteran precision, in spite of the galling fire from the bush. But just as it was completed, the gallant Thornburgh was hit by a Ute bullet. He fell from his horse on the bank of the Milk River, and throughout the days of fighting which followed his men could clearly see his body from their defenses. After his fall the troopers managed to reach the wagons. The fight was already raging there.[2]

The Utes were quick to take advantage of the natural features of the battle field. The wagon corral was wretchedly situated, its only advantage being that it was close to the river. Ridges commanded it on three sides. One of these was too far away to be of much use to the Indians

[2] The Ute strategy had been pretty. Colonel E. V. Sumner in his article "Besieged by Utes," Century Magazine, 1891, copyright by the Century Co., says that at the beginning of the battle the Indians had less than half as many men as Thornburgh, or about seventy-five warriors. Rabbit agrees with this estimate, saying there were less than a hundred. With this small force they gave the troops a bad lacing. Undoubtedly Jack and Colorow received reinforcements later.

but they occupied points of vantage on the other two. From these points the keen-eyed Ute marksmen, trained deer hunters all, kept a deadly fire on the corral. If a soldier so much as exposed an arm he was likely to feel a bullet.

Now the Indians fired the grass and sagebrush on the valley floor and creeping up under the smoke, poured in a murderous volley. But there was no charge. The Utes lay concealed, picking off the horses and occasionally a man. By nightfall not five horses were standing. As the sun set, Captain Payne of the 5th Cavalry, the senior officer now, called for volunteers to carry a message for help. Out of the several who offered, a wiry, hard-riding Irish trooper named Murphy was chosen. At pitch dark he led one of the few unwounded horses cautiously down the valley for a mile. Then he mounted and rode for his life.

AT THE AGENCY

All the afternoon while Thornburgh's men fought in Red Canyon, Meeker, twenty-five miles away, sat in ignorance that a battle was going on. An Indian runner loped in with news of the fight for the other Indians, but not one word was breathed to the whites. Meeker fatuously supposed the trouble was over. He placidly prepared a letter to Thornburgh, saying "Things are peaceable." As he wrote, the man to whom the words were addressed lay dead.

Wilmer Eskridge started to Thornburgh with the letter. Two Utes, Antelope and Ebenezer, accompanied him. Barely out of sight of the agency, two miles down the road, they killed Eskridge and hurried back.

Utterly unsuspecting any danger, the agency people went about their daily tasks. Dinner was over and Mrs.

Meeker and her daughter Josie washed the dishes, while Mrs. Price, wife of the post trader, did the week's washing outside. Shadduck Price, her husband, and a youth named Frank Dresser, were throwing dirt from a wagon on the roof of a new building, on top of which Art Thompson spread the dirt and tramped it down. Meeker and Bill Post, the carpenter, were taking an inventory in a warehouse. The others were at their usual duties.

The return of Antelope and Ebenezer was a signal. There are conflicting accounts of what followed. According to the white account, obtained from the three women who were the only survivors, twenty Indians, led by Douglas, left their teepees and ran toward the buildings, shooting and yelling. Rabbit, however, says the shooting was started by the white men who realized suddenly that things were going wrong. Whoever started it, it seems pretty clear that the Indians intended to clean out the white people in the agency. Price and Thompson were killed at the first volley. Just when Meeker met his fate is not known. Frank Dresser was shot through the leg but ran for the agency house.

Mrs. Price entered first and handed the youth her husband's gun. He was all fight. With the gun barrel he smashed out a window pane and killed Johnson's brother. Mrs. Meeker and Josie, crazed with fright, ran in. Dresser, in agony from his wound, was the only man in the house. He knew the place would soon be afire, so led a dash to the adobe milk house, near at hand. They reached it safely and remained there until nearly sundown. All that time the shooting continued. Some of the agency men had obtained weapons and were fighting. Just who these last survivors were, will never be known. After a time the firing ceased.

The Utes looted the buildings. As they emptied them

of all goods they set them afire. Smoke from the main agency house poured into the milk house in strangling clouds. They had to run for the timber.

At the first step the Utes were after them. Dresser was shot down and Mrs. Meeker slightly wounded. The bounding Indians overtook and seized the women. Mrs. Price was fearful they would be burned. "No burn white squaw; heap like-um", grinned the Indians. Mrs. Price's captor was Ahu-u-tu-pu-wit, a small, ugly Indian. Josie fell to the lot of Persune. Douglas tried to take her away, but Persune threatened to fight for her. Douglas was finally contented with the ownership of Mrs. Meeker. The three women were held as captives until October 23rd, when their release was obtained.

CHAPTER XXIV

OURAY'S PEACE

BESIEGED BY THE UTES

Up in Red Canyon, Thornburgh's men, their leader dead, still lay surrounded by the Utes. The night of September 30th was black but the wounded were begging for water. Some men volunteered to crawl down to the river and fill the canteens. Fire from the opposite bank drove them back. Again the men crawled down, this time covered by riflemen. A duel in the dark followed, the soldiers shooting at the flashes of the Indian guns while their comrades filled the receptacles. The whole party got back safely with the precious canteens full.

As daylight came, the sniping from the surrounding heights began again. Not an Indian was in sight. There would be a puff of smoke. When a soldier returned the shot, his foe was usually yards away behind another boulder or bush.[1] Payne had to conserve his ammunition so he ordered his men to reply only occasionally—just enough to prevent open attack. During the long hot day the remaining horses were killed and some of the men hit. Among the dead were Lieutenant Paddock and Surgeon Grimes.[2]

[1] The Utes who were killed were nearly all shot through the top of the head, according to Rabbit. This was because they protected themselves so well behind boulders that only a few inches of their skulls were exposed at any time, and that only when they were firing.
[2] An incident occurred during the day which almost ended several lives. A horse, frantic with wounds, furiously thrashed about and finally fell into the pit where the wounded were kept. A quick-witted trooper shot the animal dead and nobody was injured.

So exhausted were the men that evening that many of them fell asleep at the breastworks. Payne and Lawson held a council of war. Had Murphy gotten through? Was help coming? What had happened at the agency? A check showed they had lost thirteen killed and forty-three wounded, more than forty percent of the command.

As October 2nd dawned clear and bright, the sharp-shooters in the hills again began their pot-shooting. But shortly after sunrise the welcome sound of galloping hoofs was heard down the valley. There were some shots and a cheer, and a troop of the 9th (colored) Cavalry came riding in. Captain Dodge, in command, brought the cheering news that Murphy had gotten through. More help was coming.

Undaunted by the reinforcements, the Utes fought dog-dedly on. Very soon the horses of the Negro troopers joined those of their white comrades in limbo. The new arrivals dug their elbows into the dirt and settled down to the siege.

But help was really on the way. General Wesley Merritt was coming from Fort Russell with four troops of cavalry and a company of infantry in wagons. At Rawlins he was joined by four more companies of "charioteers" as the cavalry called the wagon-riding doughboys. All day October 2nd they rode and all the following night. At dawn of the 3rd they came upon the hideous sight of a civilian train, massacred to a man. A little way farther, and with glad rejoicings, they reached the entrenchments.

If anybody expected to see the Utes run at the arrival of Merritt's overwhelming force, he soon saw his error. The Indians were hard to scare. One Ute, from his eyrie, shouted in broken English: "More horses, more shoot-um!"

Merritt's skirmishers went out. The first volley from

the infantry rolled like a clap of thunder through the mountains. But the Ute fire never slackened. Merritt's men were tired and he decided to let them rest before beginning the assault on those hill tops.

He never had to charge the hills. Shortly after noon, a white flag waved. A few minutes later a white man came toward the soldiers from the Indian lines. He proved to be Joseph Brady, a miller at Los Pinos, accompanied by a friendly Indian. He carried a letter to the Utes from Ouray, who, far away on his hunt, had heard of the outbreak and now sternly ordered them to desist. Even at a distance Ouray's influence was potent. The Utes slipped away. The war was ended.[3]

GATHERING UP THE WRECKAGE

The wounded were taken from the "fort," now stinking from the putrefying bodies of dead men and horses. The dead were buried, thirteen of them. There were forty-three wounded. The Indian loss was unknown at the time. The military later claimed that thirty-seven were killed.[4] Samson Rabbit, however, says only six bodies were brought from the battle field by the Utes. The latter count is probably the nearest correct, since the Utes fought entirely from cover.

Merritt moved to the White River Agency on the 11th. All along the road were evidences of the massacre. The body of Carl Goldstein, a freighting contractor, was found in a gully six miles from the agency. Nearby was the corpse of Julius Moore, his teamster, hacked and mutilated. Far-

[3] Rabbit insists that Ouray arrived at the scene of the battle in person after riding all day across the mountains, but sent his emissaries to talk to the soldiers instead of going himself, for fear of being shot while he tried to negotiate with them. The military had no record of the presence of Ouray.

[4] "Record of Engagements," p. 91.

ther along, in a deserted mine, lay Henry Dresser, of the agency, dead. He was unmutilated and evidently crawled into the hole to die after being mortally wounded. Two miles from the agency was the murdered Eskridge, stripped and scalped. Then came the agency itself—and what a scene of desolation it presented.

Blackened heaps of ashes alone showed where the agency buildings had stood. Around the yard was strewn the débris of articles looted from the storehouses. Here and there were the bodies of the agency men. Meeker was found a hundred yards from the ashes of his home. The top of his head had been beaten in. His mouth was stretched to a horrible width by a barrel stave driven into it. His body was slashed and disfigured and around his neck was a log chain by which he had been dragged. Frank Dresser, a bullet through his heart and another through his leg, was found in a nearby field. George Eaton's body was partly devoured by dogs or wolves. The corpses of Thompson, Price and others, were gathered and buried.

There was nothing more to be done here. Merritt turned his attention to recovering the women prisoners. During the negotiations word came that Lieutenant W. B. Weir and Scout Humme had been killed in a brush with Utes October 20th, as a detachment was reconnoitring twenty miles from the White River. The Utes said this attack was provoked by Humme who shot at several peaceful Indians.

In the end the release of the three agency women was brought about largely through Susan, wife of one of the chiefs, and a sister of Ouray. Susan had been rescued from captivity among the Arapahoes by the whites several years before. She felt under obligations and boldly harangued the warriors until she convinced them the women should be released. General Charles Adams, special agent for the

Indian department, risked his life during these negotiations by going boldly to the Ute camp.

The captives were brought to Merritt on the night of October 23rd. Then the commission on Indian affairs held a fruitless session. No direct testimony could be brought against any but the ring-leaders of the uprising and those involved in the captivity of the women. The hearings dragged on for days.[5] Then suddenly came word of the death of Ouray, the great chief, the peacemaker, the white man's steadfast friend.

It was like a closing curtain. The Northern Utes were moved to the Uintah reservation in Utah. The Southern Utes were allotted reservations in the Animas and Florida valleys of Southern Colorado. Four or five of the chief offenders were punished by being sent to Leavenworth penitentiary. Among these were Persune, Douglas, Johnson, Ahu-u-tu-pu-wit, Colorow and Matagoras. The latter came back after two years in prison with his mind gone— "stir simple" to use a modern slang phrase. He was killed, according to Rabbit's account, a few months later by two Utes who were afraid he might, in his crazed condition, harm someone.

[5] A strange complication arose after the Utes voted to release the captive women. Persune, the young warrior who had captured Josie Meeker, fell in love with her. Although most Indians scorn to show such a weakness as interest in a particular way toward a woman, this brave forsook all tradition. He implored the girl to stay with him; made all sorts of extravagant promises, such as that she should never have to work, and that he would give her all his possessions; and wept in quite un-Indian way when she refused. Persune was inconsolable after her departure. He always considered her his squaw, so much so that when she died some years later in Washington, D.C., where she was employed in the Treasury office, the other Indians thought he should have painted his face black and gone into mourning for her as a man would ordinarily mourn for a dead wife.

X.

THE WAR WITH THE MESSIAH
1889–1891

CHAPTER XXV

THE GHOST DANCERS

SITTING BULL RETURNS

MUCH water, historically speaking, passed under the bridge in the decade between 1880 and 1890. In the Southwestern deserts, the long and bloody war with the Apaches was fought to a conclusion. Cochise, Victorio, Nana and Geronimo had taken turns raiding and burning or leading the troops in fruitless chases through Arizona and New Mexico, until finally the Apaches were pursued across the line and run to earth deep in Mexico itself. There were some troubles in the mountains, notably the Bannack and Sheepeater wars of Idaho. The plains themselves, although the major Indian wars were ended, were far from peaceful. Small bands of Sioux continued to defy the government, to attack small parties of white men, and to run off stock and commit other depredations.[1]

Sitting Bull continued to live with several hundred of his Sioux north of the Canadian border. He got along well with the "Red Coats," as he called the British, and was respected by them. During his entire residence in Canada, from May, 1877, to July, 1881, his band was charged with only one depredation, the theft of one hundred horses

[1] In the two years 1880 to 1881, the war department records show ten troop movements after Indian war parties, with nine skirmishes, four soldiers or scouts killed, fifteen hostile Indians killed and the surrender of one thousand, seven hundred and seventy-nine Sioux in Montana and the Dakotas. The last figure includes Sitting Bull's large following which surrendered at Fort Buford in 1881.

from some neighboring Canadian Indians. Sitting Bull restored the horses to their owners and severely punished the guilty braves when he was notified of the affair by the mounted police.

In spite of this exemplary record, he was suspected by the United States of stirring up the trouble which kept detachments on the move pursuing vagrant bands of irresponsible Sioux. The Dominion officers also were anxious to get rid of their unbidden guests. At last, after negotiations were opened by "Fish" Allison, a scout and interpreter, and Major Walsh, of the Dominion police, Sitting Bull was persuaded by a French trader, Louis LeGare, to return to the United States. His surrender was at Fort Buford, Montana, July 19th, 1881. For two years he was a virtual prisoner at Fort Randall, but in 1883 was allowed to return to his old home near the Standing Rock Agency, where Major William McLaughlin was agent.

The old chief remained bitter. So an attempt was made to "break" him by recognizing other Indians as chiefs. It did not work. In 1883, shortly after his arrival at Standing Rock, a commission appeared to try to induce the Indians to take up agriculture. Sitting Bull arose to speak. The chairman tried to put him in his place, as the saying is, by telling him that he was no longer a chief, but a common Indian with no rank, and therefore had no right to speak.

Sitting Bull merely waved his hand. Every Indian got up and left the room. The commission realized it could "recognize" whomever it wished. But the Sioux still recognized Sitting Bull. At the next sitting, the old chief's remarks were listened to at great length and with marked respect.[2]

When General Crook and another commission came in

2 Vestal, "Sitting Bull," p. 247.

the summer of 1889 to try to buy a big block of Sioux lands for a song, Sitting Bull stopped the whole negotiation for a time. Agent McLaughlin, however, finally managed to get most of the Indians to sign it and the deal went through. That was the first time the Sioux went against the wishes of Sitting Bull. His power was waning.

THE BEGINNING OF THE CRAZE

In the winter of 1889 a new spirit possessed the Sioux. For the first time in years they looked with hope to the future. Their lot was no easier to bear. Dishonesty on the part of many Indian agents; cheating of the red man right and left; and white crooks acquiring fortunes by thefts for which they were never punished—these all continued as before. But the Indians were seized with a strange religious fervor.

Far to the west the Ogalallas had heard that an Indian Messiah had arisen. The news spread like wildfire. Not only the Sioux but practically every other tribe in the West caught the inspiration. It was similar to scores of the religious crazes which break out from time to time among more civilized people. But to the Indian, prostrate under the heel of the white conqueror, it was doubly significant, because it held out a hope to him of freedom from oppression—divine help in his extremity.

It is a weird circumstance that the last hope and belief of the unfortunate red race was founded upon the doctrines of the Christian religion which it had fought for more than three hundred years, from the Atlantic coast to the Pacific.

Harassed, not knowing which way to turn, the Indians hearkened to the words which had been ceaselessly poured into their ears by white missionaries. They had heard of the second coming of Christ, how He would return to His own people; that the meek and lowly, the downtrodden and oppressed would be exalted and redeemed. They had also been taught that the generations gone before would be restored to life; and that evil would be banished from the world. But it was a strange, bizarre interpretation which the red man put upon these teachings.

As the rumor of the Messiah grew among the despairing Indians, a great religious revival appeared among them. No "protracted meeting" of the white man ever approached it for awful sincerity of conviction. Night by night, day by day, the ceaseless throb of the tom-toms echoed from every Indian camp in Montana and Wyoming, Nebraska and the Dakotas, Texas and Oklahoma.

The strange, half-Christian, half-savage belief spread silently and swiftly. Almost overnight it was flourishing, full-blown. The Messiah was coming, they said. He had come once to save the white race but they had despised and killed Him. Now He rejected them and would come to destroy the whites and save His red children. All who believed in Him were to wear a peculiar kind of dress and to practice the Ghost Dance as often and as long as they could. The Ghost Dance, in common with many Indian dances, notably the Sun Dance, was a test of endurance.[3] It was believed that if anybody died of exhaustion during this dance he would be taken directly to the Messiah and enjoy the company of those who had gone before.

Word was brought by the Arapahoes in the fall of 1889 that the Messiah's camp could be found near Walker Lake, Nevada. The news aroused to concert pitch the religious fervor of the Sioux. Two of their trusted warriors

[3] Mrs. J. A. Finley, wife of the post trader at Pine Ridge, described a Ghost Dance participated in by 480 Indians, which lasted from Friday noon until Sunday at sundown. During that time none of the dancers touched food or water. Scores succumbed to exhaustion or the trances typical of the dance. Seven or eight died as a result of another dance held near Wounded Knee.

were elected emissaries to the holy one, representing two great divisions of the Dakota Nation. One of them, Kicking Bear, was an Ogalalla. The other, Short Bull, was an Unkpapa.

Knowing little English and with only vague directions of rumor to guide them, the two men started west, and travelled until they reached the Shoshone country—lands in which their people had not travelled without bloodshed in the memory of tradition. But now, in the shadow of the new common interest, they were received with honor, feasted and sent on their way with new directions. They took train to the country of the Paiutes. And now they entered lands so far distant that the farthest wanderings of their forefathers had never carried them thither. Among tall mountains, with lovely lakes and forests interspersed with burning deserts, again they found welcome and new tidings which set their feet southward. Everywhere as they progressed they met Indians who bore tidings that the Messiah had actually come. Finally they reached their destination. They saw the Messiah himself.

THE MESSIAH

His name was Wovoka, but he had lived for a time in his youth with a white family named Wilson, and the whites in the vicinity of Walker's Lake, Nevada, knew him as Jack Wilson. He was unknown and insignificant up to the time of his great vision. When the Sioux visited him, he was about thirty-five years old. He was a full-blooded Paiute, affecting white man's clothing and distinguished by tattoo marks on both wrists. He had never been out of Mason Valley in which he was born and spoke only Paiute, except for a smattering of English.

Wovoka's great "revelation" occurred about two years before he talked to Short Bull and Kicking Bear. At that time the "sun died" (an eclipse) and he went into a trance, being taken to the other world. He said he saw God, together with all those who had died before, engaged in their favorite occupations, all happy, and all young. After these things were shown to him, he said, God told him to return to his people, "tell them they must be good and love one another, have no quarreling, and live in peace with the whites; that they must put away all the old practices that savored of war; that if they faithfully obeyed his instructions they would at last be reunited with their friends in the other world." He was then given the dance which he was commanded to give in turn to his people.[4]

This was the man whom the emissaries met. He received them with cordiality but severe formality. The prophet proclaimed that the Messiah promise had been fulfilled. He said that they were only a few of many who had come to hear the words of truth.[5] Then he announced that he was about to move eastward, when there would be driven before him vast herds of wild horses, buffalo, deer, and elk, and as he came the dead Indians would rise and join the living. Finally, he taught them various mystic rites unknown to them and charged them to go before him and announce his coming.

Kicking Bear and Short Bull returned to their homes after a journey of more than two thousand miles among strange peoples. At a great council the emissaries expounded the story of the Messiah's coming. It was received with profound rejoicing.

[4] James Mooney, 14th Annual Report of the Bureau of American Ethnology, 1892–93, personal description of Wovoka whom he saw and interviewed, pp. 771-72.

[5] Porcupine, a Cheyenne, made a similar pilgrimage shortly before the Sioux. He told Lieutenant Robertson of the 1st Cavalry that fifteen or sixteen tribes were at the council at Walker Lake which he attended. Among those he named were Cheyennes, Arapahoes, Gros Ventres, Utes, Navahos, Bannacks, Shoshones, Crows and others who left before he came. The mention of these widely scattered tribes shows how far the belief had spread.

Bureau of American Ethnology

The Ghost dance. The Indian in the foreground is going into the trance typical of the dance.

Courtesy of Prof. C. W. Grace

Sitting Bull, in foreground, is addressing the land treaty commission in 1889. General Crook, with the army cap and gray beard, is at left of table. Agent McLaughlin, with beard and black hat is second to his right.

Thus far the Messiah craze had been purely a religious mania. "The Ghost Dance was entirely Christian—except for the difference in rituals." [6] But it needed only a spark to convert it into a roaring explosion of slaughter. That spark was furnished by a green "tenderfoot" agent, R. F. Royer, at Pine Ridge.

Alarmed by the growth of the religion and the reports, prejudiced and untrustworthy, that the Indians were on the "verge of a big outbreak," Royer wired for troops. They reached Pine Ridge October 19th, 1890. Thousands of Indians immediately took to the Bad Lands. Overnight the newspapers of the nation began printing the Ghost Dance on their front pages. Settlers in the Sioux country deserted their homes and fled to the cities.

Sitting Bull stayed quietly at his home on the Grand River. He was credited all over the country with being the high priest of the new religion, but it seems that he took little, if any part in it. Major McLaughlin, at Standing Rock, gave out a statement that there was no danger from his Indians. Still the name "Sitting Bull" was a name of menace. The attention of the whole United States was fixed on the great Unkpapa's movements.

Thanksgiving Day dawned ominously. The government sought to quiet the Indians by an issue of beef at Pine Ridge. But Plenty Bear, a friendly Sioux, brought word that in the camp of Big Foot on the Cheyenne River, there were three hundred and sixty-four lodges, or more than two thousand Indians, and others were coming in every hour. Agent Royer [7] was scared silly.

General Miles, still in command of the department, had to do something. He resolved on a two-fold plan: To arrest Sitting Bull; and to disarm the rest of the Indians.

[6] Vestal, "Sitting Bull," p. 279.

[7] The Sioux called him Lakota Kokipa-Koshla, or "Young-Man-Afraid-of-the-Indians," which is eloquent testimony to their opinion of him.

CHAPTER XXVI

THE LAST INDIAN BATTLE

THE DEATH OF SITTING BULL

BUFFALO BILL CODY, the circus man, came to Fort Yates, November 28th, with an order to "capture" Sitting Bull. Cody and Sitting Bull were friends. The chief had been an attraction in Buffalo Bill's wild west show one year. Now Cody proposed to take him a wagon load of presents and induce him to come in and surrender of his own free will.

McLaughlin opposed the move on the ground that the weather was too pleasant, giving the Indians an advantage if conflict developed. He recommended a delay, saying he would attend to Sitting Bull and the other Indians as soon as cold weather arrived. Cody's order was countermanded.

But McLaughlin's hand was forced. Short Bull, near Pine Ridge, claimed to have received a revelation that because of white interference the Messiah was speeding up his coming. Sitting Bull was interested. On December 12th he asked for a pass from Standing Rock to Pine Ridge.

The request may have been perfectly innocent. The fact that he asked for a pass instead of slipping away without permission, lends color to that theory. But Agent McLaughlin thought that Sitting Bull was about to go to the "hostiles." The same day Miles ordered Sitting Bull's arrest.[1]

McLaughlin had built up a fine body of Indian police. Couriers that night notified all of these Sioux policemen to assemble at Sitting Bull's village on the Grand River. Loyally they responded. Some of them rode forty miles that night to be at the rendezvous on time. Captain E. G. Fechet, with one hundred men and a Hotchkiss gun marched from Fort Yates, arriving near the village at daybreak.

The sun was not yet up when the Indian police, led by Lieutenant Bull Head and Sergeants Shave Head and Red Tomahawk, surrounded Sitting Bull's cabin. Bull Head and a small squad entered. The old chief was asleep on the floor. He was aroused and told to get into his clothes.

Although he complied, wrath blazed in the old man's eyes. Here was an indignity which he could ill brook. Like any common felon he was hustled out of the house, with Bull Head and Shave Head on each side of him and Red Tomahawk behind.

By this time Sitting Bull's warriors were swarming about like angry hornets. Winchesters were in evidence everywhere. Cries of anger, threats, and taunts filled the air. The women began wailing.

Suddenly Sitting Bull's voice was heard above the tumult.

"I am not going!" he shouted. Then he began giving directions for his own rescue. A war whoop screeched out. From close at hand a rifle crashed and Bull Head collapsed, shot by Sitting Bull's friend, Catch-the-Bear. As he

[1] Charges have been made that there was an understanding between the agent, the officers of the Indian police, and the military that Sitting Bull should be "put out of the way". The New York Herald, December 17th, 1890, said so in plain words. The charge was also asserted on the floor of the United States Senate. Miles and other officers with the expedition, strenuously denied these charges.

fell, Bull Head turned and shot his prisoner through the body. Two more shots rang out close together. Red Tomahawk had fired into the chief's back. Sitting Bull pitched into a huddled heap. Either of the bullets in his body would have killed him.

On that frosty morning air a sudden cachinnation of rifle shots rose. Everybody was firing. Shave Head dropped, hit by a bullet from Strikes-the-Kettle's gun. Several more police went down. Surrounded, they fought like tigers and beat back the furious Unkpapa. Sitting Bull's cabin door stood open. It was the only refuge and they ran toward it, carrying their dead and wounded. In the house they found Crowfoot, Sitting Bull's seventeen-year-old son, cowering. They killed him without mercy.

Captain Fechet galloped up. His Hotchkiss gun took a hand and began spraying death. At first the shells fell close to the police. But Fechet altered his range. The hostiles caught the full impact.

Their chief was dead and Sitting Bull's people scattered across the river.

Four police were dead. Two more were dying and two others were wounded. Besides Sitting Bull, eight Unkpapa warriors were killed, including Catch-the-Bear, Jumping Bull, the chief's adopted brother, and his son Crowfoot.

The dead police were buried in a common grave at Standing Rock. Sitting Bull's body, the head smashed in by the angry police after the fight, was dumped into a wagon and carried to the agency, where it also was buried —in quicklime.

So passed Sitting Bull. At his hour of glory he was a figure of almost epic splendor. In his death he bequeathed to his people a legend of grandeur, and to the world the spectacle of one more man who chose death rather than submission.

WOUNDED KNEE

Sitting Bull was dead. Now came the more difficult of Miles' two measures—the disarming of the hostiles.

At news of the chief's death the whole Sioux Nation became tense. Within three days after the killing on Grand River, there were two fights on or near Cheyenne River, where Big Foot's village stood. On the other hand many of the Indians returned to their agencies. For example, a thousand Ogalallas returned to Pine Ridge on October 18th. Six days later, Hump's band, numbering two hundred and twenty-four, gave up at Fort Bennett.

But there was still one big band at large—Big Foot's village on the Cheyenne. The remnants of Sitting Bull's people had joined that chief.

Colonel E. V. Sumner of the 8th Cavalry, tried diplomacy and talked with Big Foot. The chief said he wanted to be friendly. In proof of this three hundred and thirty-three of his people surrendered on December 21st. Then orders came to arrest the chief. That order stopped the movement toward peace.

Big Foot's band fled to the Bad Lands on the night of December 22nd. Nearly three thousand troops began at once to close in on them. On December 28th Major Whiteside of the 7th Cavalry, found the village on Wounded Knee Creek and called upon the Indians to surrender.

Big Foot tried to parley.

"We want peace," he said. "I am sick and my people——"

"I will not parley with you," said Whiteside. "You must surrender or fight. Which shall it be?"

"We surrender," answered Big Foot. Then he said something which tells a story of the despair and perplexity of the Sioux: "We would have done it before, if we had known where to find you."

That afternoon the whole band of about two hundred and fifty men, women and children, was marched to the 7th Cavalry camp down the creek. The Indians camped near the tents of the soldiers.

Next morning Colonel J. W. Forsyth, commanding the 7th, formed his five hundred men around the Indian village, with four Hotchkiss guns trained on the Sioux. Then he ordered the prisoners disarmed. Big Foot's statement the day before that he was sick was no exaggeration. He lay in his tent suffering from pneumonia.

The braves, sullen and uncomprehending, failed to obey the orders of Whiteside as quickly as he believed they should. Only a few rifles were given up. The major grew irritated. At last, after consulting with Forsyth, he brought the cavalry closer, formed them into a hollow square, and sent squads into the teepees to look for weapons.

Into the lodges strode the soldiers, shouldering their way in, driving forth the women and children, throwing over beds and other camp furniture, intensifying the mounting anger of the watching warriors. A medicine man, Yellow Bird, began haranguing the Indians, calling out that the ghost shirts nearly all of them wore were bullet proof and urging them to resist. A trooper grabbed the edge of a warrior's blanket to jerk it away. Yellow Bird stooped and tossed a handful of dust into the air. Sharply a rifle shot rang out.

It was what the 7th Cavalry was waiting for. For fourteen years they had wanted to wipe out the Custer disaster in blood. This was too good a chance to miss.[2] Right into

---

[2] General Miles brought charges against Forsyth for his conduct of this affair, mentioning specifically the circumstance of the slaughter of women and children three miles from the scene of the engagement. Forsyth was, however, exonerated by the secretary of war, Redfield Proctor,

the crowd of sitting and standing warriors, many of them so close to the muzzles of the carbines that they could nearly touch them, the soldiers discharged a shattering volley. Nearly half the warriors in Big Foot's band were killed or wounded by that first discharge.

Like wildcats the survivors leaped to their feet and threw themselves against the cordon. Most of them were unarmed, but they seized knives, clubs, anything to fight with. They were outnumbered nearly four to one, and far more than that in arms, yet they charged right at the throats of the troopers with desperate bravery. The squaws and even children took part. Captain Wallace fell with a wound in his leg. Before he could rise, he was clubbed to death by a swarm of Indian women.

The Hotchkiss guns went into action. Rapid-fire shells burst among the Sioux with terrible execution. Within a few minutes the field was strewn with the bodies of dead and wounded Indians. A handful broke through and fled in wild panic down a deep ravine. The blood-mad soldiers pursued, and the Hotchkiss guns never ceased to hurl their shells into the helpless, fugitive crowd. This was massacre in all its horror.[3]

The bodies of some of the women and children were found two and three miles away, where they had been pursued and killed by the human blood hounds.

The killing was over by nine o'clock although some parties of soldiers still hunted fugitives in the hills. Twen-

[3] The attitude of the 7th Cavalry is reflected in a conversation between a scout and an unnamed officer of that body right after the fight. This officer said, "with much gluttonous thought in his voice: 'Now we have avenged Custer's death,' and this scout said to him: 'Yes but you had every chance to fight for your lives that day; these poor Indian people did not have that opportunity to protect and fight for themselves'." This quotation is taken from the statement of the Rev. C. S. Cook, a half-breed clergyman of the Episcopal Church, which was made before the Secretary of the Interior, and members of the Indian Bureau, at Washington, D.C., February 7th, 1891.

ty-nine whites were dead and thirty-three wounded. The Indian loss will never be known. A blizzard set in that night and it was three days before the soldiers returned from Pine Ridge where they had taken their prisoners and wounded. How many helpless Indians, shot and unable to move, perished in the cold, it is impossible to guess, but there must have been many. Two or three little children were even found alive, protected through those three bitter days and nights by the bodies of their dead mothers.

By the time the soldiers returned to the scene, the bodies of many of the Sioux had been carried away by their relatives. But plenty of corpses still remained. The burial party reported sixty-four men and boys, forty-four women, and eighteen young children, or one hundred and twenty-six. General Miles, in his final report, however, says that not less than two hundred were killed. Among the dead was Big Foot, who was found lying in front of his tent.

Dr. Charles Eastman, who visited the battle field after the blizzard, before the burial of the bodies, thus describes it:

"It was a terrible and horrible sight to see the women and children lying in groups, dead. Some of the young girls wrapped their heads in their shawls and buried their faces in their hands. I suppose they did that so they would not see the soldiers come up to shoot them. At one place there were two little children, one about a year old, the other about three, lying on their faces, dead, and about thirty yards away from them a woman lay on her face, dead. These were away from the camp about an eighth of a mile. In front of the tents, which were in a semi-circle, lay dead most of the men. . . . This was where the Indians were ordered to hold a council with the soldiers."

AFTER THE MASSACRE

The guns of Wounded Knee could be clearly heard at Pine Ridge, nine miles away as the crow flies. There was intense excitement among the Indians at the agency as they heard the distant roar of firing and knew a fight was going on. Many of the warriors jumped on their ponies and rode to the scene, but the soldiers forced them back. Then a big body of Indians appeared on the ridge several hundred yards to the west of the agency and began to shoot at it. General Brooke ordered the Indian police to reply. They doubled past the agency school, and lay in line along the fence, their faces inscrutably calm, shooting at the Sioux who were now thick on top of the ridge.

The attacking Indians were not Ogalallas, but Brulés, led by Two Strike, Kicking Bear and Short Bull. After losing a man or two, they withdrew.

The situation was extremely grave. The troops had several skirmishes in the succeeding days. The very day after the massacre the Sioux almost trapped Forsyth and his men who were saved only by the prompt arrival of the 9th (colored) Cavalry.

By January 5th, 1891, the general situation was about this: Of the twenty-five thousand Sioux Indians on the northern reservations, twenty-one thousand, five hundred, were living in peace, while only thirty-five hundred were out. Of this number, less than one thousand were warriors. With the constant arrival of more troops, Miles now had eight thousand soldiers in the theater of war. It was the largest force ever assembled in one place to fight Indians.

But even with this army the outlook grew daily graver. All night the signal fires twinkled on the horizon and through the days constant puffs of smoke, dotting the air over practically every high bluff or ridge, showed where the Indians were telling each other of the movements of troops and other information.

Skirmishing continued constantly. Yet day after day passed and the great battle was postponed. On January 7th, Lieutenant Edward H. Casey, with a company of Cheyenne scouts, tried to pacify a band of Sioux. He was shot and killed by Plenty Horses, a Brulé.[4]

Miles worked day and night to avert the explosion. He counted on the sensible Indians, by now disillusioned of the miraculous powers of their Messiah priests, to bring the people to peace.

Slowly his soldiers pressed the great body of hostiles on three sides, moving them toward the Pine Ridge Agency, where it was planned to disarm and keep them. The Indians, sullen and restless, travelled slowly and grudgingly. At any moment an unfortunate act might have precipitated a general battle. But fortune was with Miles as it had been so many times before. In two days, during which he moved the hostiles thirty miles, the general scarcely slept.

Within sight of the agency, the Indians halted and said they would go no farther. Double guards walked in the army lines that night. Miles and his officers, tense, watchful, gazed toward the red flicker of the Sioux campfires.

The moon rose. Suddenly rifles began to speak. Furious yelling broke out among the teepees. Every soldier snatched his gun, convinced that the battle had come at last. But nothing happened. The noise ceased. Dawn came peacefully.

Next morning the extraordinary occurrence was ex-

---

[4] An interesting after-act of the war was the trial of Plenty Horses for the murder of Casey. On May 28th, 1891, Federal Judge Shiras peremptorily stopped the proceedings and ordered the jury to bring in a verdict of "not guilty". He held that a state of war existed between the whites and the Sioux and that under the laws of war Plenty Horses was justified in killing an enemy officer.

plained. True to Miles' surmise, the calm element in the Sioux camp had at last convinced the others that to fight would be suicide. Despairing, enraged, heart-sick, the bitter-enders sought wildly for something on which they could vent their pent up feelings. They rushed out with their rifles and ran amuck, shooting down their own dogs and horses.

It was relief of a sort. Next day the thousands of recent hostiles, eagle feathers fluttering, paint and beadwork gleaming, rode sullenly to the agency and camped. Thirty years of war was ended.

.   .   .   .

The other day, unnoticed in his squalid hut, died Wovoka, the Indian Messiah. Without honor even in his own tribe, his death created not a ripple in the land his influence once dominated. His body was buried in a sandy grave on the shores of Walker Lake.

No thumping drums, no spirit song accompanied his passing. Symbol of the red man's last hope, once worshipped by fanatical thousands, the news of his demise, on October 4th, 1932, served only to recall a troubled day in the West—the final, tragic stand of the retreating red man; the swan song of his race.

The Ghost Dance was dead long before its prophet.

BIBLIOGRAPHY

Bourke, Captain John G., "On the Border With Crook," New York, 1891.

Brady, Dr. Cyrus Townsend, "Indian Fights and Fighters," Garden City, 1912.

Brady, Dr. Cyrus Townsend, "Northwestern Fights and Fighters," Garden City, 1910.

Branch, E. Douglas, "The Hunting of the Buffalo," New York, 1929.

Brininstool, E. A., "A Trooper With Custer," Columbus, 1925.

Brininstool, E. A., "Chief Crazy Horse, His Career and Death," Nebraska History Magazine, December, 1929.

Brininstool, E. A., "Fighting Red Cloud's Warriors," Columbus, 1926.

Brininstool, E. A., and Hebard, Dr. Grace Raymond, "The Bozeman Trail," Cleveland, 1922.

Bronson, E. B., "Reminiscences of a Ranchman," Chicago, 1910.

Carrington, Frances Courtney, "My Army Life," Philadelphia, 1910.

Carter, Captain R. G., "The Old Sergeant's Story," New York, 1926.

Cook, James H., "Fifty Years on the Old Frontier," New Haven, 1923.

Cook, John R., "The Border and the Buffalo," Topeka, 1907.

Custer, E. B., "Boots and Saddles," New York, 1885.

Custer, General George A., "My Life on the Plains," New York, 1874.

De Barthe, Joe, "Life and Adventures of Frank Grouard," Sheridan, 1894.

Dixon, Olive K., "The Life of Billy Dixon," Dallas, 1927.

Dodge, Colonel Richard I., "Our Wild Indians," Hartford, 1885.

Dunn, J. P., "Massacres in the Mountains," New York, 1886.

Finerty, John F., "Warpath and Bivouac," Chicago, 1890.

Folwell, Dr. William Watts, "A History of Minnesota," publication of the Minnesota State Historical Society.

Forsyth, Colonel G. A., "Thrilling Days of Army Life," New York, 1900.

Grinnell, George Bird, "The Fighting Cheyennes," New York, 1915.

Grinnell, George Bird, "Two Great Scouts and the Pawnee Battalion," Cleveland, 1928.

Hare, Bishop W. H., "Chief Joseph's Own Story," North American Review Magazine, April, 1879.

Heard, Isaac V. D., "The Great Sioux War," New York, 1863.

Hodge, Frederick W., "Handbook of American Indians," Bulletin 30, Bureau of American Ethnology.

Jackson, Helen Hunt, "A Century of Dishonor," Cambridge, 1885.

Johnson, W. Fletcher, "Life of Sitting Bull," Chicago, 1891.

Kansas State Historical Society Reports.

King, Captain Charles, "Campaigning With Crook," New York, 1890.

Laut, Agnes C., "Pioneer Women of the West," Outing Magazine, March, June, July, 1908.

Linderman, Frank, "American," New York, 1930.

Manypenny, George W., "Our Indian Wards," Cincinnati, 1880.

Miles, General Nelson A., "Personal Recollections," Chicago, 1896.

Minnesota State Historical Society Collections.

Mooney, James, "The Ghost Dance Religion," Bulletin 14, Bureau of American Ethnology.

Nebraska State Historical Society Collections.

Parkman, Francis, "The Oregon Trail," Boston, 1872.

"Record of Engagements With Hostile Indians," Official Compilation.

Reports of the Secretary of War, 1862–1891.

Shields, G. O., "The Battle of the Big Hole," New York, 1889.

Standing Bear, Chief Luther, "My People, the Sioux," Brooklyn, 1928.

Sumner, Colonel E. V., "Besieged by the Utes," Century Magazine, October, 1891.

Vestal, Stanley, "Sitting Bull, Champion of the Sioux," Boston, 1932.

Wheeler, Colonel Homer W., "Buffalo Days," Brooklyn, 1923.

Wood, Major C. E. S., "Chief Joseph the Nez Percé," Century Magazine, May, 1884.

Wright, Robert M., "Dodge City, the Cowboy Capital," Wichita, 1913.

INDEX

Note: When the same name is used by more than one Indian, the different individuals are numbered (1), (2), etc., in the order of their appearance in the book.